CITY SECRETS

FLORENCE, VENICE & THE TOWNS OF ITALY

ROBERT KAHN

SERIES EDITOR

THE LITTLE BOOKROOM

NEW YORK

© 2001 Robert Kahn
Series Editor: Robert Kahn
Editors: Dave King and Nalini Jones
Fact checking and Editor's Notes: Paul Pascal, Professor Emeritus of Classics,
University of Washington, Fellow of the American Academy of Rome, 1952
Book design: Katy Homans with Christine N. Moog, Homans Design
Original series and imprint design by Red Canoe, Deer Lodge, TN, Caroline
Kavanagh and Deb Koch.
Maps: Jenny King
Key: Based on a design courtesy of E. R. Butler & Co., New York
Chapter divider pages: Collection of Claudia Cohen

Cover: *View of an Ideal City*, attributed to Piero della Francesca, Galleria
Nazionale delle Marche, Urbino, Italy. Alinari/Art Resource, New York

The passage on pages 133–134 is excerpted from *Provoked in Venice* by Mark
Rudman, Wesleyan University Press, 1999, and appears courtesy of the author.

The editors acknowledge with appreciation Adele Chatfield-Taylor, Pier Consagra,
Alan Feltus, Tia Fuhrmann, Beatrice Guthrie, Fiona Duff Kahn, Elizabeth Kogan,
Karen Marshall.

First Printing: June 2001
Printed in Hong Kong by South China Printing Company (1988) Ltd.

Library of Congress Cataloging-in-Publication Data

Florence, Venice, & the Towns of Italy / Robert Kahn, series editor.
    p. cm. — (City secrets ; 2)
    Includes bibliographical references and index.
    ISBN 1-892145-01-4
    1. Art, Italian—Guidebooks. 2. Art, Modern—Italy—Guidebooks.
    I. Kahn, Robert, 1950– . II. Series.
    N6914.F59 2001
    914.504'93—DC21

00-051846

Published by The Little Bookroom
5 St. Luke's Place
New York NY 10014
(212) 691-3321
(212) 691-2011 fax
book-room@rcn.com
editorial@citysecrets.com
www.citysecrets.com

Distributed by Publishers Group West; in the UK by Macmillan Distribution Ltd.

HOW TO USE THIS BOOK

This is a highly subjective guidebook which reflects the personal tastes and insights of its contributors. Our editors asked architects, painters, writers, and other cultural figures—many of them fellows of the American Academy in Rome or members of Save Venice— to recommend an overlooked or underappreciated site or artwork, or, alternatively, one that is well-known but about which they could offer fresh insights, personal observations, or specialized information. Respondents were also invited to describe strolls, neighborhoods, events, shops, and all manner of idiosyncratic and traditional ways of spending time in Italy.

These recommendations have been organized into three primary sections: Florence; Venice; and the Towns of Italy. (Not included is Rome, which is the subject of the first volume in the series, *City Secrets Rome.*) The sections on Florence and Venice include city maps with the location of each entry coded according to the text; the third section has been divided into four general geographical areas, then further divided by province. In addition, four icons appear throughout the book to reference restaurants ⑪, shops ⑱, hotels ⋈, and (in the case of Venice) vaporetto stops ⚓.

The editors feel proud of the high number of unusual and delightful "secrets" included here. At the same time, we acknowledge that Italy provides an endlessly rich travel experience, and that this book, though full, is not exhaustive. It is our hope that readers will be inspired by the enthusiasm of our contributors to explore even further and perhaps discover a few secrets of their own.

Finally, every care has been taken to ensure the accuracy of the information in this book. However, the publisher is not able to accept responsibility for any consequences arising from use of the guide or the information it contains.

TABLE OF CONTENTS

9   PREFACE

10   FLORENCE / FIRENZE & ENVIRONS
16   **Historic Center**
26   **Oltrarno**
36   **City Center West**
39   **City Center North**
48   **City Center East**
51   **Colli**
53   **Outside City Center & Environs of Florence**
       Arcetri, Campo di Marte area, Carmignano, Fiesole,
       Galluzzo, Impruneta, Montughi, Settignano

60   VENICE / VENEZIA
64   **San Polo & Santa Croce**
76   **Cannaregio**
86   **Castello**
102   **San Marco**
115   **Dorsoduro**
135   **Venetian Islands**
       Giudecca, San Giorgio Maggiore, San Michele,
       Torcello, San Lazzaro degli Armeni

144   NORTHWEST ITALY
148   **Piedmont & Valle d'Aosta**
       Rivoli, Stupinigi, Varallo
153   **Liguria**
       Genoa/Genova, Portofino, Portovenere
157   **Lombardy**
       Castelseprio, Castiglione Olona, Como, Desenzano
       del Garda, Lecco, Mantua/Mantova, Milan/Milano,
       Monza, Pavia

169 NORTHEAST ITALY

172 Veneto & Trentino—Alto Adige
Asolo, Bassano del Grappa, Casella d'Asolo, Fanzolo,
Lonigo , Masèr, Mestre, Padua/Padova, Portogruaro,
Possagno, San Vito d'Altivole, Solighetto, Trento,
Treviso, Verona, Vicenza

187 Friuli—Venezia Giulia
Aquileia, Castello di Miramare, Cividale del Friuli,
Grado, Udine

190 CENTRAL ITALY

194 Emilia-Romagna & Marche
Bologna, Maranello, Parma, Piacenza, Ravenna,
Riola, Urbino

208 Tuscany / Toscana
Arezzo, Bagni di Lucca, Barga, Cavriglia, Chiusi,
Colonnata, Cortona, Lucca, Lucignano, Magliano
in Toscana, Manciano, Montefollonico, Abbazia di
Monte Oliveto Maggiore, Montepulciano, Monterchi,
Montevarchi, Pienza, Pietrasanta, Pisa, Pitigliano,
Poggio a Caiano, Rofelle, Abbazia di San Galgano,
San Gimignano, San Giovanni Valdarno, Sansepolcro,
Abbazia di Sant'Antimo, Seravezza, Siena, Sovana,
Trequanda, Viareggio, Volterra

247 Umbria
Assisi, Bevagna, Burano, Castiglione del Lago, Città di
Castello, Deruta, Foligno, Gubbio, Lerchi, Niccone,
Norcia, Orvieto, Pissignano, San Presto, Spello, Todi

271 Lazio
Bagnaia, Bomarzo, Caprarola, Cerveteri, Civita di
Bagnoregio, Abbazia di Fossanova, Genzano di Roma,
Licenza, Monte Circeo, Norchia, Ostia Antica, Palestrina,
Abbazia di San Benedetto, Abbazia di Santa Scolastica,
Sermoneta, Sperlonga, Tarquinia, Terracina, Tivoli, Viterbo

297   SOUTHERN ITALY

300   **Abruzzo & Molise**
       Alba Fucens, Fossacesia, Pietrabbondante, Saepinum

303   **Campania**
       Campi Flegrei, Capri, Caserta, Cumae, Ercolano,
       Ischia, Naples/Napoli, Padula, Paestum, Pompeii,
       Ravello, Sorrento, Torre Annunziata, Vietri sul Mare

329   **Basilicata & Puglia**
       Castel del Monte, Maratea, Matera, Rionero in
       Vulture, Venosa

339   **Sicily / Sicilia**
       Gibellina Vecchia, Mozia, Noto, Palermo, Piazza
       Armerina, Selinunte, Syracuse/Siracusa

347   **Sardinia / Sardegna**
       Nuraghe su Nuraxi, Santu Antine, Serra Orrios

349   INDEX OF RECOMMENDED READING

352   INDEX OF CONTRIBUTORS

361   INDEX

PREFACE

Imagine, when you travel, asking a great painter what painting you should see or inviting a renowned classicist to join you in visiting an ancient site. Suppose you were looking for the perfect local meal and a writer whose novel you had just read suggested her favorite restaurant—and at the end of that meal a Poet Laureate accompanied you on his favorite stroll home. This is what it is like to be a fellow at the American Academy in Rome. Many years later, my memory of this remarkable experience inspired the idea for City Secrets. In our first book, *City Secrets: Rome*, we asked those who knew the city best to recommend both well-known and undiscovered places. Their contributions were sometimes profound, often humorous, and always insightful.

The response to *City Secrets: Rome* was overwhelming. Readers, critics, and our generous contributors encouraged us to continue on with the rest of Italy—and so, we have. This book is not comprehensive, nor would we want it to be; there are already a number of fine general guides that cover the country as a whole. Ours is a record of those places that our contributors (many from the American Academy in Rome and Save Venice) have found important, entertaining, or sometimes even just odd and overlooked. It is a record of hidden treasures, lesser-known destinations, and some well-known places described in unusual ways. For those new to Italy, think of this book as a companion—an opinionated friend who knows a little too much, but whose presence makes the ordinary extraordinary. For those of you who know Italy, we hope this book will be a reminder that there is always so much more to see.

My best advice is to get lost . . . wander down a quiet street or follow your own thoughts while spending far too long sitting in a small village piazza. Discover something that you can call your own, and when you do, let us know. We would love to hear about your city secrets—in any city, anywhere.

Robert Kahn
New York City

FLORENCE & ENVIRONS

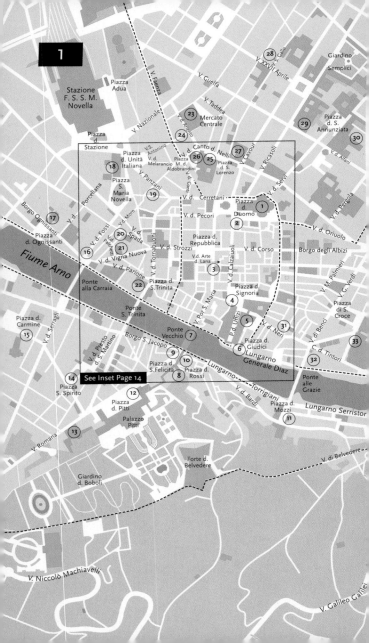

1

Stazione
F. S. S. M.
Novella

Piazza
Adua

V. Fienna

V. Guelfa

V. Taddea

V. XXVII Aprile

28 Gullo

Giardino
d.
Semplici

V. Nazionale

V. d. Ariento

23 Mercato
Centrale

24

29

Piazza
d. S.
Annunziata

30

V. d. Alfani

Piazza d.
Stazione

Piazza
d. Unità
Italiana

18

V. d.
Melarancio

VS
Antonino

Piazza
M. d.
Aldobrandini

26 Canto d. Nelli
25

27

V. Cavour

V. Ricasoli

Piazza
S.
Maria
Novella

V. Panzani

19

V. d.
Conti

Piazza
d. S.
Lorenzo

V. d. Servi

V. d. Oriuolo

V. d. Pergola

Borgo Ognissanti

17

V. d.

Porcellana

V. d. Cerretani

Piazza
d.
Duomo

1

2

Piazza
d. Ognissanti

Fiume Arno

16

V. d. Fossi

V. d. Moro

20

21

V. d.
Spada

V. Tornabuoni

V. d. Strozzi

V. d. Pecori

Piazza d.
Repubblica

V. d. Arte
d. Lana

3

V. d. Corso

V. d. Calzaiuoli

Borgo degli Albizi

V. M. Palmieri

V. G. Verdi

V. d. Vigna Nuova

V. d. Parione

22

Piazza d.
S.Trinita

V. P. S. Maria

Piazza d.
Signoria

4

Piazza
di S.
Croce

33

Piazza d.
Carmine

15

V. d. Serragli

Ponte
alla Carraia

Ponte
S. Trinita

Borgo S. Jacopo

Ponte
Vecchio

7

P.za Uffizi

5

V. d. Neri

31

V. d. Benci

C. d. Tintori

32

Lungarno
Generale Diaz

6

Lungarno

Piazza d.
Giudici

V. di Presto
d. S. Martino

9

10

Piazza d.
S.Felicita

8

Piazza d.
Rossi

Torrigiani

V. d. Bardi

Ponte
alle
Grazie

Piazza d.
Mozzi

11

Lungarno Serristor

Piazza
S. Spirito

14

See Inset Page 14

13

12

Piazza
d. Pitti

Palazzo
Pitti

V. Romana

Giardino
d. Boboli

Forte d.
Belvedere

V. di Belvedere

V. Niccolò Machiavelli

V. Galileo Galilei

FLORENCE AND ENVIRONS
HISTORIC CENTER

1 Santa Maria del Fiore (Duomo)
2 Arciconfraternità della Misericordia
3 Orsanmichele
🍴 4 Caffè Rivoire
5 Galleria degli Uffizi
6 Società Canottieri, or Circolo Canottieri
7 Ponte Vecchio

OLTRARNO

8 Santa Felicita
🎁 9 Madova
🍴 10 Le Volpi e l'Uva
11 Museo Bardini
12 Boboli Garden / Giardino di Boboli
13 Museo La Specola
🍴 14 Piazza Santo Spirito
15 Santa Maria del Carmine

CITY CENTER WEST

🎁 16 N'uovo
17 Refettorio della Chiesa di Ognissanti
18 Santa Maria Novella
🎁 19 Beltrami
🍴 20 Trattoria Garga
🍴 21 Il Latini
22 Santa Trinita

CITY CENTER NORTH

🎁 23 Mercato Centrale
🍴 24 Antica Gelateria il David
25 San Lorenzo
26 Cappelle Medicee
27 Palazzo Medici-Riccardi
🛏 28 Albergo Splendor
29 Opificio delle Pietre Dure
30 Museo Archeologico

CITY CENTER EAST

31 Flood Marker
32 Fondazione Horne
33 Santa Croce
🍴 34 Dolci e Dolcezza

COLLI

35 Piazzale Michelangelo
36 San Miniato al Monte

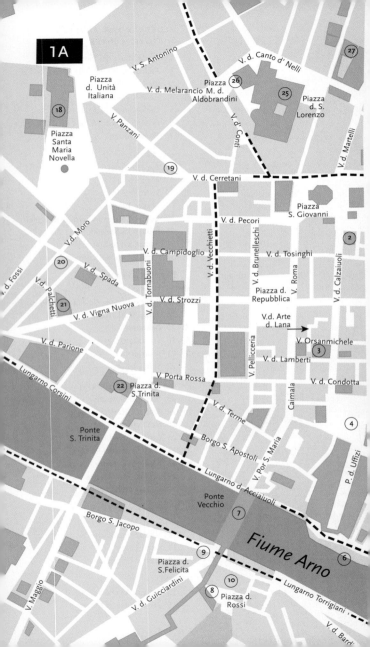

FLORENCE AND ENVIRONS
HISTORIC CENTER DETAIL

1 Santa Maria del Fiore (Duomo)
2 Arciconfraternità della Misericordia
3 Orsanmichele
4 Caffè Rivoire
5 Galleria degli Uffizi
6 Società Canottieri, or Circolo Canottieri
7 Ponte Vecchio

OLTRARNO

8 Santa Felicita
9 Madova
10 Le Volpi e l'Uva

CITY CENTER WEST

18 Santa Maria Novella
19 Beltrami
20 Trattoria Garga
21 Il Latini
22 Santa Trinita

CITY CENTER NORTH

25 San Lorenzo
26 Cappelle Medicee
27 Palazzo Medici-Riccardi

CITY CENTER EAST

31 Flood Marker
32 Fondazione Horn

HISTORIC CENTER

1.1 Santa Maria del Fiore (Duomo)
Piazza del Duomo

Dome

1418–1468, Filippo Brunelleschi

How does one begin to describe the achievement that this structure represents? It is no less than the most innovative architectural solution since (and probably including) antiquity. I know of no other building in which form and function are so completely unified.

Brunelleschi inherited certain problems and dimensions from the existing cathedral plan, begun by Arnolfo di Cambio in 1296. His solution was technologically unprecedented, while succeeding, at the same time, in harmonizing an existing Gothic structure with an uncompromisingly modern form. The expanse at the crossing was equivalent to that of the Pantheon, but the Pantheon was a simple poured-concrete dome (a negative form was built in wood, and then cement, mixed sequentially with travertine, brick, and pumice, was poured in). Even though the Pantheon supports no weight at the top—the oculus not only supplies the sole source of light, but also neatly avoids the problem of carrying weight at the most critical point— it developed serious cracks soon after completion.

Brunelleschi instead proposed to build his dome in masonry—the largest ever attempted until that point— and he proposed to do it *without the use of any template forms or scaffolding*. It was to be self-supporting during the construction and surmounted by a massive lantern whose enormous weight is unmatched in any dome before or since, including Michelangelo's for Saint Peter's in Rome. Brunelleschi understood that hemisphere domes tend to fail consistently at around thirty degrees (he had walked to Rome to study the Pantheon) and deduced that sixty degrees, the curvature of Santa Maria del Fiore, was the maximum arc that could support weight from above without deforming.

Brunelleschi's early decision to retain the octagonal perimeter shape left by Arnolfo was critical, and several important features of the construction derive from this choice. The raising of the *tamburo*, or drum section, not only emphasized the importance of the corners, it also made possible the insertion of the huge circular windows in the center of each bay. These windows obviously increase the light to the interior, but more importantly, the upper curves act as blind arches which transfer the weight of the dome to the corners and down through the piers to the ground. The three smaller domes of the transepts and apse, together with their solid buttresses, help to contain the outward thrust.

Many architects and architectural historians have overlooked the importance of the corners to the dome's engineering. A certain herringbone bricklaying technique, characteristic of circular 'rotation' domes, has led to the erroneous conclusion that the dome really functions by virtue of the circle inscribed within the octagon. The herringbone bricklaying technique consists in laying some bricks flat and, periodically, others on edge. Each successive layer is shifted to fit against the previous edge-laid brick, and so on. The adjacent rows of edge-laid bricks result in several vertically spiraling courses through the walls, which converge at the top; the weight of the lantern then tightens the entire structure. An added feature of this technique is that two edge-laid bricks can act as stops, which prevent the other bricks from falling into the void during construction. The edge-laid rows can occur at intervals roughly equivalent to the arm span of a single worker and can greatly expedite the construction—especially in this case, where no scaffolding was used.

The bays between each of the eight ribs of the dome are flat, and this is a fundamental principle of the building

system Brunelleschi devised here. It is based upon straight-
line transmission of the forces. The weight of the materials
is pulled in towards the void from the corners but it is
opposed by the straight line of force through the flat bays
to the rib on either side. If each bay had been curved outward (to form a circular dome), the opposing forces would
tend to rupture the wall between the ribs. Corners, then,
and flat bays are essential to the support of the dome. This
building is a machine that constantly generates the forces it
needs to support itself.

Aesthetically, the lantern gathers the major formal
lines of the structure, but it also serves an important static
function, as noted above. The average marble block for
it weighs over six thousand pounds. Brunelleschi realized
the importance of the lantern for the stability of the dome.
Although he was present at Signa for the arrival of the first
block shipped from Carrara and accompanied it to Florence
to be hoisted and set in place, he feared he would not live
to see the lantern's completion. Before his death in 1446,
he entrusted the plans to his rival, Michelozzo—who had
beaten him in the competition to build Palazzo Medici—
because he knew he was the only other person capable of
the job.

The cupola occupied Brunelleschi from the earliest
models in 1417 until his death; he supervised every aspect
of its design and construction. He was not merely an aes-
thetician (like Alberti, the architect of Santa Maria Novella
a generation later, who couldn't be bothered with the
mechanics of the building process and simply handed over
his drawings to Rossellino to get the work done.) Brunelleschi designed the shape of the bricks (the wooden forms
still exist in the Museo dell'Opera del Duomo) and rou-
tinely inspected them for quality as they came out of the
ovens in the morning. He designed tools and templates for
construction details and even invented several ingenious
systems with pulleys for hoisting material up to the building site, since there was no scaffolding from the ground.

(Fifty years later, Leonardo da Vinci drew copies of these mechanical devices, and he is often miscredited with their invention). He made special allowances for drainage and the eventual settling of the ground. The 72 holes (three rows of three in each of the eight sections) serve to equilibrate the temperature inside and outside the dome, so that different expansion and contraction rates of the materials would not cause fissures. He even had kitchens installed between the inner and outer domes so that less time would be lost to meal breaks.

Brunelleschi met with considerable resistance along the way. His drawings and plans were notoriously sketchy because he was afraid they would be copied, and twice he nearly lost competitions for this reason. Even though he won the dome competition, Ghiberti was initially named *capomaestro* with him. After numerous disagreements about the construction, Brunelleschi famously feigned sickness and told Ghiberti to go ahead alone. It quickly became apparent that without Brunelleschi, construction would have to cease. Brunelleschi agreed to return only if he was given complete authority over all aspects of the construction. Unbelievably, in 1433, after thirteen years as *capomaestro*, Brunelleschi was arrested for working as a builder without having been matriculated in the mason's guild.

The construction of the dome dominated the civic landscape for fifty years, and it could be seen from as far away as Prato. Even today it inspires awe, especially as one approaches it from the narrow via dello Studio, where it looms above the rooftops, or gazes at it from the lush lawn at the Forte di Belvedere at sunset. Few extant buildings come anywhere near symbolizing civic pride and ambition, or, indeed, human potential and nobility, as much as this great dome.

GEORGE BISACCA
Conservator of paintings

Roman Roads

ITINERARY

a Via Torta and via
Bentaccordi
City center east,
near Santa Croce

b Piazza della
Repubblica
Historic center

c Via Calimala
Historic center

How easy it is to overlook ancient Roman Florence as one strolls through the Renaissance city! Yet the ancient city is very much in evidence in the urban layout: via Torta and via Bentaccordi outline a portion of the Roman amphitheater, and the ancient *cardo* and *decumanus* survive as streets that meet at the site of the ancient Roman forum, now the 19th-century Piazza della Repubblica. On via Calimala, near the corner of via Por Santa Maria, ask the *portiere* to see the *strada romana*; in the basement of this apartment house not far from Ponte Vecchio you can see the ruts in the ancient Roman road at the gate that led south out of Florence, toward Rome. This fragment of ancient life was discovered after World War II, when this area was excavated after being mined.

ANN THOMAS WILKINS
Classicist

Editor's Note: On August 3, 1944, the retreating Germans mined and blew up all the bridges across the Arno. Only the Ponte Vecchio was spared, though at the cost of leveling the streets at both ends.

Staircase
1420–1436, Brunelleschi

The best 463 steps to climb in Florence are those ascending Brunelleschi's dome of the cathedral. There is no elevator, but one is amply rewarded for the physical exertion. A small display on one of the landings exhibits Brunelleschi's pulleys and scaffolds used to construct the massive *cupolone*. Upon arriving at a catwalk at the base of the dome, one can view Vasari's painted *Last Judgment* in terrifying proximity. Scaling the spiral staircase toward the summit, notice the herringbone pattern of the brickwork, used to reinforce the dome. The staircase is sandwiched between two interlocking shells, another of Brunelleschi's architectural inventions to make the dome less heavy and self-supporting. The view from Michelozzo's lantern at the top is unequalled in all of Florence. One can see Alberti's Renaissance façade of Santa Maria Novella attached to the Gothic church behind it; the open, square atrium of Palazzo Medici; the Romanesque church of San Miniato perched high on a hill on the other side of the Arno; and the dome of the Synagogue, all with crystalline clarity.

KATEY BROWN
Art historian

1.2 Arciconfraternita della Misericordia
Piazza del Duomo 19/20

I was curious about the Brotherhood of the Misericordia, and it has become my custom to look for them outside their headquarters whenever I visit Florence. Seeing the members emerge from their building in black, hooded robes is certainly a throwback to the brotherhood's founding more than 750 years ago. The hoods help both male and female members remain anonymous as they go about their altruistic work, which includes providing ambulance service in the city.

MARY ANN HAICK DINAPOLI
Genealogist

Editor's Note: The order's Italian name, in its full sonorous majesty, is Venerabile Arciconfraternita della Misericordia di Firenze. In a manuscript (still extant) of 1361, the founding of the Confraternity is reported as being in 1244, which is 21 years before Dante was born. Besides their absolutely state-of-the-art medical services, one of their avowed missions is still to provide dowries for poor girls. They have several branches in other parts of Florence.

1.3   Orsanmichele
1361
Via dell'Arte della Lana

Tabernacle
1349–1359, Andrea Orcagna

Though 1337 is the date of Orsanmichele's foundation
stone, the building (a granary) was constructed in 1307-
1308 and repaired in 1321 and 1332. The critical date,
however, is 1361, when the grain market was moved elsewhere and the ground floor transformed into a Marian
oratory. (The upper two storeys continued in use as granaries. Years ago, a colleague told me that while she was
scrambling around up there, examining the structure, she
found some kernels of grain.)

Orcagna's tabernacle has now been gloriously restored;
it includes reliefs of Mary's life, including the death and
Assumption of the Virgin. Inside the tabernacle, on the
altar, is Bernardo Daddi's *Madonna Enthroned*. The outside of Orsanmichele has some of the greatest works of
15th–century Florentine sculpture (though some have now
been replaced by replicas, with the originals moved to the
Bargello.) Among the most notable are Ghiberti's *John the
Baptist*; Donatello's *Saint George* and *Saint Mark*, the latter of which Michelangelo praised as representing an
honest man—evidently something noteworthy in his experience; Verocchio's *Doubting Thomas* group; and Nanni's
Four Crowned Saints. The niches themselves are wonderful, especially George's, with its (copy of) Donatello's
schiacciato, or flattened (the word is also used to describe
certain kinds of sandwich) relief of Saint George and the
dragon. (The original is in the Bargello.)

RONA GOFFEN
Art historian

RECOMMENDED READING
Diane Finiello Zervas, *Parte Guelfa, Brunelleschi and Donaello*,
J. J. Augustin, 1987.

1.4   Caffè Rivoire
Piazza della Signoria

Each time we return to Florence we stop at the elegant
Caffè Rivoire on Piazza della Signoria for *cioccolata con
panna,* piping hot chocolate with heavy whipped cream
spread on the top. It's scalding, thinner and less creamy
than you might expect, and exceptionally rich in flavor.
It's great on a damp winter day and refreshing on a chilly
summer evening, but whatever the weather, it's a treat not
to be missed; if you stand rather than sit, you can afford
to come back for a second.
DAVID G. WILKINS AND ANN THOMAS WILKINS
Art and architectural historian and classicist, respectively

Stop at the renowned cafe on the Piazza della Signoria to
enjoy a hot chocolate. It has the most amazing consistency,
like the Arno when the water is low.
SUSAN KLEINBERG
Artist

1.5   Galleria degli Uffizi
Piazzale degli Uffizi

Il Corridoio Vasariano
1565, Giorgio Vasari

The corridor can accommodate only a limited number of visitors.
Tickets available at the Uffizi ticket office; ☎ 055 238 86 51

The corridor of Vasari is a most unusual moment of architecture. Constructed in only five months for a Medici
wedding in the year 1565, it was, in effect, devised as
a "skyway" or elevated corridor to connect the Palazzo
degli Uffizi (formerly the official administrative offices for
the Medicis) to the grounds of the Palazzo Pitti on the
other side of the Arno.

Elusive and almost disguised—unless one is aware of
it—the *corridoio* snakes around and negotiates Florence,
transforming itself as it comes into contact with the urban

fabric. So where does one find access to this linear architecture? One must go to a stair between Room XXV and
Room XXXIV of the Uffizi (make a reservation at the ticket
booth). The stair descends through a part of the Uffizi, and
suddenly one realizes one is on an enclosed bridge crossing
over the Lungarno, with traffic charging along below. This
bridge makes a right angle turn and transforms into the
upper, enclosed, level of a portico that parallels the Arno!!
You've probably walked through this portico looking to
the Arno, but not realized that above is a passageway for
people. And what is more amazing is that the corridor/por-
tico makes yet another sharp turn, to the left this time, to
metamorphose into an upper level to the Ponte Vecchio!
Once the corridor/bridge traverses the Arno, it 'disappears'
into a medieval house and emerges to wrap around a
medieval tower. And if this isn't enough, the corridor
straightens out again and adheres to the front of the
Church of Santa Felicita to be incorporated into the
church's exterior façade; inside the church, the corridor
presents itself as a viewing loggia, so that the Medici
princes could see into Santa Felicita. From here the corridor embeds itself between medieval buildings paralleling
the via Guicciardini to descend and transform into a staircase that mysteriously becomes a doorway leading out into
the Boboli Garden of the Palazzo Pitti. Interestingly
enough, one emerges to the sound of water, adjacent to a
rather fantastically shell-encrusted grotto. Think about it:
the city and garden are joined by a 'line' that wiggles and
changes its identity (stair, portico, bridge, church façade
from without, church viewing box from within, stair
again) as it maneuvers the views of a city to become the
views and sounds of a garden.

The corridor is lined with not-so-exciting portraits, but
this is really not important. What is significant is to make
the journey and become part of a portico, part of a bridge
(and what a bridge!), part of a church; a line transforming.

JUDITH DIMAIO
Architect

RECOMMENDED READING
Henry James, *The Portrait of a Lady*, Viking Penguin, 1984.
Originally published in 1881.

1.6   Società Canottieri, or Circolo Canottieri

Early 20th century
Lungarno Maria Luisa de'Medici 8

Built at beginning of the 20th century beneath Giorgio
Vasari's 16th-century Piazzale degli Uffizi, the Società
Canottieri (known more commonly as the Circolo Canottieri)
is one of the most fascinating spots to experience Florence
from a different point of view. This is not the view of the
river from the Ponte Vecchio, nor the cityscape from Piazzale
Michelangelo, nor the aerial panorama from the Campanile
di Giotto in Piazza del Duomo, but relaxing in the sun in this
flowered garden, one has the privilege of watching the city
as if from its belly-button. It's no coincidence that among
rowing club members the place is called *l'ombelico*.

The club was established at the beginning of the last
century and holds some prestige in international rowing
circles. It occupies the undercrofts of the Uffizi Palace,
and the beautiful wooden boats run under the Loggia
degli Uffizi and along the river toward the Ponte Vecchio.
Although most of the club is open only to members, no one
will stop you from having a drink at the bar or from taking
a picture of the fascinating boat-gallery or Ponte Vecchio,
where groups of envious tourists might watch you!
FRANCESCA DELL'ACQUA
Art historian

1.7   Ponte Vecchio

If you wander across the bridge in the early morning or late
evening when the shops are closed, you can see how the
Florentine symbol of the stylized lily has been adapted as the
decorative pattern for the hinges on the wooden shutters.
DAVID G. WILKINS
Art and architectural historian

OLTRARNO

1.8 ### Santa Felicita
Piazza Santa Felicita

Annunciation and Deposition
1525–1528, Jacopo Pontormo
Cappella Capponi

On the way to the Palazzo Pitti, immediately after crossing
the Ponte Vecchio, one finds the unassuming church of
Santa Felicita. The church, originally built in the middle
ages and remodeled in the middle of the 18th century, sits
in Firenze's quieter Oltrarno neighborhood, a neighborhood that is still populated by many of the city's finest
craftsmen and artisans. After entering Santa Felicita, look
into Brunelleschi's marvelous Cappella Capponi immediately on the right. It is difficult to avoid swooning when
confronted with Jacopo Pontormo's stunning frescoes. The
colors in the *Deposition* are a sumptuous array of pinks,
greens, ochres and blues. The dead Christ appears to be in
a peaceful slumber as He is passed down to a crouching
figure whose torso magically changes hue from fuchsia to
lime green. Pontormo's wonderful *Annunciation* is also
located in this chapel. The rapport between hovering angel
and Virgin is sublime!
FRED WESSEL
Artist and professor

*Editor's Note: Brunelleschi was commissioned by
Bartolomeo Barbadori to design the chapel about 1420,
and it was originally called the Barbadori Chapel.
Pontormo did the paintings between 1525 and 1528 for
Ludovico Capponi; hence the current name.*

In Santa Felicita, in the heart of Florence, art lovers will
find an unlikely oasis of peace and solitude in which to
reflect on two beautiful Pontormos. The tiny chapel, just
inside on the right, houses both the *Annunciation* (fresco),

and the *Deposition* (oil). Here, in one spot, are the first and last chapters of a great religious tale.

The works reveal Pontormo's genius with color, going from hot pink to cool blue, passing from acid green to warm purple, and creating *chiaroscuro*—a sense of light and dark—by juxtaposing warm and cool colors without using black.

In an exhibit a year after the 1966 flood of Florence, the *Annunciation* was shown in the Fortezza da Basso. The angel Gabriel and Virgin Mary, on separate sections, were placed side by side as they are in the chapel. As I looked at the two figures I had a disturbing sensation, because I had never noticed before that the two figures are illuminated by different light sources. Gabriel is illuminated from the right and Mary from the left. In their proper settings in the Cappella Capponi, there is a window between them which illuminates the two figures in such a natural manner that one never even considers the light source. Seeing this fresco out of its proper space distorted the artist's intent and prompted me to wonder how often we encounter works of art out of their original contexts.

Happily, in this chapel, we can enjoy these great treasures as the artist intended.

SWIETLAN NICHOLAS KRACZYNA
Artist and printmaker

Pontormo's *Deposition*, a monument of mannerism in Cappella Capponi (the first chapel on the right). You can pay the custodian to turn on the lights.

RICHARD L. FEIGEN
Art dealer

In spite of the iron fence rail which partially blocks your view, a visit to Pontormo's *Deposition* of Christ in Santa Felicita is a revelation. Christ's heavy body sinks downwards as He is lifted and carried. The Virgin swoons.

If you tip the watchman, he may open the cage and let you in to gaze unfettered by the fencing. He likes it best if you pre-book the opportunity—drop by in the morning to enter the chapel later the same day.

DANA PRESCOTT
Artist and writer

In my opinion, Pontormo's *Pietà* (also called *Deposizione*) is possibly the greatest single work in Florence, the *Primavera* of Botticelli notwithstanding. Note too the surrounding frescoes.

JOHN C. LEAVEY
Painter

The brilliant and shocking colors, the beautifully strange faces, and the evocative subject matter contribute to this painting's fascination.

LIDIA MATTICCHIO BASTIANICH
Restaurateur

This church is right across the Ponte Vecchio; on a hot day, after lunch, it's a great spot for a visit, and the painting is fabulous! The vivid colors, the beautiful and harmonious composition. It's a wow. I take everyone who visits us to see it. (It's in the Cappella Capponi, to the right of the entrance.) There's nothing else to see in this church—what a relief!

Lunch, of course, is at Cammillo (Borgo San Jacopo 57R, ☎055 21 24 27), or the new and trendy Beccofino (Piazza degli Scarlatti 1R, ☎055 29 00 76), where the food is great (though the service can be glacial).

KATHE DYSON
Traveler

1.9 Madova

Via Guicciardini 1/R, ☎055 239 65 26

After you've visited Santa Felicita for Pontormo's frescoes and *Pietà* altarpiece—and perhaps had a bite to eat at one of the two quite good restaurants to the left and right of the square next to the church—it's an easy stroll to the Palazzo Pitti. On your way there, be sure to stop at Madova, the best glove store in Florence.

RONA GOFFEN
Art historian

1.10 Le Volpi e l'Uva
Piazza dei Rossi 1/R, ☎ 055 239 81 32

🍴🍷 After drinking in Pontormo's dazzling colors go to the Volpi e l'Uva, a quiet wine bar, and drink in some of Italy's other great art, a glass of its magnificent *vino*. This tranquil oasis is located in the Piazza dei Rossi right next to the church. Sit under an umbrella and order a glass of Tignanello, Barolo, Brunello or one of the fifteen or so bottles that are opened daily and are available by the glass. Complement this with an order of assorted bread or *focaccia*, an order of assorted salami, and an order of assorted cheeses.

FRED WESSEL
Artist and professor

1.11 Museo Bardini
Piazza dei Mozzi
Currently under restoration; reopening January 2002

Part of the collection of the early 20th-century antiquarian Stefano Bardini, in a handsome setting near the Arno, the Museo Bardini is one bridge down from the Ponte Vecchio, half a block in from the bank opposite the Uffizi. The collection includes carvings, sculpture and decorative art from the medieval period to the baroque.

HELEN COSTANTINO FIORATTI
Interior designer

Shopping Spree

ITINERARY:

a ⌁ Hotel Lungarno
Borgo San Jacopo 14
☎ 055 272 61

b 🏺 Castorina
Via Santo Spirito
13/15R
☎ 055 21 28 85

c 🏺 Romanelli
Lungarno Acciaiuoli
74/R
☎ 055 239 60 47

d 🏺 Peter Bazzanti
and Son
Lungarno Corsini
46/R,
☎ 055 21 56 49

e Museo Salvatore
Ferragamo
Via Tornabuoni 2
☎ 055 336 04 56

f 🍴 Cantinetta
Antinori
Piazza Antinori 3
☎ 055 292 234
Closed Saturdays
and Sundays

I always check into the Hotel Lungarno.
It's a charming, ever-so-discreet and wonderfully located hotel paralleling the Arno
on the Palazzo Pitti side, between the
Ponte Vecchio and Ponte Santa Trinita.
After checking in, I always follow the
same route to a divine sequence of shops.
First I go to Castorina, artisans of wood
objects since 1895. The shop is on the via
Santo Spirito, an extension of the Borgo
San Jacopo, so only a slight distance from
the Hotel Lungarno. Anyway, it is chock
full of architectural details, moldings, sim-
ulated marble frames in all shapes and
sizes. . . circles, ovals, squares, frames for
fans. Gilded reading stands, spheres and
obelisks painted to simulate malachite,
and a thousand other intriguing objects
can be found in this special shop.

Departing this shop, I retrace my steps
and cross to Ponte Santa Trinita. When I
reach the other side I always turn right
and go to Romanelli. For those who love
marble and stone, from malachite to lapis
lazuli, this store is bliss. There one can
find boxes, paperweights, pyramids, urns,
spheres, obelisks of the most beautiful
craftsmanship, and in the most exquisite
marbles, alabasters, and stone. The shop
has been around for a very long time, and
survived the great flood of 1966. Ask for
Adele, or Romanelli himself.

Once I am able to make the retreat
from this shop, which closes for lunch, I
retrace my steps to the Ponte Santa Trinita
and continue along the Arno to Peter
Bazzanti and Son. This is the bronze store

where all ancient Roman bronzes from Pompeii, Herculaneum, and just about any other site can be found in
reproduction. These bronzes at Bazzanti are of great quality.
There are bronze fauns, satyrs, pans, gods, goddesses, busts
of Socrates, Homer and emperors, and bronzes of Antinous
and Mithras, to name a few. If you love antiquity and the
figural material that populated ancient Roman architecture,
you will be in heaven in this wonderful Florentine *bottega*.

Yet my walk is still not complete. There is one more
stop—the large medieval palace at the end of the via
Tornabuoni that is closest to the Ponte Santa Trinita. This
palazzo is the home of Salvatore Ferragamo, the great shoe
designer. Although the store is wonderful, my true interest
is in the Museo Salvatore Ferragamo. You must make an
appointment at the store to visit the museum, which
exhibits all of his great shoe designs and their lasts (blocks
or forms in the shape of someone's foot). There, beautifully
displayed on the top floor, are shoes that belonged to
Audrey Hepburn, Wally Simpson, Judy Garland, Marlene
Dietrich, citizens and travelers who found their way to
Ferragamo. It is a beautifully appointed museum, and if
you love shoes you will not be disappointed.

I always end this walk, or take a luncheon *intermezzo*
before Ferragamo, and it is always to the most lovely
Cantinetta Antinori, which is at the opposite end of the via
Tornabuoni from the Ponte Santa Trinita. One must pass
through a huge arched doorway into a large room much
like a *cantina*. The menu is special everyday and it is not
a large menu, but once one discovers this delightful Tuscan
ambience, it will be hard to go elsewhere.

It is quite amazing when one realizes that in such a
small area as I have described, so many varied and intriguing
places exist. But this is Florence.

JUDITH DIMAIO
Architect

RECOMMENDED READING
Iris Origo, *Images and Shadows: Part of a Life*, David R. Godine,
1999.

1.12 Boboli Garden / Giardino di Boboli
Piazza de'Pitti

Pack a picnic and spend an afternoon in the Boboli
Garden. Allow at least a few hours.
JOHN L. WONG
Landscape architect

Grotta Grande del Buontalenti
1557, begun by Vasari; 1583–1588, completed by Buontalenti

Grotticina di Madama
1553–1555, Davide Fortini and Marco del Tasso

The artificial grotto or *nymphaeum*—a supernatural grotto
space dedicated to the nymphs or muses—was an architectural folly of the Renaissance which took as its reference
the ancient *nymphae* of Rome. Artificial grottoes of the
Renaissance were designed by the leading architects of the
day and incorporated shell encrustations, stalactites, mosaic
and fantastic sculptural elements. Fountains and water
jokes were integral to the plan, most often placed in
remote parts of the gardens of villas and *palazzi*. Two of
the most well-known, the Grotta Grande and the Grotta
delle Capre in Giardino di Madama, are hidden in the corners of the Boboli Garden and are well worth seeking out.
Just outside the city, the Villa and Parco Demidoff has
another of the most fabulous grottoes of this kind: the
Apennine fountain and grotto, a giant figure of stalactite
and stone emerging from a small pond, complete with a
shell- and stone-decorated interior.
LESLIE RAINER
Conservator

1.13 Museo La Specola
Via Romana 17
Closed Mondays

Tucked into a side road south of the Palazzo Pitti, through
a dark courtyard, and up three flights of stairs: La Specola—

"the Observatory." Florentines know it: they come as schoolchildren to this surpassingly strange, disconcerting museum unlike any other. Part is a hodgepodge collection of taxidermy, gorillas and quetzals and tapeworms in one silent room after another. The eerie displays smell faintly of preservative, and the visitor wanders in solitude. But this is only the beginning; La Specola's true treasure is waxworks. Since the collection's beginning in 1775, past the death of its founder, Grand Duke Pietro Leopoldo di Lorena, in 1792, and through much of the 19th century, the collection has continued to grow. The Grand Duke founded the museum as a way to teach anatomy without using corpses. The result is far more violent, a fantasy of vivisection. Beautifully and artfully made models of naked, serene people—disemboweled, dissected, skinned, decomposing—gaze with open and expressive eyes at the visitor. In one corner are perfect dioramas of plague-filled streets and syphilis wards. A man's head, eyes open, goatee, half his skull peeled away. Bring the kids.

SALLIE TISDALE
Writer

Editor's Note: Grand Duke Pietro Leopoldo di Lorena spent years in the political and intellectual life of Florence and has a prominent role in the history of the city, though he was actually Austrian. The waxwork collection is sometimes referred to as "La Collezione Lorenese."

Museo La Specola is in the *sezione di zoologia* of the Museo di Storia Naturale dell'Università di Firenze. It houses 26 full-length wax models and hundreds of anatomical parts in an 18th-century gallery. The collection is staggering: exquisite and awe-inspiring.

GERALDINE ERMAN
Artist

A fascinating museum of the history of science. *Specola* in Italian means "astronomical observatory."

HELEN COSTANTINO FIORATTI
Interior designer

1.14 Piazza Santo Spirito

Osteria Santo Spirito
Piazza Santo Spirito 16/R, ☎ 055 238 23 83

Pensione Sorelle Bandini
Piazza Santa Spirito 9, ☎ 055 21 53 08

A walk through Piazza Santo Spirito, especially at dusk, provides one of the most inspiring combinations of space with architecture, as the strange and austere façade of the church fills the space. The Osteria Santo Spirito, on the corner, serves delicious, affordable food in a dark, intimate, shabby-chic atmosphere. Pensione Sorelle Bandini, in a lovely 15th-century palazzo, is perfectly placed. The rooms are as big as you can get in Florence, some with a great view over the Arno to the mountains. Cats roam freely through the *pensione*, and a loggia overlooks the piazza.
LESLIE RAINER
Conservator

1.15 Santa Maria del Carmine
Piazza del Carmine 14
Closed Tuesdays

Cappella Brancacci
15th–century frescoes

A visual experience that cannot be missed is the extraordinary Cappella Brancacci in Santa Maria del Carmine. Literary types will know Masaccio as the "Hulking Tom" at the end of Browning's "Fra Lippo Lippi," a painter who far surpassed the speaker of the poem. Masaccio's frescoes in this chapel were instantaneously legendary for their use of perspective, and if one is to believe the unreliable Vasari, "all the most celebrated sculptors and painters who lived from his day to our own, have become excellent and famous by exercising themselves and studying in this chapel. . . to learn and to grasp the precepts and the rules for good work from the figures of Masaccio." The chapel also contains works by Masolino and, after the deaths of both Masolino and Masaccio, was finished by Filippo Lippi's son, Filippino. In honor of the millennium, a chart now tells you which fresco is which and by whom, but you won't go wrong if you use a method along the lines of Emily Dickinson's litmus test for poetry: if you feel physically as if the top of your head were taken off, you know it's Masaccio. His Adam and Eve expelled from Paradise is as heartbreaking a representation as anything in Western art. And I can never get enough of Saint Peter's curing the sick with his shadow or distributing alms to the poor, though *The Tribute Money* is generally considered the chapel's masterpiece. Masaccio's self-portrait appears underneath it, in a doorway to the right of Saint Peter enthroned. He's the curly-headed one who looks like a wrestler—true to his name, "hulking" or "big bad" Tom.

JACQUELINE OSHEROW
Poet

CITY CENTER WEST

1.16   ## N'uovo
Via dei Fossi 21/R, ☎ 238 22 90

Furniture and accessories, gifts, all objects of great imagination and style combining traditional Florentine workmanship with eclecticism and wit. They will make custom pieces and individual items.
HELEN COSTANTINO FIORATTI
Interior designer

1.17   ## Refettorio della Chiesa di Ognissanti
Piazza Ognissanti 42

The Last Supper
1480, Domenico Ghirlandaio

Although close to many hotels, the Ognissanti is one of the lesser-visited sights in Florence, yet it also contains one of the city's marvels. In the refectory of the monastery is one of Ghirlandaio's most majestic masterpieces, and with any luck you'll have it all to yourself. As was common in refectories, it is a Last Supper that covers the entire end wall. The lush colors, the delicate details (notably the flowers that place the scene in an eternal spring), and the grace of the figures make it a work of art that can enthrall the spectator for many a long, lingering visit. It is one of the most peaceful yet enlivening places in the entire city—an immediate refreshment for even the weariest tourist.
THEODORE K. RABB
Historian

1.18   ## Santa Maria Novella
Piazza di Santa Maria Novella

Trinity
ca. 1426, Masaccio
North Aisle

Last Judgment
1354–1357, Nardo di Cione
Cappella Strozzi

Visit Santa Maria Novella for Masaccio's *Trinity* and
Nardo di Cione's *Last Judgement* frescoes. The Strozzi
altarpiece by Nardo's older brother Orcagna is still *in situ*
in the chapel.
RONA GOFFEN
Art historian

RECOMMENDED READING
Rona Goffen, ed., *Masaccio's Trinity*, Cambridge University Press,
1998.

1.19   **Beltrami**
Via Panzani 1/R, 055 21 26 61

Readers with small shoe sizes may be happy to learn that
the Beltrami shoe outlet carries tiny sample sizes, such as
34 and 35. You can even call ahead to Chiara and tell her
the sizes you want to try, and she'll have a mountain of
cardboard boxes waiting for you.
DANA PRESCOTT
Artist and writer

1.20   **Trattoria Garga**
Via del Moro 48, 055 239 88 98

Fun, great food.
RICHARD L. FEIGEN
Art dealer

1.21   **Il Latini**
Via dei Palchetti 6/R, 055 21 09 16

Slather olive oil on the *ribollita* and devour a steak at a
communal table at Il Latini. No menus, just grouchy wait-
ers and well-dressed Florentines. Rough, but. . .
ROSS ANDERSON
Architect

Cenacoli

ITINERARY

a Museo di San Marco
Piazza San Marco 1

b Ognissanti
Piazza Ognissanti 42

c Sant'Apollonia
Via XXVII Aprile 1

d Sant'Onofrio
Via Faenza 42

e San Michele a
San Salvi
Via di San Salvi 16

f Il Convento della
Calza
Piazza della Calza 6

I recommend searching out the *Cenacoli* (*Last Suppers*) of Florence, the frescoes that adorn the refectories of Renaissance monasteries and nunneries. Some are easily accessible, like the two magnificent and well-preserved Ghirlandaio *Last Suppers* in San Marco and Ognissanti. Some are worth seeking out, such as that by Andrea del Castagno in the still cloistered nunnery of Sant'Apollonia. And then there are the lesser known examples by Perugino in the Convent of Sant'Onofrio, and the marvelous Andrea del Sarto in the church of San Salvi. And if you are lucky, or very persuasive, you might talk the nuns of the Calza near Porta Romana into letting you briefly glimpse their precious *Cenacolo* painted by Franciabigio.

WILLIAM E. WALLACE
Art historian

1.22 **Santa Trinita**
Piazza di Santa Trinita

Frescoes and Altarpiece
ca. 1422, Lorenzo Monaco

Cappella Sassetti
1479–1485, Domenico Ghirlandaio

Visit Santa Trinita for the frescoes and altarpiece, which are the late work of Lorenzo Monaco—and for the Sassetti chapel by Ghirlandaio, likewise with frescoes and altarpiece *in situ*.

RONA GOFFEN
Art historian

CITY CENTER NORTH

1.23 **Mercato Centrale**
Via dell'Ariento 10–14

Walk through San Lorenzo market early in the morning, visiting the fishmongers, butchers, and fruit and vegetable vendors. There is such energy and enthusiasm here. Then head over to the church of San Lorenzo and relax in Brunelleschi's masterpiece.
LIDIA MATTICCHIO BASTIANICH
Restaurateur

RECOMMENDED READING
Mary McCarthy, *The Stones of Florence*, Harcourt Brace, 1989.

1.24 **Antica Gelateria il David**
Via Sant'Antonino 28/R, ☎055 21 86 45
Closed Sundays

As you leave the Mercato Centrale di San Lorenzo—a fascinating place and worth seeing (only in the mornings)—there is a tiny hole-in-the-wall ice cream shop, all plastic and seemingly uninviting, on the via Sant'Antonino (it's on the left, going towards the Piazza Unità Italiana and Santa Maria Novella.) It is called Antica (though remodeled) Gelateria il David. Stop there and try their *nutella* ice cream. (Nutella is the commercial name of the beloved Italian hazelnut paste. During a Nutella strike several years ago, the newspapers wrote of desperate mothers who did not know how to deal with *merenda*, or snack time. I know depressed ladies who lie in bed and eat it with a spoon.) Il David's flavors, when compared to the most famous ice cream shops in Florence, are a revelation! Also less expensive and with much bigger scoops, but that's not the point.
HELEN COSTANTINO FIORATTI
Interior designer

Editor's Note: There is also a street market outside the Mercato Centrale di San Lorenzo, which is in operation all day.

1.25 San Lorenzo
Piazza di San Lorenzo

Biblioteca Mediceo-Laurenziana
Begun in 1524, Michelangelo
Enter from Cloister

In the sprawling monastic complex of San Lorenzo, visitors sometimes have difficulty locating Michelangelo's Laurentian Library. From a convoluted approach through an unexceptional cloister and up a dark and narrow stair, the unwary visitor steps into an expansive and impressive volume of vertical space—the Laurentian Library vestibule. As with the nearby Medici Chapel, a dense exterior architecture has been brought indoors. Rising from the shoulders of peculiarly anthropomorphic consoles, paired monolithic columns soar to meet sections of broken entablature.

A casual visitor is rendered small in such stately company. The oft-described sense of enclosure and compression in the vestibule is felt mainly when, like a servant, one stands to the side of the monumental staircase or climbs its side wings. To mount the central flight—reserved, said Michelangelo *per il signore*—is to feel like a prince and to experience the grandeur of the Medici, whose purposes Michelangelo well served. From the center of the broad staircase, the vestibule is capacious, the prince its center, the columns his ordered retainers. The consoles genuflect. The vestibule organizes human experience and helps shape the person within it. It is an architecture for princes.

WILLIAM E. WALLACE
Art historian

The overblown scale of the stair in the vestibule, the wall reversal, and the gigantic scale of the columns and volutes make this one of the most compact and rich spaces of the Renaissance.

ROBERT LIVESEY
Architect

Like the Scala Regia in the Vatican, this staircase provides the most elegant statement in entry.

JOHN L. WONG
Landscape architect

One of the most extraordinary moments in architecture, Michelangelo's corner of the stair hall leading to the Laurentian Library is packed with more architectonic power than most entire buildings. A corner that puts Mies van der Rohe to shame, here "more is more" with an almost inexpressible series of spatial operations. Just to name a few: folded space, mirrored space, inside-outside space, layered space, negative space, positive space, warped space. For an architect, the details are literally breathtaking; the mind can barely grasp the way this corner was conceived, let alone built for all to see—and to feel.

ALEXANDER GORLIN
Architect

1.26 ## Cappelle Medicee
Piazza di Madonna degli Aldobrandini

New Sacristy / Sagrestia Nuova
1521–1524, Michelangelo

The rough exterior of irregular brick courses of the New Sacristy of San Lorenzo in Florence looks like it was stripped of its façade, but in fact it was never finished. Michelangelo's design remains one of the great unbuilt projects of the world, a complex, interlocking, sculptural façade of columns, pilasters, moldings, and panels. Stand before the façade with a photograph of the original wooden model and imagine the lost grandeur of the absent masterpiece.

ALEXANDER GORLIN
Architect

The space is truly inspiring! Perfectly proportioned and finely detailed. A space that soars and enlightens the viewer. Try to go there early, when it is quiet. Check with the guard to see whether access can be granted to a side door to see some sketches and line works on a plaster wall.

JOHN L. WONG
Landscape architect

Sotterraneo

1529–1530, Michelangelo

By appointment at the ticket office. Hours vary;

☏ 055 238 86 02

Each year I bring groups of artist to Italy to paint and study the Italian Renaissance. One of the visits that moves the romantics among us to tears is the little-known *sotterraneo* under the Sagrestia Nuova at San Lorenzo. Here are recently discovered wall drawings in the secret passageway where Michelangelo hid from the Medici for three days during the 1530 siege of Florence. Having sided with the Republic against the exiled Medici (another chapter in the love-hate relationship between Michelangelo and the most famous art patrons of all time) he feared the consequences of his perceived betrayal. While in hiding he took some pitch from a wall torch and, as he later wrote, "to forget my fears I fill these walls with drawings."

Standing among the drawings, sketches and doodles (yes, even doodles!) that cover the walls and ceilings of this tiny cave-like structure, one feels as if one is on tour inside Michelangelo's mind. It is "virtual Michelangelo."

To enter, you must ask for an additional ticket to the *sotterraneo* when purchasing the standard ticket to the

Medici Tombs. The ticket you receive will be a timed
admission to the passageway. Upon entering the Sagrestia
Nuova you will notice, at the far side of the room, a small,
plain-looking door with a guard standing next to it. At the
designated time present him with the second ticket and
enter this most magical of places.

FRED WESSEL
Artist and professor

The drawings were made by Michelangelo and a few others during the Spanish invasion of 1529–1530. It's wonderful to scan the walls, seeing what you can and imagining
the rest, while footsteps echo overhead.

SUSAN KLEINBERG
Artist

1.27 **Palazzo Medici-Riccardi**
*15th century, Michelozzo; major addition at the end of the
17th century*
Via Cavour, ☏ 055 276 03 40

Procession of the Magi
1459–1463, Benozzo Gozzoli; recently restored
Admission to the chapel in small groups

Years ago, before the restoration, when there was no ticket
booth, no gift shop, and no locked wrought-iron gate in
the entryway, I used to find it impossible to be on the via
Cavour, or, indeed, anywhere near the Palazzo Medici-
Riccardi, without running into the courtyard and up the
steps to spend at least a few minutes taking in Benozzo
Gozzoli's *Procession of the Magi*. There I'd be at the bus
stop, late for someone or something, but I'd decide that I
couldn't live until I remembered how many cheetahs
appeared in the procession (two—but one looks a little like
a bobcat), or refreshed my mind as to the precise nature of
the golden discs hanging from the ornamental regalia on
Cosimo de'Medici's horse.

Everyone responds to these frescoes. I've brought nine-teen-month-olds ("See the horsey? See the monkey?") and I've brought sober senior-citizen attorneys who couldn't contain themselves. There are certainly greater works of art to be seen in Florence, but I know of none more delightful. (The only one that might give it any competition at all is Luca Della Robbia's choir loft in the Museo dell'Opera del Duomo, and by all means don't miss that either.) There's an undeniable charm in such elaborate and loving detail; besides, it's always a thrill to see a landscape at the edges of a fresco that looks precisely like the place where you took a walk that very morning . . . (For a view of countryside just like Gozzoli's, follow signs to the Museo delle Porcellane in the Boboli Garden (see p. 32); there's a lovely view from the grounds right beside it.) And even a rather entrenched non-Christian like myself can get into the spirit of this over-the-top procession. Who doesn't love to bring gifts to newborn babies, even when they're nothing more than human? By the way, Gozzoli himself appears twice in these frescoes. On the east wall, he wears a red hat inscribed with gold block letters, the closest thing the chapel has to a signature: OPUS BENOTTI (a Latin pun on his name, suggesting that his work is "well-noted" or, perhaps, that the viewer should "note it well." I'm indebt-ed to Diane Cole Ahl, who notices this pun in her book *Benozzo Gozzoli*.) On the west wall, he wears a blue hat, with a white band, his fingers displayed in an odd config-uration reminiscent of a salutation out of *Star Trek*.

JACQUELINE OSHEROW
Poet

RECOMMENDED READING
Diane Cole Ahl, *Benozzo Gozzoli*, Yale University Press, 1996.

I always stop by the Medici palace to see the *Procession of the Magi* in the little chapel. It's one of my son's favorite stops in all the world, a kind of "Where's Waldo" fresco, abundant with exotic animals and birds.

DANA PRESCOTT
Artist and writer

1.28 Albergo Splendor

Via San Gallo 30, ☎ 055 48 34 27

Though I have stayed in all levels of accommodations in Florence, from student *pensioni* to elegant five star hotels, my favorite is the lovely Hotel Splendor, on via San Gallo. The breakfast room of this patrician palace makes me never want to leave, and I have often painted and sketched on the adjoining terrace, which looks out on the Piazza San Marco.

DANA PRESCOTT
Artist and writer

1.29 Opificio delle Pietre Dure

Via degli Alfani 78, ☎ 055 28 94 14

Florentine mosaics, the *pietre dure* whose traditional combination of marble and precious stones goes back to antiquity, nearly died out during the Middle Ages, at which time the craft was revived by Lorenzo the Magnificent. By the end of the 19th century, the popularity of the *pietre dure* had begun to fade again, until the late 1930s when it died out almost completely.

In 1947, Richard Allmand Blow (1904–1985) set up a workshop on his property to revive the art form. (Blow was an American painter who spent several months a year at Villa Piazza Calda, a Renaissance structure he'd bought and restored in 1927; it stood on a hilltop in Santa Margherita a Montici, across the Arno from Florence.) Because of general shortages of materials Blow came to use, and ultimately favor, the gray and ochre stone dug from the riverbed of the Arno, and it became a trademark of some of the more beautiful pictures, boxes, obelisks, and tabletops that survive. Standing on any bridge across the Arno, especially on a wintry day, one can see the same color and opacity of the stone in the water itself.

To see the stone, and the mosaics, visit the Opificio delle Pietre Dure on the via degli Alfani, which had been the Monastery of San Niccolo until 1853; it now contains many worthwhile examples, as well as the evidence that *pietre dure* is again a thriving industry in Florence. Richard Blow was a link in this chain.

ADELE CHATFIELD-TAYLOR
President of the American Academy in Rome

1.30   ## Museo Archeologico

Via della Colonna 38, ☎ 055 235 75
Hours vary

Once a dusty, rather unorganized repository of objects Greek, Roman, Etruscan, and Egyptian, Florence's Archaeology Museum is in the process of being refurbished so that its treasures can be viewed in their cultural contexts. The Greek red- and black-figured vases—the best-known being the intricate François krater—and the Etruscan funerary monuments are among my favorites. I am especially drawn to the solemn, enthroned mother-and-child cinerary urn from Chianciano (limestone, circa 400 BC). We don't know when it was discovered, but it or a similar urn surely influenced some artists when they depicted the theme of the Madonna and Child.

ANN THOMAS WILKINS
Classicist

Perhaps the only great museum in Florence where the harried tourist can enjoy peace, quiet, and unobstructed views of the art is the National Archaeological Museum. Very much off the beaten tourist track in this Renaissance-centered city, the museum is nonetheless home to major monuments that every undergraduate has seen in art history textbooks. There's the dramatic, snarling Chimera of Arezzo; the portrait statue of that worthy, weather-beaten Roman citizen Aulus Metellus, aka L'Arringatore; the François vase with its visual encyclopedia of Greek legend

in Attic black-figure painting; and the Etruscan cinerary
urn of a young man accompanied by a kindly but imposing
death-daemon. In addition to the well-known works, there
are also dozens of hidden treasures in the cases of bronze
statuettes and pottery that anyone with an interest in antiquity will be delighted to discover.

SUSAN E. WOOD
Art historian

CITY CENTER EAST

1.31 **Flood Marker**
Northwest corner of Via dei Neri and Via San Remigio

The Arno flood of November 4, 1966, was only the most
recent in a series of six inundations that date back to 1177.
For an original *trecento* marker of the flood of November 1,
1333, go to this corner and look up. A 14th-century hand
reaches up through the waves, an outstretched finger just
touching the high water mark. For another set of flood
markers, see those on the façade of Brunelleschi's Pazzi
Chapel, in the cloister at Santa Croce.
DAVID G. WILKINS AND ANN THOMAS WILKINS
Art and architectural historian and classicist, respectively

1.32 **Fondazione Horne**
Via dei Benci 6, ☎ 055 24 46 61
Closed Sundays

Between the Arno and Santa Croce is the personal collection of an expatriate in his former house which boasts
among its treasures a superb *Saint Stephen*, tentatively
attributed to Giotto.
HELEN COSTANTINO FIORATTI
Interior designer

1.33 **Santa Croce**
Piazza di Santa Croce

Santa Croce is the great Franciscan church of Florence, and
one goes there for just everything—Michelangelo's tomb;
the Bruni monument (he was buried with a copy of his
History of Florence), and Giotto's Bardi and Peruzzi
chapels, *inter alia.*
RONA GOFFEN
Art historian

RECOMMENDED READING
Rona Goffen, *Spirituality in Conflict: Saint Francis and Giotto's Bardi Chapel*, o.p.

Frescoes, Bardi Chapel
1371, Giotto

I'd hate for anyone to miss Giotto's depiction of the confirmation of the stigmata in the Bardi Chapel in Santa Croce. Of course, visitors already have innumerable reasons to visit this blockbuster church: the tombs of Michelangelo and Galileo, among other luminaries; Brunelleschi's gem of a Pazzi Chapel and his beautifully proportioned courtyard; not to mention what one of my landladies once referred to as that *poverino*: Cimabue's crucifix, irreparably damaged in the 1966 flood. I'd certainly encourage everyone to see them all—I've spent entire afternoons daydreaming in the Pazzi Chapel—but, for me, what's most affecting in the entire Santa Croce complex are the looks on the faces of Giotto's monks as they hover in attendance on their wounded saint.

JACQUELINE OSHEROW
Poet

Second Cloister
Completed in 1453, after a design by Brunelleschi, who died in 1446

I had always admired Brunelleschi's famous dome and Pazzi Chapel in Florence, but emotionally they had never done much for me, seeming mostly like feats of engineering. In Santa Croce's second cloister, I saw how this extraordinary Renaissance architect adapted his style to the Franciscan vision of life, and I began to love his work. Often missed by tourists, it is just a few steps from the Pazzi Chapel.

For me, this cloister is the perfect architectural expression of Franciscan poverty, that lack of things which generates plenitude. The second (higher) register of slender columns frames the air, creates pure squares of space, and etherealizes the square cloister below, whose form they echo.

These squares and the solid Romanesque arches with their peaceful rhythm below (in the first register), teach us somehow about Franciscan simplicity, the solidity of simplicity.

After this, one's compelled to reconsider other Brunelleschi structures. The Pazzi Chapel seems a hymn to mind, and the Romanesque arches of the Spedale degli Innocenti, one of Brunelleschi's earlier works, strike us with their rhythm, which seems both beautiful and healing. The dome, of course, is Florence's signature and an expression of her lucky, happy hubris.

JANE OLIENSIS
Cultural historian

`1.34` Dolci e Dolcezza
Piazza Cesare Beccaria 8/R

Pastries, gifts and delicious desserts; refined and a real cut above the others. Run by a young man who found himself by founding an unusual place for Italy.

HELEN COSTANTINO FIORATTI
Interior designer

The Work of Benedetto da Maiano

ITINERARY:

a Palazzo Vecchio
Piazza della
Signioria, Sala
d'Udienza

b Santa Croce
Piazza di Santa
Croce

c Bargello
Via del Proconsolo 4

Walking through the Palazzo Vecchio, I looked up and saw a beautiful doorway by Benedetto da Maiano. I searched for more of his work and found the pulpit in Santa Croce and a marble bust of Mellini at the Bargello.

BETH VAN HOESEN ADAMS
Artist and printmaker

COLLI

1.35 **A Stroll to the Piazzale Michelangelo**
Bus to Piazzale Galileo, walk the Viale Galileo, stop at San Miniato al Monte, and on to Piazzale Michelangelo

Everyone knows about the drop-dead gorgeous view of the city from the Piazzale Michelangelo, but getting there can be half the fun if you take a bus up to the Piazzale Galileo and walk from there. Stroll at a leisurely pace up the curving viale Galileo, enjoying many brief glimpses of the city. In spring, the gardens along this route are filled with Florence's trademark irises. Near your destination, pause for a visit to San Miniato al Monte, one of the finest surviving examples of Romanesque architecture in the Tuscan black-and-white style, which for my money is the most beautiful of the Romanesque regional styles in Europe. The church also boasts a stunning apse-mosaic and marble intarsia floors. When you reach the Piazzale Michelangelo, give your feet a well-earned rest and enjoy the view from a café or *gelateria*. Guilty pleasures include the kitschy but colorful souvenir stands.

SUSAN E. WOOD
Art historian

1.36 **San Miniato al Monte**
Via Monte alle Croci 34

The combination of view and architecture make this an ideal spot to begin or end a visit to Florence. High on a hill overlooking the city, the view encompasses the Arno River, flowing westward towards Pisa, as well as the outlines of the city's major monuments. The green and white marble Tuscan Romanesque façade of the church and the Renaissance Chapel of the Cardinal of Portugal inside reveal the continuing impact of classicism in Florentine architecture. Try to visit in the late afternoon, when the sun is setting.

DAVID G. WILKINS
Art and architectural historian

Chapel of the Cardinal of Portugal
Luca della Robbia, Antonio Rossellino, Alesso Baldovinetti, Antonio and Piero del Pollaiolo

It's hard to imagine a more serene burial chapel than this one, erected in the 1460s to honor a young cardinal, a prince from the royal house of Portugal, who died in Florence in 1459. The chapel is perhaps the most harmonious decorative ensemble of the 15th century, with contributions by della Robbia, Rossellino, Baldovinetti, Pollaiolo, and others. Notice how the design of the ceiling matches that of the floor, how the walls are coordinated, and how the wrought-iron gate is repeated in the painted altarpiece. Best of all, the landscapes in the paintings echo the same views we see today as we stand outside the church and look out over the meandering river and cypress trees of the local landscape.

DAVID G. WILKINS
Art and architectural historian

OUTSIDE CITY CENTER & ENVIRONS OF FLORENCE

Medici Villas

A good day outing is to see the nearby recommended villas—all within the environs of Florence. Don't forget to pack a picnic.
JOHN L. WONG
Landscape architect

One of the wonders of Florence is how accessible the countryside is. I always make at least one foray to see one of the nearby gardens. These are great locations to sketch or paint undisturbed. Easily reached by bus, too.
DANA PRESCOTT
Artist and writer

a. **Villa Medicea della Petraia,** *1576–1589, Buontalenti*
   Castello, 7 km north of Florence; closed first and last Monday of each month
b. **Villa Le Balze**
   Fiesole, 8 km northeast of Florence; ☎ 055 592 08; gardens only
c. **Villa Medici** (see also p. 55), *1458, Michelozzo*
   Fiesole, 8 km northeast of Florence; ☎ 055 239 89 94
d. **Villa Gamberaia** (see also p. 58), *1610, Zanobi Lapi and others*
   Settignano, 9 km northeast of Florence; ☎ 055 69 72 05
e. **Villa Medicea,** *1596, Buontalenti*
   Artimino, 20 km west of Florence; ☎ 055 879 20 40; Tuesdays by appointment only
f. **Villa Medicea,** (see also p. 231), *1479, Giuliano da Sangallo*
   Poggio a Caiano, 23 km northwest of Florence; ☎ 055 87 70 12; closed Tuesdays and second and third Mondays of each month.

ARCETRI

2 km south of Florence; see map p. 210

Trattoria Omero
Via Pian dei Giullari 11/R, ☏ 055 22 00 53

🍴 Real Tuscan food, no frills.
RICHARD L. FEIGEN
Art dealer

CAMPO DI MARTE AREA

3.5 km northeast of historic center

Buscioni
Via Cento Stelle 1/R, ☏ 055 60 27 65
Closed Mondays

🍴 En route to the main road to Fiesole, Buscioni, on the via
Cento Stelle, has the most marvelous warm raised doughnuts.
They are light as a feather and filled either with apricot
preserves or pastry cream; they're available in the morning,
summer and winter, and after 4:30pm in the winter. They're
so good that my steering wheel has had to be treated with
handi-wipes before I've driven even a few yards.
HELEN COSTANTINO FIORATTI
Interior designer

CARMIGNANO

25 km west of Florence; see map p. 210

Chiesa di San Michele
Visitation
1530, Jacopo Pontormo

After you've seen Pontormo's *Annunciation* in Santa
Felicita, take an afternoon and drive out to Carmignano
where in San Michele you can see his splendid *Visitation*.
🍴 After that, have a great meal at Da Delfina (via della
Chiesa, 1, ☏ 055 87 18 074) in Artimino (looking directly

at a Medici villa). This is the best Tuscan cooking I know. Carlo Cioni, the owner, is really wonderful. (Delfina is his mother's name.) Sunday lunch is a great time to do this.
KATHE DYSON
Traveler

FIESOLE
8 km northeast of Florence; see map p. 210

Villa Medici
1458, Michelozzo

A Renaissance villa of the Medici sited on the hillside overlooking the city of Florence. A magnificent example of a 15th-century villa where the landscape and architecture are as one. A series of terraces steps down the side of the hill connected by gardens, pathways, and stairs. Various views of the city of Florence and surrounding countryside are unveiled along this informal walk. The entrance is inconspicuous; it is a side door on the street side of a walled garden.
JOHN L. WONG
Landscape architect

Museo Bandini
Via Giovanni Duprè 1, ☎ 055 594 77
Closed the first Tuesday of every month

This two-room museum can be seen while visiting Fiesole and the *teatro Romano*, as it is open during the day without interruption. It shows small, gold-background, jewel-like, primarily Tuscan paintings of the 14th and 15th centuries, and also a handsome nuptial chest, called a *cassone*.
HELEN COSTANTINO FIORATTI
Interior designer

GALLUZZO
5 km southwest of Florence; see map p. 210

La Certosa del Galluzzo
1342, Niccolò Acciaioli
Colle di Montaguto, ☎055 204 92 26
Outside the village of Galluzzo; a 20-minute ride on bus #37
from Piazza Santa Maria Novella. Closed Mondays.

Frescoes
1522–1525, Jacopo Pontormo
Palazzo degli Studi

For more Pontormo *capolavori* and for a tourist-free art
experience, escape to La Certosa Monastery. It is set in a
peaceful landscape where even on the hottest day in
August you will find a fresh breeze.

La Certosa was built by Niccolò Acciaioli in 1342,
and occupied by the Carthusian monks until 1958. Now it
is occupied by a dozen or so monks of the Cistercian order,
a subgroup of the Benedectines. It can be visited for free,
although a good tip will make the trip worth your while.
A monk will be your guide.

In the picture gallery of the Palazzo degli Studi are five
Pontormo frescoes, painted in the 16th century, after he
fled to La Certosa to escape a plague in Florence.

Pontormo's five lunettes depict the stages of Christ's
Passion. The cycle was originally in the outside courtyard
and the paintings have badly weathered; much detail has
disappeared. What the frescoes do reveal is the artist's
incredible concept of abstract design. To eyes accustomed
to 20th-century art, Pontormo's abstract shapes and his
unusual combinations of color are a pure delight.

If you finish your visit at La Certosa and find yourself
in search of lunch or dinner, I suggest that you walk back
to Via Senese. A further four hundred meters south
(towards Siena) will bring you to a group of houses—the
hamlet of Bottai. The trattoria, La Bianchina (via Cassia
36, ☎055 237 46 23), is well-known for its *bistecca*

Fiorentina and *pappardelle al cinghiale* (noodles with a heavy wild boar sauce). After the meal, cross the street and take the bus back to Florence.

If your Certosa excursion is by car, you can drive back to Galluzzo for dinner. Head towards Florence, and at the first traffic light turn left onto via Volterrana. Wind your way up for about two kilometers and on the right side, just before the Pieve Giogoli, is a trattoria called Bella Ciao (via Volterrana, ✆055 74 15 02). There is no sign, and actually, it is not classified as a trattoria but as a *circolo recreativo* named after two local partisans. Bella Ciao has good wood-baked pizzas, excellent meats, and greaseless, deep-fried vegetables. But their specialty is tripe. If you are into tripe, this is the best place in all of Florence. You can eat tripe as antipasto, *primo*, main course, and I think also as dessert, while you sit outside on a large terrace overlooking the Florentine hills. Keep in mind: they are open only in the evenings, are closed Mondays and Tuesdays, and do not take credit cards.

SWIETLAN NICHOLAS KRACZYNA
Artist and printmaker

IMPRUNETA
14 km south of Florence; see map p. 210

Bar Italia
Piazza Buondelmonti 33, ✆055 201 10 46
Closed Tuesdays

The ice creams are intensely flavored; I recommend the very dark chocolate and delicious nut flavors and all the fruits, or the hot chocolate in winter. If you get sticky or need to use the bathroom, it's an unexpected dream of marble and luxury.

Impruneta has been famous for terra cotta for centuries. Try to see the Luca della Robbias in Santa Maria all'Impruneta on Piazza Buondelmonti.

HELEN COSTANTINO FIORATTI
Interior designer

MONTUGHI

3 km north of historic center

Museo Stibbert

Via Stibbert 26, off the via Vittorio Emmanuele (northwest of Piazza della Libertà); closed Thursdays

Set in an outlying area surrounded by parks, this villa is a good place to take children. You'll immediately recognize the taste of a collector of one hundred years ago—a true time warp—with the late owner's love of arms and armor and full-scale horse models, with their trappings.

HELEN COSTANTINO FIORATTI
Interior designer

SETTIGNANO

10 km northeast of Florence; see map p. 210

One fascinating spot for enjoying Florentine atmosphere is the hill where the village of Settignano lies. Take the #10 bus from the Piazza San Marco; the bus winds up narrow roads and past Tuscan gardens, depositing you finally in a silent and enchanted little square with a small church, a newsagent, and a single bar. Walk around and admire Florence from above.

Settignano is the birthplace of many marble sculptors, the most famous certainly Desiderio. His extraordinarily delicate works can still be seen in Santa Croce, Santa Maria Novella, and other Florentine sites.

For an unconventional descent, try the stone-paved stairs of the pedestrian via Vecchia di Settignano. At the bottom is Ponte a Mensola, and if you can walk another ten minutes, follow the via di Vincigliata to the fabulous Villa I Tatti. Here the art historian Bernard Berenson spent his life studying Renaissance art and gathering around him not only magnificent artworks of the past, but also the most brilliant intellectuals of his own day.

FRANCESCA DELL'ACQUA
Art historian

Villa Gamberaia
1610, Zanobi Lapi and others
Via Rossellino 72, ☎ 055 69 72 05
Closed Sundays; open weekends by appointment only

The Villa Gamberaia is well worth the visit, if only to
stroll along the cypress-lined Philosopher's Walk and enjoy
the framed view of the Florentine landscape beyond. The
giardino segreto and axial relationships of the garden and
villa deserve particular scrutiny.
D. B. MIDDLETON
Architect

The Stones of Italy

The cities of Italy are extrusions of the local geology.
Fashioned from materials readily at hand, every town has
a distinctive character and color: the pervasive salmon of
Assisi, the burnt red of Siena, the terra cotta of Bologna,
the motley, molding assemblage that is Venice. Florence is
brown, opaque and unyielding. The streets are canyons of
local *pietra forte*, an unforgiving, roughhewn stone. In this
monochromatic and fundamentally medieval environment,
the new outdoor sculpture of the Renaissance—heroic classical figures in marble and gilt bronze by Ghiberti and
Donatello—must have been dazzling, colorful, modern.

Tucked into the Vincigliata hills near Bernard Berenson's Villa I Tatti is the Luogo delle Colonne, the Renaissance stone quarry where Giorgio Vasari obtained the
monolithic columns that adorn the Uffizi. The abandoned
quarry became a favorite watering hole of Victorians who
dammed the stream, laid out paths, and constructed a
pseudo-gothic tower in the midst of the glen. Queen
Victoria favored this idyllic retreat, a cool respite from the
Florentine summer. Now, one trespasses private property to
find the crystal pool defiled by trash and stagnation.
WILLIAM E. WALLACE
Art historian

VENICE

Ponte della Libertà

CANNAREGIO

Canal Grande

SANTA CROCE

San Polo

San Marco

Bacino d. Stazione Marittima

Canale di Fusina

DORSODURO

Canale della Giudecca

GIUDECCA

ITALY

TORCELLO

BURANO

MURANO

SAN ERASMO

SAN
MICHELE

VENICE

Porto di Lido

LIDO

GIUDECCA

CASTELLO

Canale Di San Marco

SAN
GIORGIO
MAGGIORE

SAN POLO & SANTA CROCE

1.1 **Istituto Universitaria di Architettura di Venezia**
Campo dei Tolentini
⚓ Piazzale Roma

Entrance
1985, Carlo Scarpa

The career of the quixotic 20th-century Venetian architect
Carlo Scarpa can be traced in a day's tour of his native
city: the deft installations of artifacts in the Accademia
and Museo Correr; the early homage to Frank Lloyd
Wright at the Olivetti showroom on the Piazza San Marco
and the Venezuela Pavilion on the Biennale grounds; and
the liquid material renderings and dense narrative strate-
gies of the Querini-Stampalia Foundation (later deployed
on a grander scale at the Brion Family Cemetery not far
away in San Vito d'Altivole—see p. 180). A final, often
overlooked, chapter in this strange *oeuvre* is found on the
Campo dei Tolentini at the entrance to the Istituto
Universitaria di Architettura di Venezia, where Scarpa
taught for years. Completed by Sergio Los after Scarpa's
untimely death in 1978, the entrance and the garden it
shields combine to gently reveal the unsettling, often
repressed, undertow of Venice.

Facing the Campo, then, a massive concrete wall delib-
erately evokes the plinth of the neighboring church of San
Nicolò da Tolentino. The wall, however, eerily flips the
steps of San Nicolò to the vertical and mysteriously supports
a hooded canopy through an endless series of concatena-
tions—the canopy itself often cradles giggling schoolchildren
(how did they get up there?). Gliding silently on one glim-
mering muntz metal roller, the entry gate has an elegant
black steel structure with an Istrian stone plaque engraved
with Vico's phrase, *verum ipsum factum*.

Yet Venice is the home of strange truths. For passing
through the plinth to the netherworld inside, we find our-

selves walking in a canal bordered by islands that crest above the entry wall. The islands are articulated as verdant earth (grass), sky (terra cotta roofing tiles), and water (the ancient sunken aquatic portal). We do not know where we are yet we seem to be hovering, suspended, beyond terra firma. We are in Venice.
MICHAEL CADWELL
Architect

Editor's Note: Vico was an 18th-century Italian philosopher. Verum ipsum factum, *in obscure Latin, is popular with architects. Literally, it can mean either "the thing constructed is itself the truth," or "the truth itself is the thing constructed."*

1.2 ## Santa Maria Gloriosa dei Frari
Campo dei Frari
 San Tomà

It really is glorious, with some of the greatest works by Bellini, Titian, Donatello, Paolo da Venezia, and the Vivarini. Donatello's *Saint John the Baptist* was made for his fellow Florentines who maintained a chapel in the Frari. Bellini's triptych in the sacristy was endowed as the altarpiece of the woman buried in the pavement in front of the altar; her son (one of Bellini's patrons) is buried in the grandiose tomb that frames the entrance to the sacristy from the church. Their kinsman was a patron of Titian's Pesaro Altarpiece—Pesaro's tomb is on the wall next to it; and Titian's sublime *Assumption of the Virgin* on the high altar commemorates the dedication of the church. ("Santa Maria Gloriosa" means "Saint Mary assumed into heaven.") Titian himself is believed to have been buried here, and a rather undistinguished neoclassical monument marks the spot; and opposite is the tomb of the heart of the great sculptor Canova (other body parts are in the Accademia and in Possagno, the sculptor's birthplace: a man of parts).

VENICE

SAN POLO AND SANTA CROCE

1 Istituto Universitaria di Architettura di Venezia

2 Santa Maria Gloriosa dei Frari

3 Scuola Grande di San Rocco

4 Scuola Grande di San Giovanni Evangelista

5 San Zan Degolà

6 Campiello del Pistor

7 Osteria Da Fiore

8 Mascari

9 Alla Madonna

While you're at the Frari, you can easily visit the Scuola Grande di San Rocco and its church, which are literally next door. The Scuola is decorated top to bottom with some of Tintoretto's greatest works.

RONA GOFFEN
Art historian

RECOMMENDED READING
Rona Goffen, *Piety and Patronage in Renaissance Venice: Bellini, Titian, and the Franciscans*, o.p.
Rona Goffen, *Giovanni Bellini*, Yale University Press, 1989.

No matter how often I go, the progress through the architecture to the Titian is always a remarkable journey.

SUSAN KLEINBERG
Artist

1.3 Scuola Grande di San Rocco
Campo di San Rocco
 San Tomà

Paintings
1564–1587, Tintoretto

In Italy there are several storehouses of greatness: buildings which house the most intense production of the works of great masters: these include the Arena Chapel in Padua (Giotto), San Marco in Florence (Fra Angelico), the Sistine Chapel in Rome (Michelangelo), and the Scuola San Rocco in Venice (the treasures of Tintoretto).

   Begun around 1517 to honor San Rocco, the saint who ministered to Plague victims, the building contains many of the most outstanding works of the painter Jacopo Robusti, known to us as Tintoretto. In 1564, the Confraternity held a competition to decide which artist would be chosen to make the first important painting in the building. Tintoretto, breaking the rules which called for the artists to submit drawings, instead made a painting, installed it, and gave it to the Confraternity. He was then chosen to make all the paintings for the building. Accepting this responsibility gave him the impetus to make his greatest works, and the Scuola contains more than a hundred—some decorative, some mythological, others of the most devout religious passion—but all meant to inform and entice the viewer. In sum, it is one of my favorite places on this earth.

Jean-Paul Sartre's essay entitled "The Prisoner of Venice" has caused me to love Tintoretto even more. It's collected in *Situations I*, a book of his essays.

JACK BEAL
Painter

RECOMMENDED READING
Jean-Paul Sartre, "The Prisoner of Venice" in *Situations I*, Schoenhofs Foreign Books, 1989.

Annunciations

ITINERARY:

a Scuola Grande di
San Rocco (see p. 68)
Campo di San Rocco
⚓ San Tomà

b San Salvatore
Campo San Salvatore
⚓ Rialto

If Last Suppers are among the special treasures of Florence, the Annunciation is a subject inventively addressed by Venetian artists. Particularly wonderful are those by Titian and Tintoretto in the Scuola di San Rocco, but most startling of all is the explosive apparition that adorns a dark side altar in the church of San Salvatore. Thanks to Titian, the mystery of revelation is made visible. And should you ever find your way to the Cathedral San Pietro in the northern city of Treviso, you will be rewarded by one of Titian's earliest and strangest variants on the theme.

WILLIAM E. WALLACE
Art historian

1.4   Scuola Grande di San Giovanni Evangelista

Campiello della Scuola 2454

⚓ San Tomà

Even if you don't go in, the entranceway is worth the visit—my favorite eagle, in honor of Saint John.

RONA GOFFEN
Art Historian

1.5   San Zan Degolà

ca. 10th century

Campo San Zan Degolà

⚓ Riva di Biasio

Frescoes

ca. early 13th century

Outside of Torcello, there are few places in Venice where one can still see the splendid work of medieval fresco artists. Most Venetian churches were long ago assaulted by the Renaissance or baroque movements and now stand dressed up in their finery. To get a glimpse of the medieval Venetian past in an atmosphere of peace and solitude, head straight for the church of San Zan Degolà (Saint John the Baptist Beheaded). The church itself probably dates back to the tenth century and was beautifully decorated with frescoes in the early 13th century. After that, however, it fell on a long history of hard times, and the parish itself was closed in 1810. In 1983, a project to uncover and restore the medieval frescoes began. It was only in 1994 that the doors were finally opened to the public. This serene structure still breathes the austerity and religious devotion of the medieval parish church. Best of all, no one goes there. You will likely have this jewel to yourself, and you'll be free to think, pray, or admire the frescoes at your leisure. Next, walk out into the open campo, at all times devoid of tourists, where you can drink in the peace and simple charm that is fast becoming extinct in modern Venice.

THOMAS F. MADDEN
Historian

Recently restored, including an original fresco of the period. Nearby, Campo San Giacomo Dall'Orio is one of the most "Venetian" playing grounds for children and a place where the elderly gather as well . . . my Venetian home.

GIANFRANCO MOSSETTO
Merchant banker

Santa Croce Walk

ITINERARY:

a San Zan Degolà
Campo San Zan
Degolà
⚓ Riva di Biasio

b San Giacomo
dell'Orio
Campo San Giacomo
dell'Orio
⚓ Riva di Biasio

c Campo Sant'Agostin
⚓ San Stae

d Campo San Stin
⚓ San Tomà

e Santa Maria Gloriosa
dei Frari (the Frari)
Campo dei Frari
⚓ San Tomà

The walk from San Zan Degolà to San Giacomo dell'Orio (a beautiful church and campo) to Campo Sant'Agostin to San Stin to the Frari: this takes you past the houses of the great Venetian diarist Marino Sanudo, the greatest-ever printer Aldus Manutius (see also p. 72), and a very beautiful relief attached to a building as you approach Campo Sant'Agostin.

RONA GOFFEN
Art historian

1.6   **Campiello del Pistor**
Beginning at Campo Sant'Agostin
 San Tomà

Right-angle intersections are rare in Venice. An approximate example is where the canals of Sant'Agostin, San Stin and San Polo meet. Three of the corners are brick walls, flush on the water, but the fourth is an open *campiello*, a little courtyard. Called Campiello del Pistor (*pistor* is an old Venetian term, via Latin, meaning a bread baker or *fornaio*), this small courtyard offers an intimate sense of how truly this city is a cluster of islands, separated and connected by canals. The only foot access is from Campo Sant'Agostin: Calle del Pistor starts where Calle de la Chiesa and Rio Terrà Secondo meet, then it turns right after a few meters, leading to Corte del Pistor. Here, on the left, the narrow, dark Sottoportego del Pistor—a covered passageway—continues the Calle until it dead-ends in the Campiello. Directly across is Palazzo Donà delle Rose (16th-century, restored early 1800s), today an elementary school. The large palazzo diagonally to the right belonged to the Almateo d'Oderzo family, now extinct, which boasted poets, literary figures, and a famous medical doctor. To the left can be seen a bit of the pink Palazzo Corner Mocenigo's main façade (designed by Michele Sanmicheli and completed in 1564, five years after his death), today the Guardia di Finanza, also visible from Campo San Polo. Just beyond is the cone-shaped top of the Church of San Polo's bell tower.

Of historical interest: a stone plaque on the Gothic palazzo, Rio Terrà Secondo 2311, recalls the printing press of Aldo Manuzio, and around the corner, Ramo Astora 2313, is the site of the home of Daniele Manin, Venice's great leader of the 1848 uprising against the Austrians.

SALLY SPECTOR
Artist

1.7   Osteria Da Fiore
Calle dello Scaleter 2202/a, ☎ 041 72 13 08
Closed Sundays and Mondays
⚓ San Silvestro, San Stae

🍴 The place to go for Venice's most exquisite seafood. In Patricia Wells's list of the world's ten best restaurants that

appeared in the *International Herald Tribune*, Da Fiore placed fifth. Try lunch if you can't get a table for dinner.
MARCELLA HAZAN
Cookbook author and educator

1.8   Mascari

Ruga dei Spezieri 381, Rialto Market, ☏ 041 522 97 62
⚓ Rialto, San Silvestro

🎁 Finest quality dried porcini; true pine nuts; whole candied citron; saffron; dried *lamon* beans, the best for making *pasta e fagioli*. Mascari also carries a fine variety of condiments produced with white truffles. If you are going in the fall, you must take home at least one jar of *mostarda veneta* by Lazzari. This quince mustard is a great specialty from Vicenza. Use it on meats, but most sublimely, mix it with mascarpone.
MARCELLA HAZAN
Cookbook author and educator

Bacari

The sole aspect of authentically Venetian life that has yet to be altered by tourism is snacking at a *bacaro*. A *bacaro* is a small, cheery, crowded food-and-wine bar where, although tables are available, habitués usually stand by the counter and consume liberal amounts of young, good wine by the glass while maintaining sobriety with a variety of succulent, freshly-made tidbits known as *cicheti* (chee-keyh´-tee), the Venetian version of *tapas*. These may include *baccalà* whipped to a creamy consistency with olive oil and milk; *folpeti*, tender braised baby octopus; sardines in *saor*; baked eggplant; artichoke bottoms; risotto with cuttlefish ink; *soppressa*—the indigenous soft Venetian salami; thick, hand-sliced prosciutto; *musetto*—the Venetian version of *cotechino*, an incredibly tender cooked salami; *polpette*, little meatballs; spiced sliced tongue; *nervetti*—boiled, tenderly chewy bits of calf's feet served with olive oil, parsley, and sliced raw onion; and *tramezzini*, the Venetian sandwich which encloses between small triangles of soft bread an infinite variety of stuffings, often laced with mayonnaise. Not every *bacaro* has all of these choices; the assortment varies from place to place and each has some specialty it does better than anyone else. The visitor endowed with gastronomic curiosity and an unbiased palate will nowhere in Italy spend a more savory and convivial hour or two than in a Venetian *bacaro*. Most *bacari* open early in the morning, close for three hours or so in the afternoon, and reopen for what is usually a short evening, some closing as early as 8:30pm. There are exceptions, however. There are a dozen or more *bacari* in every neighborhood. Our current favorites are:

Osteria da Alberto

Calle larga Giacinto Gallina, Castello 5401, ☎ 041 523 81 53
Open 9am–2:30pm, 5:30pm–9pm; closed Sundays
⚓ Rialto

🍴 Alberto sold his immensely popular *osteria* in 1977, but Marco and Andrea, his successors, have started off on the right foot. Good variety of simple wines by the glass.

Antico Dolo

Ruga Rialto, near Rialto Market, San Polo 778,
☎ 041 522 65 46
Closed Sundays
⚓ Rialto

🍴 One of the oldest and most atmosphere-laden *bacari*. Stays open until 11pm or later, depending on business, and serves good hot food at table.

Do Mori
Calle dei do Mori, near Rialto Market, San Polo 429,
📞 041 522 54 01
Closed after 8:30pm, Wednesday afternoons, and Sundays
⚓ Rialto

🍴 It is Venice's most celebrated *bacaro*, famous for its
ambience, an admirable selection of superb red wines
available by the glass, and exquisite little toasted sandwiches stuffed with truffles or goose breast or topped with
musetto. It too has recently changed hands and we have yet
to try it under its new management. Stand-up service only.
MARCELLA HAZAN
Cookbook author and educator

1.9 Alla Madonna
Calle della Madonna 594, Rialto Market, 📞 041 522 38 24
Closed Wednesdays
⚓ Rialto, San Silvestro

🍴 A large, lively, busy place, popular for decades for its reli-
able cooking and affable but rather brisk service. We prefer
more intimate surroundings and a kitchen that is geared to
a small production, but the restaurant can nonetheless be
recommended for consistently good fish.
MARCELLA HAZAN
Cookbook author and educator

CANNAREGIO

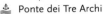 2.1 San Giobbe
Campo San Giobbe
⚓ Ponte dei Tre Archi

San Giobbe is well worth a visit, especially for its beautiful
decorative reliefs by the Lombardo in the chancel; the
Della Robbia-style chapel in the left aisle (a Florentine
interloper in a very Venetian church); and the Savoldo in
the sacristy.
RONA GOFFEN
Art historian

2.2 Sant'Alvise
Campo di Sant'Alvise
⚓ Sant'Alvise

Among the plethora of things that pack this picturesque,
medieval church, there are three spectacularly great
Tiepolos—the *Way to Calvary, Christ Crowned with
Thorns*, the *Flagellation*—that look ahead to Delacroix.
The church is not open on a regular basis, so you should
check hours before you trek out to it.
KEITH CHRISTIANSEN
Curator

Food Shopping

🏛 Food shops are open from 9am to 1pm, and 5pm to 7:30pm;
on Wednesdays they open only in the morning; on Sundays
they are closed all day. Other shops stay open from 9am to
12:30pm, and 3:30pm to 7pm, and those that cater to the
tourist trade even stay open on Sunday.
MARCELLA HAZAN
Cookbook author and educator

The Venice Ghetto

An absolute must is to walk very long and very far and get as lost (and as removed from the crowded strip between San Marco and the Rialto) as is humanly possible. This strategy is likely to bring you, sooner or later, to the ghetto, where a tour of the synagogues—a must for any Jew—is an interesting experience for anyone; there's nothing quite like them anywhere in the world. On my last visit, I eavesdropped on a priest from Vicenza who was taking his parishioners on a tour; in the museum, he made a special point of showing them my own two favorite items: two remarkable embroidered ark curtains, one representing the gift of manna in the desert and the other depicting the Waters of Salvation [Isaiah 12.2–3] engulfing Jerusalem, making it look remarkably like Venice.

JACQUELINE OSHEROW
Poet

2.3   ## Madonna dell'Orto
15th century
Campo Madonna dell'Orto
⚓ Madonna dell'Orto

Saint John the Baptist and Four Saints
ca. 1493, Cima da Conegliano

Adoration of the Golden Calf and The Last Judgment
1562–1564, Tintoretto

Venice is an endless discovery, and there is scarcely a church that does not give pleasure for either its site, architecture, paintings, or the effect of accumulation. The walk to Madonna dell'Orto, occasionally referred to as Santa Maria dell'Orto, will introduce you to an altogether quieter Venice than the area around San Marco. It takes you through the ghetto to a workers' quarter that was the parish of Tintoretto, whose father was a dyer. The large,

Sant' Alvise

Rio d. Riformati

F. d. Riformati

Rio d. S. Alvise

Campo S. Alvise

F. d. Coletti

F. d. Sensa

Rio d. Sensa

Canale d. Cannaregio

Ponte d. Tre Archi

F. d. Cappuccine

Rio d. Girolamo

F. d. Oremesini

Campo S. Giobbe

F. S. Giobbe

Corte d. Vedei

Campo Ghetto Nuovo

C. d. Pistor

Rio d. S. Giobbe

F. Savorgnan

C. d. Forno

Ghetto Vecchio

Rio d. S. Marcuola

Rio d. Crea

Rio d. Crea

C. Riolo

Rio Terà S. Leonardo

Campo Geremia

Campo S. Marcuola

S. Marcuola

C. Misericordia

C. Cavaletti

Lista d. Spagna

Canal Grande

Riva d. Biasio

Riva Biasio

Rio Mago

Rio Cà Tron

Stazione S. Lucia

Rio S. Zan Degola

Campo S. Giacomo da l'Orio

Ferrovia

Rio Marin

Campo N.Sauro

P.le Roma

F. S. Simeon Piccolo

C. d. Scaleter

C. d. Cristo

Campo S. Agostin

Parco Publico Papadopoli

CANNAREGIO

1 San Giobbe
2 Sant'Alvise
3 Madonna dell'Orto
4 Scuola Nuova Della Misericordia
5 Gesuiti
🎁 6 Tuttocasa

🍴 7 Fiaschetteria Toscana
8 San Giovanni Crisostomo
🎁 9 Pastificio Giacomo Rizzo
🍴 10 La Colonna
11 Santa Maria dei Miracoli

airy church is 15th-century Gothic with a fine, flamboyant entrance door. Immediately to the right, upon entering, is a hauntingly beautiful altarpiece by Cima da Conegliano of Saint John the Baptist. It's in its original frame. Tintoretto is buried in the apse, which is in all respects a monument to his ambitions and achievement. The lateral walls are filled with two spectacular and enormous canvases— Tintoretto's response to Michelangelo's *Last Judgment* in the Sistine Chapel. One shows the *Adoration of the Golden Calf*, the other his own vision of *The Last Judgment*. The first contrasts an aristocratic picnic in the lower half to a vertiginously placed Moses receiving the tablets of the Ten Commandments from a God the Father who seems, literally, to swim through the heavens accompanied by wingless angels. *The Last Judgment* is an over-the-top and spellbinding cataclysm. This is pictorial rhetoric at its most hypnotic. You will either be swept up in the movement (correct response) or turn away disappointed at the lack of interest in individual psychology (wrong response). The spandrels of the apse are filled with images of Temperance, Justice, Prudence, and Strength, and there are two other large canvases, the *Vision of Saint Peter of the Cross* and the *Martyrdom of Saint Paul*—also Tintoretto. Over the door to the sacristy is another beautiful large canvas by Tintoretto of the Presentation of the Virgin in the Temple that scintillates in the afternoon light, and in the aisle on the opposite side of the church is an altarpiece showing Saint Agnes resuscitating a youth. Another altar used to have a lovely painting of the Madonna and Child by Bellini. It was stolen a few years back and as of this time has not been retrieved.

KEITH CHRISTIANSEN
Curator

2.4   Scuola Nuova Della Misericordia
Begun ca. 1532, Jacopo Sansovino
Fondamenta della Misericordia 3599
⚓ Ca d'Oro, Foundamente Nuove, Madonna dell'Orto

The largest hall of an existing fraternity *scuola*, built
according to a Sansovino design but never completed.
Formerly used as a basketball court, notwithstanding its
16th-century frescoes.
GIANFRANCO MOSSETTO
Merchant banker

2.5   Gesuiti
Campo dei Gesuiti
⚓ Fondamenta Nuove

The tiled floor rolls as if the sea itself shaped it. It's quiet,
ancient, private and idiosyncratic.
SUSAN KLEINBERG
Artist

Vaporetto Ride

My favorite thing to do in Venice—aside, perhaps from
going to see the Carpaccios in the Scuola di San Giorgio
degli Schiavoni—is to go to Piazzale Roma and get a seat
outside in the front of the slower-than-slow number one
vaporetto, which makes every stop on the Grand Canal.
This ride is a pleasure at any time of day, though it's perhaps especially lovely at dusk.
JACQUELINE OSHEROW
Poet

*Editor's Note: The Linea #1 is scheduled to run all day
about every ten minutes and the trip takes approximately
forty minutes to the San Marco stop, or an hour all the
way to the Lido.*

2.6   Tuttocasa

Campo dietro la Santi Apostoli 4518, ☎ 041 523 85 85

 Ca d'Oro

 A very well-stocked neighborhood kitchen and housewares shop near the Strada Nuova thoroughfare. A good place to go for two of those items indispensable to Marcella's kitchen: *retine*, wire net flame spreaders for gas burners, and peelers. They have a nice assortment of handsomely designed Italian lucite and brightly colored plastic ware.

MARCELLA HAZAN
Cookbook author and educator

2.7   Fiaschetteria Toscana

San Giovanni Crisostomo 5719   ☎ 041 528 52 81

Closed Mondays for lunch and Tuesdays

 Rialto

 Despite the name, it has been an authentically Venetian restaurant for decades, with a varied menu that includes some meat but specializes in fish. Their signature dish is *Fritto della Serenissima*, a perfectly fried mixture of seafood and vegetables. If you like white truffles, ask for their *tagliolini coi tartufi*. Excellent wine list. Try for Roberto or Claudio as your waiter, and leave room for one of Mariuccia's own desserts.

MARCELLA HAZAN
Cookbook author and educator

2.8   San Giovanni Crisostomo

1497-1504, Mauro Coducci

Campo San Giovanni Crisostomo

 Rialto

A beautiful building by Mauro Coducci, his last work, with one of Bellini's last works, the *Saints Jerome, Christopher and Louis of Toulouse*, dated 1513. Opposite this, a relief altarpiece by Tullio Lombardo of the *Coronation*

of the Virgin, neoclassical in style *avant la lettre*. On the high altar, a great early work by Sebastiano Veneziano (before he got his papal title *del Piombo*), representing the titular saint with three lovely female saints.

RONA GOFFEN
Art historian

Cannaregio to San Marco

When I found myself crossing Rio San Giovanni Crisostomo in the Cannaregio section of Venice, I knew I had crossed the bridge from west to east. Saint John Chrysostom, whose liturgy continues to be used in Eastern Christian churches today, was once Patriarch of Constantinople. And no sooner had I entered Saint Mark's Basilica than I felt transported to Byzantium. At Saint Mark's one is completely and warmly enveloped in icon-like mosaics, all depicting the great stories and saints from the Old and New Testaments on glistening gold backgrounds.

MARY ANN HAICK DINAPOLI
Genealogist

2.9 **Pastificio Giacomo Rizzo**

San Giovanni Crisostomo 5778, ☎ 041 522 28 24

🚢 Rialto

🎁 Balsamic vinegar; white truffle paste; olive oil (ask to see the Lake Garda oil from the Riviera Bresciana). All their best products are on display in the window, with their respective prices, so you can browse and decide what to ask before going in. Rizzo is near Venice's only department store, COIN.

MARCELLA HAZAN
Cookbook author and educator

Nocturnal Circumnavigation
Board #1 boat at San Marcuola to San Zaccaria
Board #82 for return to San Marcuola
Last run at 11pm in summer

I take my favorite guests for an enchanting night-time boat ride down the Grand Canal on the *vaporetto*, the public water bus. Armed with luscious *gelati* from Il Gelatone (Rio Terrà della Maddalena, Cannaregio 2063, ✆39 04 172 06 31—near the Casinò on Strada Nova), we board the number one boat at San Marcuola and try to score a seat out front, where there's nothing between us and the dark water. We cruise past magical palaces and under the Rialto and Accademia bridges to magnificent Saint Mark's. Disembarking at San Zaccaria, we cross the nearby bridge for the landing stage for line number 82 (the one via San Giorgio, not Rialto.) This transports us via the broad Giudecca Canal and then the vast silent port precincts, eventually looping back to the railway station and San Marcuola.

GILLIAN PRICE
Writer of hiking guides

Editor's Note: The vaporetti *of Venice have their own beautifully detailed, intelligently designed, and easy-to-use Internet site: www.actv.it The ACTV stands for* Azienda Consorzio Trasporti Veneziano.

2.10 ### La Colonna
Fondamenta Nuove 5329, near Calle del Fumo
✆ 041 522 96 41
Closed Sunday evenings and Mondays
⚓ Fondamenta Nuove

🍴 When Bruno Paolato was a partner chef in Ai Mercanti (San Polo 1588, ✆041 524 22 82), that establishment was one of our favorite hangouts. Bruno fell out with his partners and ensconced himself in this small, charming trattoria.

It has tables for outdoor dining in clement weather and it is happily off the tracks that tourists usually beat. Do ask for Bruno.

MARCELLA HAZAN
Cookbook author and educator

2.11   Santa Maria dei Miracoli

ca. 1481-1489, Pietro Lombardo with his sons, Tullio and Antonio
Campo dei Miracoli
 Rialto

Perhaps the most beautiful little church in Venice, if not in all Italy, this is a favorite church of Venetian brides. From 1988–1998, Save Venice restored the entire church and everything in it. To my knowledge, it is the only Italian church in such pristine condition.

BEATRICE H. GUTHRIE
Former director of Save Venice, Inc.

CASTELLO

3.1 **Colonna**
Calle della Fava 5595, ☎041 528 51 37
⚓ Rialto

🎁 A wine shop with a very fine assortment of grappas. Also
carries one or two good olive oils.
MARCELLA HAZAN
Cookbook author and educator

3.2 **Didovich**
Campo Santa Marina 5987/a, ☎041 523 91 81
Closed Sundays
⚓ Rialto

🍴 If you are on the way to visit the great church of Santi
Giovanni e Paolo and its monumental campo with the
celebrated equestrian statue of Bartolomeo Colleoni, stop
at Didovich in Campo Santa Marina. They also make
Venice's tastiest *salatini*, little vegetable tarts.
MARCELLA HAZAN
Cookbook author and educator

3.3 **Scuola Grande di San Marco**
Campo Santi Giovanni e Paolo
⚓ Ospedale Civile

Façade
*1487-1490, Pietro Lombardo and sons and Giovanni Buori
Completed 1495 by Mauro Coducci*

A piazza with a most unusual architectural façade in perspective reliefs. Located next to the side canal, the building
façade was designed to relate to the viewer approaching
the space. Each elevation and section is revealed as one
moves forward and turns the corner.
JOHN L. WONG
Landscape architect

3.4   Monument to Bartolomeo Colleoni
1481-1488, Andrea del Verrocchio
Campo di Santi Giovanni e Paolo
⚓ Fondamente Nuove, Ospedale Civile

One of the greatest equestrian monuments stands in the
Campo di Santi Giovanni e Paolo: Verrocchio's *Colleoni*.
A *condottiere* who had served the Venetian Republic,
Colleoni provided funds in his will for the monument to
be made and erected in the Piazza di San Marco, the ducal
basilica. (There is only one piazza in Venice; every other
square is a campo.) Such a site was of course unthinkable
for the Venetians, who willfully misinterpreted the testa-
mentary bequest to refer to the campo in front of the
Scuola or Confraternity of Saint Mark—that is, the Campo
di Santi Giovanni e Paolo. (The *scuola* is now the Civic
Hospital, and you don't want to go there.)

Because Colleoni's name sounds like the Italian word
coglioni—cullions or testicles—he used them as an emblem;
this kind of crude punning is typical of Renaissance humor.
(I think it's funny, too.) The *coglioni* are represented
throughout the statue and its base, looking like plump
quotation marks.

RONA GOFFEN
Art historian

RECOMMENDED READING
Andrew Butterfield, *The Sculptures of Andrea del Verrocchio*, Yale
University Press, 1997.

3.5   Santi Giovanni e Paolo (San Zanipolo)
Campo Santi Giovanni e Paolo
⚓ Fondamente Nuove, Ospedale Civile

Not the easiest place to find in the labyrinthine alleys of
Venezia, the Church of Santi Giovanni e Paolo is on the
western border of the Castello district, away from the well-
worn paths around the Piazza San Marco and the Rialto

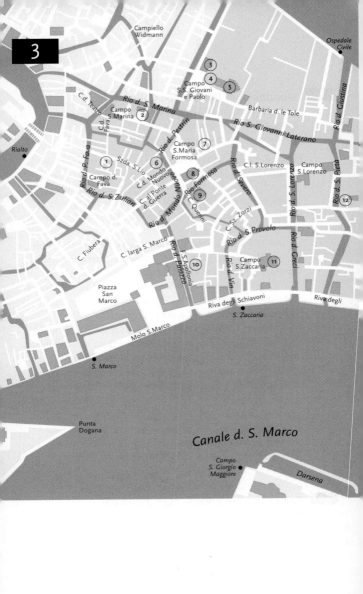

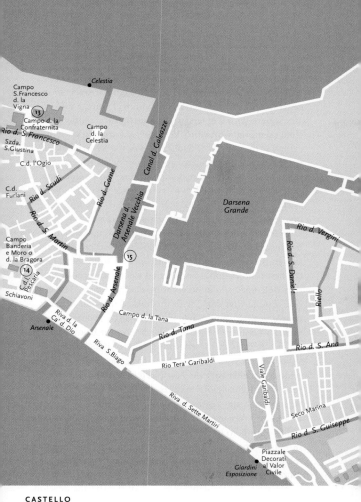

CASTELLO

🏛 1   Colonna

🍴 2   Didovich

3   Scuola Grande di San Marco

4   Monument to Bartolomeo Colleoni

5   Santi Giovanni e Paolo
     (San Zanipolo)

🍴 6   Alle Testiere

🍴 7   Al Mascaron

8   Santa Maria Formosa

9   Fondazione Querini Stampalia

10   Sant'Apollonia

11   San Zaccaria

12   Scuola di San Giorgio degli
     Schiavoni

13   San Francesco della Vigna

🍴 14   Ristorante Al Covo

15   Arsenale

Bridge. Beyond the lovely square of the Campo Santa Maria Formosa, wend your way through narrow *calli* in a generally northern direction and you will emerge into an airy square with a magisterial equestrian statue, the Colleoni memorial of Andrea Verrocchio. Looming over the campo is the church of San Zanipolo, the Venetian name for the sanctuary dedicated to two minor fourth-century saints. The church is a magnificent Venetian Gothic structure where, as opposed to so many other sites, no admission is charged and where seventy tourists aren't jostling one another to glimpse a rare Titian altarpiece.

Great Gothic churches are designed to make man feel insignificant and reverential in the presence of divine power. As large as San Zanipolo appears from the exterior, the first-time visitor is unprepared for the cavernous space that welcomes you upon entering the front door. The interior is somewhat dark, with the hushed murmur of a few people milling about while monks float by in their cassocks, a reminder of the church's important Dominican traditions. Besides the overwhelming size of the church, why should a visitor to Venezia spend the time to seek out this remote place? It isn't the best place to see paintings by renowned Renaissance masters—Bellini, Titian, and Tintoretto are better represented elsewhere. Nor is it the place to admire a Veronese or Tiepolo ceiling fresco. No, come to San Zanipolo to see the finest survey of Venetian sculpture, from the austerity of the Gothic to the exuberance of the baroque. The vast interior of San Zanipolo is the greatest repository of ducal funerary monuments in Venice. The tombs provide a valuable overview of the stylistic development of Venetian art. More importantly, they provide an unparalleled insight into the power and personalities of the Doges themselves, far more so than the sterile reception rooms of the Palazzo Ducale. Come to see the monuments, come to contemplate the lives of the powerful rulers of the Republic, come to experience the wavy, buckled mosaic

pavement, but do not come in shorts or a tank top, or one
of those apparently serene and imperturbable monks will
promptly and unceremoniously escort you to the door.
EMILIE K. JOHNSON
Curatorial Assistant

*Editor's Note: The suggestion to plan your wardrobe
accordingly doesn't apply only to San Zanipolo; Venice in
general is stricter about it than most other places in Italy.
San Marco is notorious for it, and women have occasionally been asked to cover their heads.*

I particularly like Lotto's *Saint Antoninus* and the great
ducal tombs by the Lombardo and others. Outside, at the
east end of the church (in back of the apse) is the site of
the Bellini family graves; Gentile and Giovanni were
buried there.
RONA GOFFEN
Art historian

Capella del Rosario
Ceiling paintings by Veronese

Long ago, I discovered a Veronese ceiling in the side chapel
(to the left, coming from the back entrance) and became
fascinated with its complexity and lack of predictability.
Gazing up, there is a sense of what it means to separate
from the terrestrial.
SUSAN KLEINBERG
Artist

Tomb of Alvise Diedo
Pietro Lombardo

In San Zanipolo, don't miss the magnificent floor tomb just
outside the Chapel of the Madonna della Pace. Carved by
Pietro Lombardo, this tomb is a late 15th-century example
of *niello* decoration, a sumptuous technique that involves
filling in the incised lines of the marble with *nigellum*, a

mixture of copper, sulfur, lead, and silver. The amount of
luxurious detail, contrasting the dark inlaid lines with the
radiant Istrian marble, is a measure of the astounding skill
and sensibilities of Renaissance Venetian artists. Only with
difficulty can we reconstruct the original stunning appearance of the slab before it was worn smooth by the innumerable footsteps of generations. Lorenzetti, the standard
authority on Venetian buildings and their contents, writes
of this small monument using the word *elegantissima*, and
describes the memorial as *squisita arte quattrocentesca*—
exquisite 15th-century art. English offers nothing more
precise to capture it.

EMILIE K. JOHNSON
Curatorial assistant

*Editor's Note: Alvise Diedo was a Venetian naval comman-
der in the 15th-century wars at Constantinople. Nigellum
is the Latin word for, literally, "little black stuff."*

RECOMMENDED READING
Giulio Lorenzetti, *Venice and Its Lagoon*, Istituto Poligrafico dello
Stato, Roma, 1961.

3.6   Alle Testiere

Calle del Mondo Nuovo 5801, ☎ 041 522 72 20
Closed Sundays

⚓ Rialto

🍽 You can get some of the tastiest cooking in Venice at this
miniature, twenty-seat restaurant. Bruno, the owner-chef,
trained at the legendary Corte Sconta (Calle del Pestrin
3886, ☎ 522 70 24) in the bygone days when it was
Venice's most glorious trattoria. Contact Luca, the partner
who attends to the dining room.

MARCELLA HAZAN
Cookbook author and educator

Two Ways to Pretend To Be Venetian

An expensive way: Take a room on the Grand Canal near a *vaporetto* stop and stand on the balcony. People passing in the water traffic will wave at you and act thrilled when you wave back.

A cheap way: Buy a toy cellular telephone that looks like a Nokia or a Startac and says, "*Pronto, chi parla?*" when you push a button. Talk to it while standing in a *traghetto* being ferried across the Grand Canal.

JUDITH MARTIN
Journalist

3.7 ## Al Mascaron

Calle Lunga Santa Maria Formosa 5225,   ☎ 041 522 59 95
Closed Sundays

 Rialto, San Zaccaria

🍴 Offers some of the best food served by a casual trattoria in Venice. Excellent wines. Very popular, very busy, long waits are common.

MARCELLA HAZAN
Cookbook author and educator

3.8 ## Santa Maria Formosa

Campo Santa Maria Formosa

 Rialto, San Zaccaria

Saint Barbara Altarpiece
Early 16th century, Palma Vecchio

Madonna della Misericordia
1473, Bartolomeo Vivarini

Another of these two-main-entrance churches is Santa Maria Formosa, literally, "Shapely Virgin Mary," built, according to legend, by a monk inspired by a dream of the Madonna. (You find this kind of delicious information in

Tassini's *Curiosità Veneziane*.) The Formosa has one of
Palma Vecchio's most beautiful works, the Saint Barbara
altarpiece, and one of Bartolomeo Vivarini's best, a triptych of the *Madonna della Misericordia*.

RONA GOFFEN
Art historian

RECOMMENDED READING
Giuseppe Tassini, *Curiosità Veneziane*, 8th edition reprinted by
Filippi, 1970. Originally published in 1863.

3.9 Fondazione Querini Stampalia

Calle Querini 4778
Open until midnight
San Zaccaria

Ground floor

1959-1963, Carlo Scarpa

In the fall and winter seasons, a delightfully warming experience is to visit La Biblioteca Querini Stampalia, open
until midnight, according to the stipulation of Conte
Giovanni Querini Stampalia, who made the city a gift
of his ancestral palazzo and library in 1869. A modern
Venetian architect, Carlo Scarpa, designed elements of a
purely Venetian palazzo including a private bridge, a water
entry and a garden, in a modern idiom of exquisite and
understated beauty.

MARGARET SPENCER MATZ
Architect

3.10 Sant'Apollonia

Fondamenta Sant'Apollonia 4312

 San Zaccaria

Cloister

12th century

It's late in the morning and you're heading for the Piazza
San Marco. You've survived the natives vying for *scampi*
at the Rialto markets, outmaneuvered the crowds buying
Murano glass on the Rialto Bridge, and sidestepped the
throngs milling around the McDonald's in the Campo San
Bartolomeo. You've negotiated the claustrophobic ravine of
the Merceria, stuttering along nose-to-tail in this seething
shopping artery connecting the Rialto to the Piazza. You
enter the great square under the arch of the Clock Tower
only to face a sea of humanity more intimidating than any
acqua alta—tides of polyglot tour groups flood the Piazza,
the Piazzetta, and the Riva beyond. *Magari!* The arcades
are inundated with shoppers clutching Gucci shoes, Fendi
handbags and Hermès scarves. Lines of tourists snake out
from the Basilica, the Palazzo Ducale and the Campanile.
Instigated by miscreants feeding them corn, the infamous
pigeons of San Marco are rehearsing a nightmarish scene
from a Hitchcock film. The world closes in on you and
you start to feel faint. It's too early for alcohol, and you
remember that you don't smoke. *Ma che!*

A sanctuary is not far off. Quell your panic and set
off through the Piazzetta dei Leoncini (the little square of
the lions) adjacent to San Marco. Walk around behind
the Basilica, carefully avoiding the first bridge encountered,
which, in a marketing stroke of genius, dead-ends at a
glass factory sales outlet. Turn right, then left across
a small bridge, and right again onto the Rughetta
Sant'Apollonia to a sign marked Museo Diocesano. Go
through the portal, but not to the museum, a second-storey
clutter of mundane bits salvaged from deconsecrated
churches. Your destination is the lovely cloister of

Sant'Apollonia that houses the museum's entrance. The
12th-century structure is the sole remaining example of a
Romanesque cloister in Venice, a tranquil oasis at Venetian
ground zero. Sit quietly amid the slender double columns
and the ancient wellhead, or read beneath the small semi-
circular arches that encircle the worn bricks of the pavement. A sense of calm pervades the cloister, long associated
with a Benedictine Abbey close to Torcello. After a time,
when you are refreshed, recovered from the frenetic pace
outside, you can return to the sights of the Piazza, or continue along the route to the nearby church of San Zaccaria
to see the finest Giovanni Bellini (signed and dated 1505)
in situ.

ERIC DENKER
Art historian

*Editor's Note: The Museo Diocesano di Arte Sacra (Ruga
Giuffa Sant'Apollonia, ☎041 522 91 66), a museum of
ecclesiastica, has recently been well restored, and while
hardly world-class, it contains paintings and other works
of art (Luca Giordano, Palma Giovane).*

*Also, there are 230 McDonald's in Italy, including six-
teen in Rome, thirteen in Milan, and five in Venice!*

3.11 **San Zaccaria**
*1444–1515; begun by Antonio Gambello and completed
by Mauro Coducci*
Campo san Zaccaria
⚓ San Zaccaria

Madonna and Four Saints
1505, Giovanni Bellini

The *vaporetto* ride from San Marco to San Zaccaria must
be the most spectacular single bus stop ride in the world.
And then, after you return to dry land, you need only to
wander through a short alleyway to emerge into a little
campo in front of one of the glories of Venetian architec-

ture and art, San Zaccaria. This was the doges' own church before San Marco was built, and the crypt holds the oldest tombs of doges in Venice. But the most dazzling of its attractions is the stunning Bellini altarpiece halfway up the nave. It was one of the treasures Napoleon took back to Paris; a memento of his theft remains, in the piece cut off the top so that the altarpiece would fit the location Napoleon chose for it. Stand in front of the painting when the sun is quite high in the afternoon and you will see the genius of the location as well as the painting. Only one ray of the sun can enter the church through the clerestory windows across the nave, but as the sun moves the ray picks out each of the stunning robes of the saints and the Madonna in turn. The colors glow in succession, creating a magical theater of motion, art, and devout spirituality, all fused into one by the power of both Bellini and San Zaccaria.

THEODORE K. RABB
Historian

Altarpiece by Giovanni Bellini in San Zaccaria. Must also visit Chapel of San Tarasio to south of church, descending steps to ancient crypt.

JOHN JULIUS NORWICH
Historian

RECOMMENDED READING
Salley Vickers: *Miss Garnet's Angel*, Carroll & Graf, 2001.

Cappella di San Tarasio

Aside from Bellini's ravishing masterpiece, there's also the adjacent Cappella di San Tarasio, which you enter through the sacristy. It has a frescoed vault by Andrea del Castagno, painted with the assistance of Domenico Veneziano in 1442, and splendid triptychs by the Vivarini, with their original carved and gilded frames.

RONA GOFFEN
Art historian

Reliefs

Remember to look up in Venice, because there are many wonderful reliefs attached to buildings, sometimes seemingly at random. For example (though not at random), the relief of *putti* with a coat of arms labeling the entrance to the Corte dele Pizzocare; or the relief over the entrance to the Campo di San Zaccaria.

RONA GOFFEN
Art historian

3.12 Scuola di San Giorgio degli Schiavoni

Calle Furlani
Closed Mondays
⚓ San Zaccaria

Saint George and the Dragon

1509–1511, Vittore Carpaccio

One of the often missed artistic jewels in Venice is a cycle of paintings executed by Vittore Carpaccio in 1509–1511 for the Scuola di San Giorgio degli Schiavoni, in the *sestiere* of Castello. A *scuola* was not a "school" but a brotherhood dedicated to the civic good and to performing such acts as visiting the sick, burying the dead, and providing for the material needs of less fortunate members. Many of the more than one hundred *scuole* in Venice also acted as patrons of the arts, commissioning painters to embellish their meeting houses. The Scuola di San Giorgio degli Schiavoni is an example, precious because it is the earliest *scuola* in Venice to retain its original decoration.

We enter the *scuola* building by pushing aside a velvet door-hanging that shuts out virtually all of the Mediterranean sun. Inside, the room is dark, and the paintings become our substitute for the glow of the outside world. But what a fantastical other world they conjure! Direct your eyes to the large painting to the left of the doorway, depicting *Saint George Fighting the Dragon*. The members of this brotherhood were immigrants from Dalmatia (on the opposite coast of the Adriatic Sea from Venice), and the painting depicts one of their heroic patron saints fighting for the life of a frightened princess in distant Libya.

Carpaccio, however, had never travelled to such an exotic place as Libya, and instead, he had to rely on his imagination to convincingly render the scene. Resourcefully, he looked at cheap woodblock prints of faraway architecture then circulating among the curious-minded in Venice. The imposing gateway on the distant shoreline to the left, for example, recalls an actual gate in the city of Cairo.

But the foreground scene is pure fantasy, and the artist has let his imagination run unanchored. Parts of dismembered bodies, animal skulls and lizards litter the desert landscape. Saint George spears the winged dragon right through the mouth, and blood pours down its breast. To the right, the princess clasps her hands in gratitude. We witness an exotic tale of carnage, but ultimately of saintly triumph over fear and evil. Inspiration, no doubt, to the more modestly heroic acts of this Dalmatian brotherhood in their new homeland of Venice.

BARBARA LYNN-DAVIS
Art historian and writer

3.13 San Francesco della Vigna

1534-1554, Jacopo Sansovino; 1562-1572, Andrea Palladio (façade)
Campo San Francesco
 Celestia

Madonna and Child Enthroned

ca. 1450, Antonio da Negroponte

This church has the only known work by Antonio da Negroponte, *Madonna and Child Enthroned*, circa 1450, an international Gothic extravaganza. The Giustinian chapel is decorated with elegant reliefs by the Lombardo.

RONA GOFFEN
Art historian

Badoer-Giustinian Chapel
15th century, Pietro Lombardo and his school

Don't miss the chapel of the Badoer-Giustinian family, to
the left of an altar by members of the Lombardo family.
BEATRICE H. GUTHRIE
Former director of Save Venice, Inc.

RECOMMENDED READING
John McAndrew, *Venetian Architecture of the Early Renaissance*, o.p.

3.14 ### Ristorante Al Covo
Campiello della Pescaria 3968, ☎ 041 522 38 12
Closed Wednesdays and Thursdays
⚓ Arsenale

🍴 Al Covo, by side of Hotel Gabrielli, is one of the best in
Venice. The owner's wife is Texan, his cooking Venetian.
JOHN JULIUS NORWICH
Historian

Canals

By any means possible try to come by a boat and have
someone row you, or row yourself, through the quiet, out-
of-the-way canals in the dead of night. It is a magical mode
of time travel through eons of literature and imagination.
Getting lost remains the best possible way to see Venice.
SUSAN KLEINBERG
Artist

3.15 Arsenale

Campo Arsenale

 Arsenale, Celestia

Lions

So few visitors wander on foot to the Arsenal (briefly glimpsed from the *vaporetto* on its way to the Fondamenta Nuove) that you can inspect undisturbed the lions that guard its gate. Two were brought as spoils of war from the Piraeus in 1692, and one of these (the farthest to the left) carries a runic inscription dating to the late 11th century, when the Varangian guards (ultimately of Viking origin) came to Athens from Byzantium. The inscription, however cryptic, communicates an instant appreciation of the network of travel for man and beast in medieval Europe, and the fortunes of war. Even more moving is a lion closer to the canal, whose archaic sharp-edged spine will be recognized by anyone who has seen its fellows on the Terrace of the Lions on Delos. Brought here in 1718 from Corfu, it too conveys its message of exile and melancholy.

HELEN F. NORTH
Classicist

SAN MARCO

4.1   Corte del Duca Sforza

From the Palazzo Grassi, go around the church of San Samuele and head south on Calle Malipiero, then right at Ramo Corte Teatro a few paces until you reach the Corte Sforza.

⚓ Samuele

If you do not have access to a palazzo along the Grand Canal, but you want to enjoy sitting on its banks, relaxing while you watch boatloads of tourists go by and looking like you belong there, then head for the little-visited Corte del Duca Sforza. It is just north of Ca' del Duca, a short walk from the Palazzo Grassi. The Corte is now just an open area in a relatively quiet residential district. Walk through the Corte until you reach an entryway that leads to the Grand Canal itself. There you will find classical white steps descending to the waterway, where you can sit, relax, and soak it all in. When the tourists point to you and take your picture, do your best to look like a Venetian.

THOMAS F. MADDEN
Historian

Traghetti

The *traghetti*, beat-up gondolas that are a substitute for the *vaporetti* if you only want to cross the canal, are a well-kept secret in Venice and generally used only by locals. (It is considered effete to sit down in one.) One of my indelible memories of Venice is seeing a gondolier in full dress uniform casually operating his gondola with one hand while using a cellular phone with the other.

PAUL PASCAL
Classicist

4.2   Save Venice Treasure Hunt

San Marco 2888A, ☎ 041 528 52 47
Adjacent to the Ponte dell'Accademia on the San Marco side
⚓ Accademia

Stop by the office of Save Venice and pick up a treasure hunt containing six walks, one for each *sestiere*, or section, of Venice. Prepared with the help of noted author and lecturer John Julius Norwich, the walks and map guide you on a search for each *sestiere*'s artistic and historic highlights. This is a great way to enjoy the prettiest walks in the city. Each section takes about ninety minutes to complete. My favorites are Cannaregio and Santa Croce—parts of town no one ever sees.
BEATRICE H. GUTHRIE
Former director of Save Venice, Inc.

RECOMMENDED READING
Hugh Honour, *Companion Guide to Venice*, 4th edition, Boydell & Brewer, 1998.
J. G. Links, *Venice for Pleasure*, 6th edition, Bishop Museum Press, 1999.
John Julius Norwich, *A History of Venice*, Vintage Books, 1989.
Jan Morris, *The World of Venice*, Harcourt Brace, 1995.

Editor's Note: The word sestiere *is peculiar to Venice and refers explicitly to the fact that there are six sections. They are San Marco, Castello, Dorsoduro, San Polo, Santa Croce, and Cannaregio.*

4.3   Rigattieri

San Marco 3532, ☎ 041 523 10 81
Near Santo Stefano
⚓ Sant'Angelo

🎁 An extraordinary assortment of large serving platters and other modern ceramics.
MARCELLA HAZAN
Cookbook author and educator

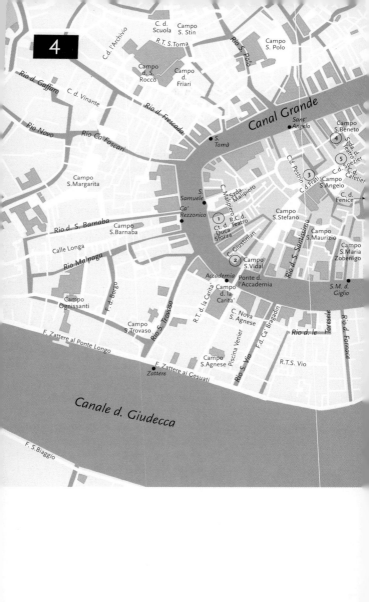

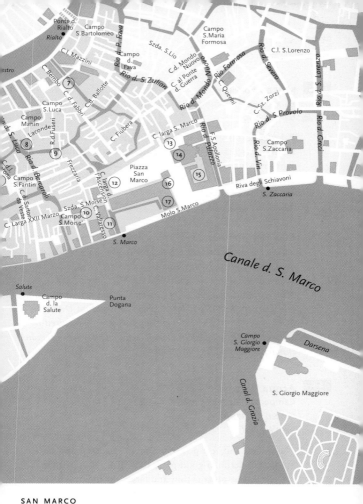

SAN MARCO

1 Corte del Duca Sforza

2 Save Venice Treasure Hunt

3 Rigattieri

4 Museo Fortuny

5 Acqua Pazza

6 Galleria Luce

7 Domus

8 Palazzo Contarini del Bovolo

9 Da Ivo

10 San Moisè

11 Harry's Bar

12 Museo Correr

13 The American Bar

14 Basilica di San Marco

15 Doge's Palace / Palazzo Ducale

16 Museo Archeologico

17 La Biblioteca Marciana,
known as La Zecca

4.4 Museo Fortuny

Palazzo Pesaro, Campo San Benedetto 3780

⚓ Sant'Angelo

Palazzo Fortuny used to be one of the palaces of the Pesaro family, patrons of Bellini and Titian. It now houses the Fortuny Museum. (Mariano Fortuny was the textile maker and designer, to whom one is particularly grateful for ravishing pleated silks.)

RONA GOFFEN
Art historian

Editor's Note: Mariano Fortuny was born in Spain in 1871 and lived in the Palazzo Pesaro for many years until his death in 1949. He was a renowned painter, theatrical costumer and lighting designer and photographer, but his principal fame was as an innovative textile manufacturer and fashion designer for such clients as Isadora Duncan. His very colorful dresses were supposed to be inspired by ancient Greek or old Venetian styles, and they were revolutionary and liberating for their day.

4.5 Acqua Pazza

Campo Sant'Angelo 3808, ☏ 041 277 06 88

Closed Mondays

⚓ Sant'Angelo

🍽 The newest and best pizzeria in town. The staff and owners are from Salerno, a good place to be from if you are making pizza. The pizza is thin and large, the mozzarella is *bufala*, the tomatoes are fresh cherry tomatoes, the oil is extra virgin, and the oven is brick. If you like chili, ask for *olio al peperoncino* that you can dispense to taste at the table. Should they put a bottle of their homemade *limoncello* on your table at the end of the meal, don't fail to fill your glass.

MARCELLA HAZAN
Cookbook author and educator

Walks

After a meal of fish and white wine, there is little that is as satisfying as a stroll among the dark and indistinctly lit *calli* and *campi* of Venice. Footsteps ring on dampened stones; light falls from warm rooms above. Occasionally one comes across a fellow traveler, usually walking more purposefully towards an unknown destination. I have memories of footsteps approaching and fading, a sound isolated by stone and then hushed by gently lapping water. Maybe one hears the plash of a gondola plying the dark waters of back canals. A bridge offers a brief glimpse of where one is and where one might go. But will you be able to get there? It hardly matters, for Venice is perhaps the only city in the world in which one enjoys getting lost.
WILLIAM E. WALLACE
Art historian

Take the walks described by J. G. Links in his superb book, *Venice for Pleasure*.
JOHN JULIUS NORWICH
Historian

RECOMMENDED READING
J. G. Links, *Venice for Pleasure*, 6th Edition, Bishop Museum Press, 1999.

4.6 Galleria Luce
Campiello della Fenice 1922, 041 522 29 49
Sant'Angelo, San Marco

Located on a corner in the Campiello della Fenice, practically next door to the work-in-progress Teatro La Fenice and the quintessentially charming Hotel La Fenice et des Artistes (Campiello della Fenice 1936, 041 523 23 33), is the Galleria Luce dell'Arte Moderna, a small gem of a gallery where works of *arte moderna* are exhibited. The stars here are Arman, Lucio Fontana and Giorgio De Chirico, but the gallery also displays quality works by lesser-known Italian and international contemporary artists. Renato Luce, who speaks fluent English, established the gallery in 1983, and it is definitely worth stopping by. One never knows what discovery one might make here— Luce has an excellent eye.

NICHOLAS ARCOMANO
Attorney

4.7   ## Domus

Calle dei Fabbri 4746, ☎041 522 62 59

⚓ Rialto

 Fancy table and kitchen ware. Ground floor is mainly gift ware, upper floor more serious cooking equipment.

MARCELLA HAZAN
Cookbook author and educator

4.8   ## Palazzo Contarini del Bovolo

Calle delle Locande 4299

⚓ Rialto, Sant'Angelo

Staircase

ca. 1499, Giovanni Candi

Wandering between Teatro La Fenice and the Campo Manin you may be lucky enough (helped by some new signposts) to come upon the Palazzo Contarini del Bovolo, which owes its name—*bovolo* means "snail"—to its 15th-century exterior spiral staircase, a unique architectural adornment and a delight to gaze upon, especially by moonlight, when its marble seems to glow pure white against the dark wall of the palace.

HELEN F. NORTH
Classicist

Follow the Calle della Vida to the entrance of the Palazzo Contarini del Bovolo, and go through the alley, Contarini del Bovolo. Here is an unexpected, astonishing and beautiful sight—especially on entering from such a dark, narrow alleyway or *calle*. The elegant circular staircase with arches above the columns repeats the rhythm of the white stone arches of the loggia. This open staircase reminds one of the Tower of Pisa. The architectural elements were reused from the demolished church of Saint Paternian.

HELEN COSTANTINO FIORATTI
Interior designer

4.9   **Da Ivo**

Ramo dei Fuseri 1809, ☏ 041 528 50 04
Closed Sundays

⚓ San Marco, Rialto

🍴🍷 Owner-chef is Tuscan. Best *fiorentina* (firm but very tasty T-bone steak for two) in town, authoritatively herb-scented pastas, a sensational mussel soup, charcoal-grilled fish, fried soft-shell crabs, roast lamb, and, in season, white truffles and grilled porcini. You might think twice about ordering the osso bucco, but you are not likely to be disappointed by anything else on the menu.

MARCELLA HAZAN
Cookbook author and educator

Caffè Corretto

🍴🍷 If you're in Venice in the winter and the cold has gone to your bones, one of the cafes will give you your *caffè corretto* with grappa (espresso "corrected" with the addition of grappa).

KEITH CHRISTIANSEN
Curator

4.10   San Moisè
Campo San Moisè
⚓ San Marco

Lovers of the baroque will enjoy the church of San Moisè,
with its 1668 façade by Alessandro Tremingnon. Inside are
two notable works: Tintoretto's *La Lavanda dei Piedi*, and
an altarfront in bronze relief by Niccolò Roccatagliata and
his son Sebastiano. Signed and dated 1633, the relief
depicts the Deposition.
DAVE KING
Writer

4.11   Harry's Bar
Calle Vallaresso 1323, ☎ 041 528 57 77
⚓ San Marco

🍴 It may not produce Venice's most ravishing cooking, but
there is no argument about its being the city's most celebrated eatery, the most clubby and glamorous, and the
most expensive. Actually, the food can be rather good. If
you want to see or be seen you must be seated downstairs
in the bar, where dinner is served after 8pm. Some of the
distinguished overflow occasionally ends up on the floor
above. If you make your reservations yourself, ask for the
maitre d', Corrado.
MARCELLA HAZAN
Cookbook author and educator

4.12   Museo Correr
Piazza San Marco 52, Procuratie Nuove (entrance in Ala
Napoleonica)
⚓ San Marco

Venice is beyond belief—more fantastic than one's most
fanciful inventions. As most of the city is well-known, I
will highly recommend one of its secret places. For reasons
I can't begin to understand, the Museo Correr has been

practically empty when I've gone to Venice, while the
Galleria dell'Accademia has been crowded. The Accademia
is a great museum, true, and it should be seen. But the
Correr is not far behind. It is in the palazzo that defines
one side of the Piazza San Marco, above Florian's, where
elegant people sit by an orchestra, watching the theater of
life. Beyond the Correr's Venetian historical collections, at
the far end and up the stairs again, there is a beautiful
collection with Bellinis and Carpaccios. Carpaccio's
Courtesans is one of the most interesting paintings around,
to my painter's eye. Easel-sized, mysterious, quiet. Felice
Casorati based his 1921 painting *Two Sisters* on this work.

ALAN FELTUS
Painter

*Editor's Note: The exhibition space for the Museo Correr
was designed by Venetian architect Carlo Scarpa in the
1950s.*

4.13 The American Bar

San Marco 302, ☎ 041 522 25 15
Beneath the Torre dell'Orologio
⚓ San Marco, San Zaccaria

🍽 Humble in appearance, the American Bar has the best
pirini and sandwiches in Venice, which, with a Campari,
makes a perfect morning pit stop. Stand-up and reasonably priced, it is streets ahead of its smart neighbors and is
surprisingly little used by foreigners. Kids can ride on the
marble lion.

JOHN CARSWELL
Curator and art historian

*Editor's Note: The clock to the left of San Marco is the
famous Torre dell'Orologio, where two Moors ring the
hour and little figures come out and dance.*

4.14 Basilica di San Marco

Piazza San Marco

⚓ San Marco, San Zaccaria

The hush of evening falls. The tourists have gone. With the lights dimmed, the dazzling beauty of the church is subdued. A few people come in before the evening Mass and whisper among themselves. Along the wall at the end of the left transept you sit on a long, plain bench, wood mounted on stone. Lean against the cool wall. Touch it. Breathe the silence. Look across the great reach of space toward the high window, where natural light fades. In the mysterious half-darkness, the *Madonna Nicopeia* looks comfortable in her niche, for she has been at home here for about eight hundred years. Just before the Mass, the lights go on everywhere, blazing on the mosaics and flooding the place with a shower of gold. At a very human level, this is death and rebirth.

MARY JANE PHILLIPS-MATZ
Musicologist and biographer

4.15 Doge's Palace / Palazzo Ducale

Piazzetta San Marco

Secret Itinerary must be reserved in advance;

☎ 041 522 49 51

⚓ San Marco, San Zaccaria

Pay for a guided tour of the "Secret Itinerary" of the palace, which takes you to the prison cells, secret passageways, inside the Bridge of Sighs, and, if the group is small enough, out onto the roof of the palace. There are no railings to speak of, and you can climb the gently sloping lead-sheeted roof for one more spectacular view of San Giorgio. Even without the roof visit, the secret stairways and chambers are a lot of fun. Ask the guide to lock the children in Casanova's grim little cell while the adults go out for a quiet lunch.

PABLO CONRAD
Writer and editor

4.16 Museo Archeologico
Piazzetta San Marco 52

 San Marco

Enter from the Piazzetta. What's fascinating here is that most of the collection was acquired in the 16th century by the Grimani, a Venetian noble family, and bequeathed to the Republic.

RONA GOFFEN
Art historian

Marble Gutters

One time, staying in a little *pensione* not far behind San Marco, I looked out the window and was amazed to see that rain gutters along the edges of the rooftops are made of marble. It isn't unbelievable enough that this city was built on stilts in the water, it even has gutters of stone to add weight to its impossible architecture! Venetian Gothic is unlike other Italian Gothic. Canals are unlike other cities' streets. Boats are unlike cars. The resulting effect is magic and quiet elegance: a beauty that makes one smile all the time.

ALAN FELTUS
Painter

4.17 La Biblioteca Marciana, known as La Zecca
1547, Jacopo Sansovino
Piazza San Marco 7

 San Marco

A secret place in Venice lies right in the center of the most celebrated piazza in Venice and perhaps the world. To experience a masterpiece of Renaissance architecture by the renowned Venetian architect Sansovino, request a day pass as a researcher or student—not a tourist—and leave a passport at the entry. The former *zecca*, or mint, of the Venetian Republic houses the national library with its literary treasure documenting all aspects of Venetian life. Enjoy sitting under an extensive skylight over the main reading room and perusing the open stacks. Select a book at random for an in-depth understanding of an aspect of a building or a painting perhaps.

MARGARET SPENCER MATZ
Architect

Editor's Note: In La Zecca were minted the famous Venetian coins called zecchini—*the source of the English word "sequins."*

DORSODURO

5.1 San Nicolò dei Mendicoli
Campo San Nicolò
 San Basilio

Gloria di San Niccolò
Late 16th century, Francesco Montemezzano

A little-known church in a poor area of the city, San
Nicolò dei Mendicoli has a superbly painted ceiling by
Francesco Montemezzano, late 16th-century, with wooden
gilded arcade filled with carved statues.
JOHN JULIUS NORWICH
Historian

5.2 Angelo Raffaele
Campo Angelo Raffaele
 San Basilio

Storie di Tobiolo
Giovanni Antonio Guardi, ca. 1750

The paintings by Guardi on the organ doors of Angelo
Raffaele are also well worth a visit.
JOHN JULIUS NORWICH
Historian

RECOMMENDED READING
Salley Vickers, *Miss Garnet's Angel*, Carroll & Graf, 2001.

*Editor's Note: The original San Angelo Raffaele goes back
almost to the origins of Venice during the Lombard inva-
sions in the sixth century. That church was destroyed by
fire in 1105 and rebuilt and reconsecrated in 1193. This
replacement was demolished in 1618 and rebuilt over the
course of a century or so. It was completed by 1735.*

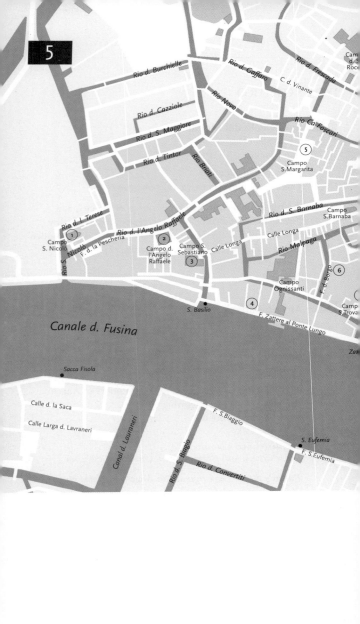

Rio d. Burchielle

Rio d. Gaffaro

Rio d. Frescada

Camp d. Roc

C. d. Vinante

Rio Novo

Rio d. Cazziole

Rio Ca'Foscari

Rio d. S. Maggiore

5

Rio d. Tintor

Campo S.Margarita

Rio Briati

Rio d. I. Terese

Rio d. S. Barnaba

Campo S.Barnaba

Rio d. l'Angelo Raffaele

Calle Longa

1

2

Campo S. Nicolò

F. d. la Pescheria

Rio Malpaga

Campo d. l'Angelo Raffaele

Campo S. Sebastiano

Calle Longa

6

Rio S. Nicolò

3

Campo Ognissanti

F. d. Borgo

4

Camp S Trova

S. Basilio

F. Zattere al Ponte Lungo

Canale d. Fusina

Zat

Sacca Fisola

Calle d. la Saca

F. S.Biaggio

Calle Larga d. Lavraneri

S. Eufemia

Canal d. Lauroneri

F. S.Eufemia

Rio d. S. Biaggio

Rio d. Conventiti

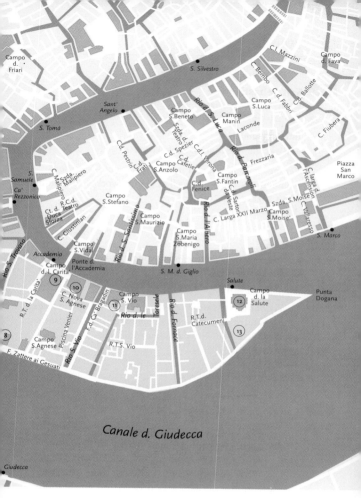

Canale d. Giudecca

DORSODURO

1   San Nicolò dei Mendicoli
2   Angelo Raffaele
3   San Sebastiano
♩♔ 4   Riviera
5   Campo Santa Margherita
♩♔ 6   Antica Locanda Montin
7   San Trovaso

♩♔ 8   Nico
9   Accademia
♩♔ 10 Trattoria ai Cugnai
11 Galleria Multigraphic
12 Santa Maria della Salute
13 Rio Terrà dei Catecumeni

5.3 San Sebastiano
Campo San Sebastiano
 San Basilio

Interior painting
Mid– to late 16th century, Paolo Veronese

Veronese's church, decorated with some of his earliest
paintings (the ceiling) as well as mature works. All beautiful.
RONA GOFFEN
Art historian

5.4 Riviera
Fondamenta delle Zattere Ponte Lungo 1473, ☎ 041 522 76 21
Closed Mondays
San Basilio, Zattere

Lovely outdoor location on embankment facing Giudecca
canal. Limited outdoor seating. Simple pastas and risottos,
good fish, chicken with cardoons sometimes, *fegato alla
veneziana* usually.
MARCELLA HAZAN
Cookbook author and educator

5.5 Campo Santa Margherita
Ca' Rezzonico

Nothing here of great historical interest, no compelling
works of art, just an exceptionally spacious and truly popular campo lined with small houses (but some date from
the 14th century), neighborhood shops and simple trattto-
rias. Plane trees and benches invite you to enjoy the shade.
Closed off at one end by a ruined campanile associated
with the church of Santa Margherita, at the other end the
Campo leads to a World War I memorial in the form of a
flagstaff surrounded by statues of the cardinal virtues. The
Antico Capon restaurant (east side of the campo) will not
disappoint you.
HELEN F. NORTH
Classicist

La Pescheria
Campo Santa Margherita
 Ca' Rezzonico

No visit to Venice is complete without a visit either to the main fish market (*la Pescheria*) near the Rialto Bridge or to the smaller but in many ways more picturesque one held on the Campo Santa Margherita, near the Carmini. This is a morning activity (they shut up by lunchtime). The Campo Santa Margherita is in a wonderful and lively popular quarter and is very animated.
KEITH CHRISTIANSEN
Curator

Campo Santa Margherita

Pick up any guide to Venice and you are directed straight to the Piazza San Marco. The façade of the Basilica is described in hallowed terms, praise is heaped on the palazzo of the Doges, the campanile, and the clock tower. Every author repeats Napoleon's description of the Piazza as the most elegant drawing room in Europe. *Feh*! How long since you had a really good time in a drawing room, the 18th century? It's the new millennium, and if you want a great experience, turn on your heels and head for the Campo Santa Margherita in the Dorsoduro district.

If the Piazza is the drawing room of Venice, the Campo is the "rec" room. In the evening in San Marco people hold hands to the overture of *The Sound of Music* played by bored musicians at old Florian's cafe. In Santa Margherita, students and adults crowd together after enjoying club concerts or classical music at the Scuola San Rocco and the Frari. In the Piazza, visitors smile nostalgically at one another while sipping the most expensive cup of coffee in Italy, while in the Campo animated conversation is fueled by fiery grappa or *sgroppino*, an ambrosia produced by whipping lemon sorbet, vodka, and Prosecco (Venetian champagne). In the Piazza, you're next to first-timers, dot-com millionaires, and Eurotrash, in the Campo you're arguing with the natives about why the city won't build the moveable barriers to protect their lagoon. San Marco is the fox trot, Santa Margherita is salsa. Don't misunderstand, the Piazza is a beautiful setting with imposing architectural monuments, but when it comes to a good time after the sun sets, there's no place like the Campo. Santa Margherita is a brash, bustling center of activity day and night, a far more accurate measure of Venetian life than the formal presentation of San Marco. One of the most extensive squares in the city, the Campo and its surroundings are a buffet of contemporary culture: everyday activities laced with the vestiges of past glories.

No need to wait for one of those crystalline Venetian days; seek out Santa Margherita on any weekday morning, sunny or overcast, or even in the rain. Enter from the north by crossing the Rio di Cà Foscari, the façade of San Pantalon at your back. You'll encounter a narrow *calle* (lane) lined with shops catering to the everyday needs of the neighborhood, including a *farmacia* and a *latteria* (dairy store) with not only milk and cheeses, but a first class selection of *vino*, too. Beyond is a lingerie and bathing suit shop (when was the last time anyone willingly entered the water in the lagoon city?) and the Vinaria Nave d'Oro, whose inexpensive table wines are dispensed by siphon from immense glass jugs, but only if you remember to bring an empty! (Okay, occasionally they'll fill up a recycled *acqua minerale* bottle for you, but not without expressing the appropriate Venetian disgust.)

The lane has modern technology, too, including a video automat dispensing tapes to local film junkies day and night. A self-declared no-smoking bar/cafe serves espresso, cappuccino, wine, and sandwiches while patrons continue to puff away. (In Venice's Marco Polo airport, authorities have placed ashtrays directly beneath the no-smoking signs.) On the truncated tower of the ex-church of Santa Margherita, now part of the university, marble

grotesques of a lion and a dragon simultaneously keep
ancient demons and truant students at bay.

The vast open space of Santa Margherita spreads to
the south, the tiles of the pavement revealing where a canal
once crossed the square. Sycamore trees, benches, well-
heads, newspaper stands and food stalls decorate the
Campo. A range of human activity is on display—shopping, flirting, children playing and riding bicycles, pension-
ers relaxing, women kibitzing. Tourists on their way to the
Accademia hurry through the square, heedless of its vitality
and hidden treasures, and students rush to class, only
returning to the Campo in the evening.

Galleries and craft shops co-exist with cafes and gro-
ceries. Within the Campo you can view photography,
hand-made pottery, and those illusionistic wooden
objects—wingtips, ties, jackets—by Loris Marazzi, himself
a cottage industry with outlets throughout Venice. More
interesting, however, are two troves of Venetian art tucked
into the southwest corner of the square. The under-visited
14th-century church of Santa Maria dei Carmini (often
called simply, "Chiesa dei Carmine," or "del Carmelo" in
the Venetian dialect) contains two marvelous 16th-century
works. On the left side in the nave is a Lorenzo Lotto
altarpiece of *Saint Nicholas and Saints* with a startling bit
of landscape below that brings to mind the early panoramic
views of Brueghel and Dürer. One of Cima da Conegliano's
most compelling paintings is just opposite, the altarpiece of
the *Nativity with Saints*, set in a limpid atmosphere that
derives from the brilliant landscapes of Giovanni Bellini.
A bronze plaque of the Deposition by Francesco di Giorgio
Martini, the Sienese Leonardo, is one of the finest of the
rare Tuscan works in the city.

Adjacent to the church is the 17th-century Scuola
Grande dei Carmini, one of the prominent confraternities
that provided cradle-to-grave care for Venetians, as well as
worthy charities such as orphanages and dowries for the
poor. The Scuola contains a striking decorative cycle by

Giambattista Tiepolo, the greatest of all late Venetian
artists. On the ceiling of the Sala Capitolare, an imperious
Virgin bestows the sacred Scapular on the Blessed Simone
Stock. Above, Mary is surrounded by a cadre of angels
showing a bit much gam, while below, the damned inhabit
a Goyesque hell. Who was the Blessed Stock, and what of
his scapular vision? According to Carmelite legend, Simon
was a 13th-century Englishman whose vision of Mary
giving him the cloak of the order was accompanied by her
promise of salvation to the wearer. The story is inconse-
quential for us, so sit back and luxuriate in Tiepolo's
grandiose taffeta fantasy, the heavenly drama set in 16th-
century costume inspired by Veronese. A smaller ceiling
canvas of an angel saving a workman from a fall depicts
an even more obscure story, yet is movingly realized.
Displayed in vitrines around the Sala, exceedingly hideous
Murano glass in the shapes of a rooster and eggs remind us
of the mystic marriage of beauty and banality that surprisingly often informs Italian taste.

However, you're in Santa Margherita for more than
Art with a capital A. Almost anything material or metaphysical is to be found within this great space. Interested in
something to drink? Try one of the half-dozen cafes that
range from the youthful hangouts of Il Caffè and the
Green Pub to the more stylish banquette and outside seating of the Bar Margaret Duchamp. A quick bite? How
about a slice on the fly at Pizza al Volo, or an outside seat
at one of the two pizzeria/trattorias, watching the ongoing
floor show of the *commedia umana*. Seeking an elegant
dinner? Try L'Incontro, an upper-crust restaurant of
Sardinian descent. Dessert? Rival ice cream emporiums
claim honors for the square, the august Gelateria Caffè
Causin (says right on the awning "founded 1928"), or the
more modern shop on the south side of the Campo with
the air-conditioned back room.

Oh, you prefer to eat in the intimacy of your room?
Of course the contemporary *supermercato* would save you

time, but how pedestrian and unromantic. Better to
patronize the local merchants, the *panificio* (bakery) with
its tortoise-shaped loaves, or the wine shops, or the coffee
and tea vendors, or the curious subterranean stall on the
east side of the Campo that sells only eggs and *acqua
minerale*. Cooking tonight? Try the beef from one of the
butchers, perhaps beneath the beautiful Moorish windows
of the palace at number 2931. Miró, a sleek black cat,
waits outside the door each morning for his owner to
return from school, hoping for a kindly scratch or scrap
of meat. Prepared *carne*, *pollo* and *coniglio* (rabbit) also
are available from the *macellaio* (butcher) at the southern
corner of the Campo.

But as this is the Queen of the Adriatic, fish is a better
bet. View the abundance at any of the three fish stalls that
occupy the center of Campo Santa Margherita, while gravel-
throated fishmongers hawk their seafood to you. Such
familiar species as shark, salmon, and shrimp are available,
or more exotic delicacies such as *canestri*, *razza*, and *coda
di rospo*, the end of the fish. Behind the stalls, on the west
wall of the free standing ex-Scuola of the Varotari (tanner's
guild) is a worn stone sign with raised metal letters:
LUNGHEZZE MINIME PERMESSE PER LA VENDITA DEL
PESCE DELLE SEGUENTI QUALITÀ—the minimum length for
the sale of different varieties of fish. Here we find the useful information (in Venetian dialect, of course) that the
legal size for *bransin*, *orada*, *dental*, *corbo*, *sparo*, *lovo*,
and *boseghetta* is at least twelve centimeters (five inches)
long, while *bisatto* must be 25 centimeters, *peocio* only
three. The sight of all this piscine flesh make you queasy?
No problem, there are several pharmacies available, including the most up-to-date *erborista*, Il Melograno.

Reading matter is as plentiful in the Campo as food,
from regular bookshops to the several *edicole* (news stalls)
with their dailies and journals and those adult comic books
that Italians love. Sundry *cartolerie* sell stationery and art
supplies, though the most prominent on the west side of

the Campo is more interested in selling Lotto tickets than
note paper. A phone shop, two hardware stores, and a
lighting shop provide other necessities. On a terrace above
the lamp store is the Scuola di Lingua e Cultura Italia,
where Venetians learn English, *senza dubbio* so that when
you attempt to speak to them in Italian they can demonstrate their Venetian superiority by answering in perfect
English. (There is, at times, a faint whiff of the Parisian
about the Venetians.) The busy Puntonet, one of the
ubiquitous Internet cafes blossoming around town, stands
on the east side of the square, just by the art deco façade
of the ex-Cinema Moderno. A nearby alley leads to the
Corte Del Fontego, with its bricked-up 13th-century arches
and columns curiously juxtaposed with the local party
headquarters of the Rifondazione Comunista.

    Exit the Campo by the southeast corner through the
Rio Terrà Canal, a designation for streets that were originally canals but have long since been filled. Window-shop
past the Mondonovo mask store, but don't be tempted—
consider how strange that mask will really look at home.
Besides, the masks are an unhappy reminder of the
carnevale today, that tame excuse intended for the mass
tourist trade rather than the gloriously wicked Carnevale
of the Republic. Daydream before the ads for weekly
apartment and palace rentals at the local realtor. Muse
over a pastry from the area's current favorite bakery, the
Mantovese Gobbetti, and carry away a characteristic
crumbcake or box of biscuits. Peruse the bidets and stylish
high-tech *portascopini* (toilet brushes) in a window displaying the latest fashion in bathroom articles. Then
mount the steps of the Ponte dei Pugni with its inlaid foot-
prints marking the site of ancient Venetian rites—on this
bridge contests were held between rival Venetian factions,
the Nicolotti and the Castellani, with each side attempting
to push the other over the sides of the un-parapeted bridge.
Now that would be an annual event worth reviving for

tourists. Maybe that bathing suit shop isn't such a bad idea
after all. . .

ERIC DENKER
Art historian

*Editor's Note: The wine shop, Vinaria Nave d'Oro, has
an unusual name since* vinaria *is not a regular word for a
wine shop all by itself. As used here, the name could con-
ceivably mean "The Golden Ship of Wine."*

*The list of fish waiting to be measured may be translat-
ed as: sea bass, gilt-head bream, dentex, Italian* corvo *(the
word* corvo *literally meaning crow, and referring to* ombri-
na, *a kind of sea perch),* sargo, *cod, and mullet.* Bisatto *is
the Venetian word for eel, while* peocio *is a small mussel.*
Coda di rospo, *translated as "toad's tail," refers to a fish
known in English as the angler fish, and it is a very popular fish in Venice, said to taste something like lobster.*

5.6   ## Antica Locanda Montin

Fondamenta di Borgo 1147, ☎ 041 522 71 51
Closed Tuesday evenings and Wednesdays
⚓ Zattere

The Antica Locanda Montin, on a quiet canal between
Accademia and the station, is a good place to stay—though
it tends to be full—and has a very nice restaurant in a vine-
covered *cortile* behind (open in summer.) The inside spaces
are hung with 20th-century paintings, lesser artists perhaps, but interesting nevertheless. Very pleasant.

ALAN FELTUS
Painter

5.7 San Trovaso

Campo San Trovaso

 Zattere, Accademia

I particularly like the Tintorettos and the Giambono, *San Giovanni Crisogono*. The Campo di San Trovaso is one of my favorite *campi*, around the corner from the Squero di San Trovaso, one of the few (perhaps by now the only) working gondola boatyards. The walk along the Rio di San Trovaso is lovely, too. The church is one of several Venetian churches with two main entrances, whether to accommodate the idiosyncrasies of the local geography or the rivalries of neighboring groups.

RONA GOFFEN
Art historian

5.8 Nico

Zattere ai Gesuati 922, ☎ 041 522 52 93
Closed Thursdays

 Zattere

🍴 To those who like any flavor of ice cream, as long as it's dark chocolate, Venice might claim to be the best *gelato* town in Italy just on the strength of Cipriani's masterpiece. For others, the city doesn't measure up to what you could get in Palermo, Rome or Bologna. However, it is not quite so poor that you have to give up *gelato* while you are here. There are many stands and *gelaterie* of which the most popular is Nico. Try their chocolate and hazelnut *gian-duiotto*.

MARCELLA HAZAN
Cookbook author and educator

5.9 **Accademia**
Campo della Carità
 Accademia

The Miracle of the True Cross at the Bridge of San Lorenzo
1500, Gentile Bellini
Room 20

I am partial to Jacopo Bellini's less talented son Gentile.
Unlike his kid brother, Giovanni, who can't take his eyes
off that strawberry blonde he keeps casting as the
Madonna, Gentile makes a polite effort to show the visitor around town, pointing out the sights and performing
introductions.

In this painting, he introduces himself (fourth from the
left among the gentlemen kneeling out front) and his rela-
tives (or maybe his patrons) and the local celebrities. The
portly lady in the left corner—that's Caterina Cornaro,
mailed to Cyprus to be its Venetian queen when she was a
teenager and yanked back after a widowhood spent under
siege from both friend and foe; lined up next to her in
strict bosom formation are her ladies-in-waiting from the
toy court at Asolo that Venice gave her as a compensation
package for early retirement. The bald chap in the water,
managing to stay decorously and effortlessly afloat in contrast to his treading and thrashing companions, is Andrea
Vendramin, the Guardian Grande of the Scuola Grande of
San Giovanni Evangelista. He has just rescued that confraternity's fragment of the True Cross, which unfortunately
fell in the canal while they were parading it around.

Now take a look at the crowd. This is our real introduction to sophisticated Venice. Everybody is standing
around marking time. Some are chatting, others are
shoving one another on the bridge, and the rest look
bored, wondering when the procession is finally going
to start up again and how the delay will affect their social
plans for the day.

What's the matter with them? Don't they understand what just happened? Someone dropped a piece of the True Cross in the canal! The True Cross! They took it out for ventilation and veneration, and somebody dropped it off the bridge! Who is responsible? How would you like to be the one who was entrusted to carry the True Cross and let go? What would you say—"I'm sorry"? "Hey, it was an accident"? "It's his fault, he pushed me"? "Look, I said I was sorry, what more do you want?" Now what? How is anybody supposed to find a piece of old wood if it sinks into all that junk that accumulates at the bottom of a canal?

Never mind—no use getting all worked up. These things happen. They found it, thanks to a miracle; the parade got going again, and people made it to their lunch dates.

The Scuola still has its relic of the True Cross. The porter told me he would have to go get the key and there really wasn't that much to look at and it was getting on to lunch time—but he would go if I insisted.

JUDITH MARTIN
Journalist

5.10   **Trattoria ai Cugnai**
Calle Nova Sant'Agnese, ☎ 041 528 92 38
⚓ Accademia

⊗ In Venetian, the word *cugnai* means brothers-in-law and sisters-in-law. Here you have both, in a plain, honest Venetian family that has run this restaurant for decades. My son and daughters were children when we first moved to Venice and began sitting at the big, family-sized tables; now they are past thirty. The *cugnai* hand you a simple menu of food that they cook in their tiny kitchen. No new cuisine; no new-fangled anything; just the same blessed Venetian fare, year after year.
MARY JANE PHILLIPS-MATZ
Musicologist and biographer

An 18th-Century Itinerary

ITINERARY

a Ca' Rezzonico
Fondamenta
Rezzonico
⚓ Ca' Rezzonico

b Scuola Grande dei
Carmini
Campo Carmini
⚓ Ca' Rezzonico

c Gesuati
Fondamenta delle
Zattere
⚓ Zattere

d La Pietà
Riva degli Sciavone
⚓ San Zaccaria

Start with the Ca' Rezzonico, the stupendous palace on the Grand Canal designed by Longhena in the 17th century, but completely decorated in the 18th and today the museum of the 18th century. There are spectacular ceilings by Tiepolo, fantastical furniture by the brilliant Brustolon, and dazzling rooms. Then head to the Scuola dei Carmini for one of the most suggestive ambiences in the city. The *scuole* were typically Venetian lay confraternities. Perhaps the most visited one is the Scuola di San Giorgio degli Schiavoni, with its wonderful series of canvases by Carpaccio. The Scuola dei Carmini is more intact and carries you into the 18th century. The ceiling of the second floor is decorated with dazzling canvases by Tiepolo. The furniture and furnishings are intact. Opposite the entrance to the Scuola is a good place to buy your supply of grappa before you head to the church of the Gesuati on the Zattere—beautiful in the late afternoon light. For those who think art stopped in Venice in the 16th century, this church serves as a warning. The work of the great neo-Palladian architect Giorgio Massari, it is grand, airy, spacious and scenographic, and in every way a worthy successor to Palladio's churches of San Giorgio Maggiore and the Redentore—the latter clearly visible from its front steps.

The Gesuati has a wonderful light in the morning and afternoon. The ceiling is divided into compartments with spectacular frescoes by Tiepolo (center scene shows Saint Dominic instituting the Rosary while the Madonna and her healthy child look on from the clouds; the smaller picture fields the Apotheosis of Saint Dominic and Saint Dominic Praying to the Virgin). On the first altar on the right is one of Tiepolo's religious masterpieces: the *Madonna and Child with Saints* (1748). It reaches all the way back to Bellini for the architectural setting of the figures, which is 15th-century and plays against Massari's 18th-century architecture. The third altar on the right has a splendid altarpiece by Piazzetta—who played Caravaggio to Tiepolo's Carracci. The church also contains an almost unique opportunity to see what Venetian sculptors were doing in the 18th century. The statues in the niches and the reliefs with Biblical stories are by Morlaiter—a contemporary of Tiepolo's and wonderfully gifted. In short, this church encapsulates 18th-century Venetian art in a way equaled only by Massari's other great ecclesiastical masterpiece, the oval-shaped church of the Pietà, which you may wish to dash over to see after having your eyes opened here (concerts are given in the Pietà, and this may be something to keep in mind, especially since Vivaldi was associated with the church, which had a famous school of female musicians and singers who performed from behind the grilled balconies). Like Ruskin, I love Byzantine Venice, medieval Venice, and Renaissance Venice, but unlike Ruskin, I would be hard pressed to think baroque and 18th-century Venice any less enthralling.

KEITH CHRISTIANSEN
Curator

5.11 Galleria Multigraphic
Campo San Vio 728, ☎ 041 528 51 59
⚓ Accademia
Closed Sundays

A few minutes' stroll from the Peggy Guggenheim
Collection at the Palazzo Venier Dei Leoni, in the direction
of the Accademia Bridge, is the unpretentious but very special Galleria Multigraphic. There is a 19th-century printing
press in one room. Owned by Luciano de March, the
gallery exhibits both original works and graphics by
contemporary Italian and European artists. Among them
are Mario Palli, whose abstract works are striking, and
Giuseppe Santomaso, a native Venetian who died in 1990
and was a friend of Peggy's. There is a photo of him in the
Guggenheim cafe. He was honored by Venice with an exhibition at the Museo Correr in 1982.

   Art is a constant, vital force in the everyday life of
Venetians. Before returning to your hotel, take a moment
for a prayer of gratitude at Santa Maria della Salute for all
this beauty—past and present.
NICHOLAS ARCOMANO
Attorney

5.12 Santa Maria della Salute
1631–1687, Baldassare Longhena
Campo della Salute
⚓ Salute

Eighteenth-century Venice is about sophisticated theatrical
artifice. It's also about lightness and delicacy and intrigue.
Baldassare Longhena's masterpiece, the perfect monument
to mark the beginning of the incomparable promenade
that is the Grand Canal, was completed in 1687 (five
years after his death), and no single monument is more
responsible for ushering in that golden period of the 18th
century than this one.

The church was actually commissioned to commemorate the city's deliverance from the brutal plague of 1630. Longhena wrote that he designed the building with a circular plan in order to symbolize a crown dedicated to the Blessed Virgin. The building is always glorious and sets the tone of your visit to Venice in any season, but it is really at its best on November 21st (the *festa della Salute*), when the main doors are wide open and the interior brightly lit in the evening light, and seaworthy Venetians hobble across the canal upon a temporary fabric-draped walkway atop a makeshift chain of boats to visit the church.

That kind of Venetian *scenografia* is nearly enough to make you forget that this elegant setting did not come about as naturally and easily as it may seem. The Venetians worked hard to achieve this lightness. Documents attest to the fact that no fewer than 1,156,627 tree trunks from the Dolomites were driven into the muck and cut off flush to create a platform on which to build the church and the entrance plaza.

Dazzling though all this may be, there is more: namely, three altarpieces by Luca Giordano (to the right as you enter) and a *Pentecost* by Titian (on the left as you enter). The Titian comes from the suppressed church of Santo Spirito in Isola, as do the others on the ceiling of the Sacristy. These date from the 1540s while the altarpiece (on panel) is one of Titian's earliest, dating from circa 1510. The Sacristy also contains Tintoretto's fine *Marriage at Cana* and two wonderfully fresh *bozzetti* by Luca Giordano for his altarpieces in the church. A small 12th-century Byzantine icon which originally hung in the Hagia Sophia in Constaninople has been removed recently for restoration.

GEORGE BISACCA
Conservator of paintings

5.13 **Rio Terrà dei Catecumeni**
Near the bridge of Santa Maria della Salute
 Salute

The living room of the San Gregorio neighborhood, this spacious square faces the Giudecca Canal. For most of the day, you sit quietly, away from noise and clutter. Partly shaded, partly sunny, Catecumeni offers peace as waves from the *zattere* break over the *fondamenta*. Then several women gather, and suddenly there is pandemonium as noisy children tumble out of the elementary school run by nuns of the Le Salesie di Padova order. Out come book bags, jump ropes and balls; dogs bark. Then gradually everyone drifts away toward the Salute or into the Calle dell'Abbazia or Calle dei Spezieri, and peace returns.

MARY JANE PHILLIPS-MATZ
Musicologist and biographer

Editor's Note: In Venice, a rio terrà *is a former canal that has been paved over.*

Echo

It's not that you're encircled by water; it's more that everything is swirling, like Tintoretto in his quest to capture everything at one time in defiance of space and time.

Perspective? Venice is the place. Street names resist. Palaces and piazzas collapse into one another. The harbor shape-shifts in the mist. Nowhere is it easier to get lost. My attention is enticed, incited, to circle, to keep roving, if not like the water itself around the fixed points of the quays, then like the palaces on the Grand Canal, the gondolas, taxis, *vaporettos*, police boats, wherries top-heavy with mounds of cement and criss-crossed planks, and other water-bound vehicles, that swirl like brush strokes in action across the canals and wider reaches of the Adriatic.

Siena, an homage to stasis; Venice an homage to kinesis.

That is why Tintoretto and Turner and Carpaccio are its truest masters and not the—however brilliant and accurate—Canaletto and Gaudi. Swollen with the remnants of ancient enthusiasms, Venice offers distraction that is not without soul. Everything that happens in Venice happens more than once. This doubling forces you to notice the slight changes that occur moment to moment, and enforces this with noises that, thanks to the acoustic richness of the place, could originate out on the water or in a bar, like this clatter of plates, the clank of spoon against cup in the (perfectly Italian) "India Cafe."

MARK RUDMAN
Poet, essayist, and translator

RECOMMENDED READING
Mark Rudman, *Provoked in Venice*, Wesleyan University Press, 1999.

VENETIAN ISLANDS

GIUDECCA

6.1 **Il Redentore**
1577–1592, Andrea Palladio
Campo del Redentore
 Redentore

The church of the Redentore, by Palladio (completed after his death), was built in gratitude for salvation from the Plague and is best visited the third Sunday in July, during the Feast of the Redeemer. You should do it right, starting on the San Marco side of the canal, and crossing the pontoon bridges built for the occasion to take you over the Grand Canal and the Giudecca Canal to the church. If you do this, you will probably not get the Plague (it's worked for me).

RONA GOFFEN
Art historian

Watching the Ships Go By

For my money, watching the ships go by is the best thing to be done in Venice, and it is best done by sitting on the quayside below the Dogana, at the tip of the Giudecca. From here you can see in your mind's eye the gilded galleons of *la Serenissima* returning from the east, trailing the ensigns of defeated enemies, and in your real eye the great, gaudy cruise ships which, sailing in hardly less splendidly, bring yet more wondering pilgrims to this seaport of delight.

JAN MORRIS
Writer

6

ITALY

TORCELLO

BURANO

MURANO

SAN
MICHELE

San Erasmo

VENICE

Porto di Lido

GIUDECCA

LIDO

F. S.Biagio

S. Eufemia

F. S. Eufemia

Canale della Giudecca

Giudecca

F. d. Ponte Piccolo

Campo
S.Cosmo

Redentore

Campo
del S.S.
Redentore

F. San Giacomo

Corte
Grande

Rio d. Ponte Piccolo

Rio Pallada

Rio d. Ponte Lungo

Rio d. S.Eufemia

GIUDECCA

1

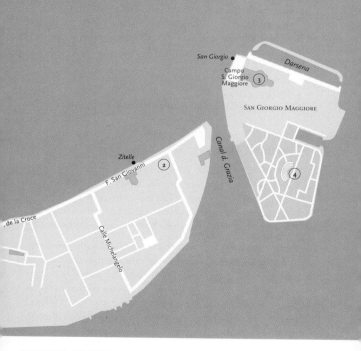

VENETIAN ISLANDS

GIUDECCA

1 Il Redentore

🍴 2 Hotel Cipriani

SAN GIORGIO MAGGIORE

3 San Giorgio Maggiore

4 Teatro Verde

6.2 Hotel Cipriani

Giudecca 10, ☏ 041 520 77 44

⚓ Zitelle

🍴 It is the place to go for the best chocolate ice cream in the world; see the recipe in *Marcella's Italian Kitchen* (p. 320 of the Knopf edition). The hotel's new casual restaurant/pizzeria is called Cip's. The tables on the embankment face Venice and offer what may be the most breathtaking view ever to come with pizza. This is the place to try the best grappas made.

MARCELLA HAZAN
Cookbook author and educator

RECOMMENDED READING
Marcella Hazan, *Marcella's Italian Kitchen*, Knopf, 1995.

Swimming Pools

⚓ Sant'Alvise, Sant'Alvise 3161, ☏ 041 71 35 67;

⚓ Sacca Fisola, Campo San Gerardo, ☏ 041 528 54 30

In Italian pools, swimmers must wear caps, and flip-flops, thongs or plastic sandals are also required for the shower room. The pools now have email: rari-nantesve@shineline.it

Being a passionate swimmer, I often travel with swimsuit and goggles. Perhaps others would be interested in Venice's two, modern, clean 25-meter public pools. They both have regularly-scheduled 45–90 minute periods of free swim (in addition to classes). Single swims cost 7,500 lire; a larger investment of 65–70,000 lire buys a ten-swim ticket good for three months. One is in Cannaregio, at Sant'Alvise, and the other is on the Giudecca at Sacca Fisola, Campo San Gerardo. Both are easily reached by *vaporetto*, and the latter has a beautiful view of the lagoon; one whole wall is glass.

SALLY SPECTOR
Artist

SAN GIORGIO MAGGIORE

 San Giorgio

6.3 ## San Giorgio Maggiore
Begun 1565, Andrea Palladio

Maybe Palladio's greatest church and one of the masterpieces of Renaissance architecture; while you're waiting for
the *vaporetto* to go back to Venice, you get a great view of
the city.

RONA GOFFEN
Art historian

6.4 ### Teatro Verde
Isola di San Giorgio Maggiore

A unique and scenic Teatro di Verzura (Theater on the
Green) to be enjoyed during summer Biennale dance and
music seasons.

GIANFRANCO MOSSETTO
Merchant banker

SAN MICHELE / ISLAND OF THE DEAD

 #23, #52

Grave of Joseph Brodsky
Cemetery of San Michele

Visit the grave of Joseph Brodsky (1940–1996) in the section set aside for foreigners in the Cemetery of San Michele
on the Island of the Dead. The 1987 Nobel Laureate in
Literature, regarded by many as the greatest Russian poet
of his generation, was as well a great English essayist and
American citizen, and was buried here according to his
own wish. Read *Watermark* (1992), which he wrote in and
about Venice.

ADELE CHATFIELD-TAYLOR
President of the American Academy in Rome

RECOMMENDED READING
Joseph Brodsky, *Watermark*, Farrar Straus, 1992

TORCELLO

 #14 from San Zaccaria

From far across the lagoon, the church of Torcello rises, linking the great horizontal expanses of low-lying marshes and lowering sky. The scene reminds us of the earliest history of Venice when a tiny, local population took refuge in the safety of the remote islands. There they built one of the gems of Romanesque Europe: the church and baptistery of Torcello with its spectacular mosaics.

WILLIAM E. WALLACE
Art historian

Santa Maria dell'Assunta
Last Judgment Mosaics / Giudizio Universale
12th century
West wall

Venice is so choked with tourists that it is a relief to wander a bit further afield. The mosaic of the *Final Judgment* in the Basilica on the island of Torcello merits a half day to itself. Of particular interest in this Byzantine epoch mosaic is the depiction of the dead souls being tormented in hell—visibly the clergy, the rich, and Turkish-looking infidel types. See how the infernal fires well up from Christ's throne and snake their way through the mosaic's panels to the scenes of torment. This Last Judgment is a worthy contrast to Michelangelo's version in every respect.

GREGORY S. BUCHER
Classicist

Excursion to the Venetian Lagoon

ITINERARY

a ⚓ Venice to Burano, take #12 from Fondamente Nuove or #4 from San Zaccaria

b ⚓ Burano to Torcello, take #14

c ⚓ Burano to San Francesco del Deserto, take local boat

A visit to the islands in the lagoon—by *vaporetto*, motorboat or *sandalo* (rowboat)—should be the crown of any Venetian sojourn, but so rich is this trip that precious details may be overlooked. Here are a few from the islands in the distant northern part of the lagoon.

When you disembark at Burano, Browning's matchless assessment of the Venetians in "A Toccata of Galuppi's" may be lurking in your memory:

> *As for Venice and her people, merely born to bloom and drop,*
> *Here on earth they bore their fruitage, mirth and folly were the crop:*
> *What of soul was left, I wonder, when the kissing had to stop?*

Look for the half-length statue of Galuppi himself, *Il Buranello*, or "the little fellow from Burano," set-up only recently in the piazza close to the landing stage. Then go into the church of San Martino on your left, seek out the oratory of Santa Barbara in the north aisle, and gaze at the young Giambattista Tiepolo's huge *Crucifixion*, a miracle of dramatic composition and somber color. Note the oval frame in the lower left with a portrait of the donor, who looks at you but points to the painting he has commissioned. Then walk a few hundred yards down the spacious via Baldassare Galuppi to the restaurant Da Romano and sample the freshest fish in the world, quite possibly presented for your choice swimming in a washtub.

A five minute ride by *vaporetto* takes you to Torcello, where—between the departure of one *vaporetto* and the arrival of the next—you may have the island not to yourself, but relatively uncrowded. Among the glories of Torcello is Santa Maria Assunta, the cathedral founded in 639 when the future Venetians fled from Altinum on the mainland before the Lombard invaders. Once you have studied the 12th-century mosaics representing the Universal Judgment on the west wall and the Byzantine Madonna on her golden ground in the central apse behind the altar, look closely at the pulpit and the fragments that support it. These are perhaps from the earliest church on this site, perhaps even from the mainland. At the base of the pulpit stair note the relief (clumsily reconstructed) representing Occasio (the Greek Kairos). His feet are planted on winged wheels, one hand holds a set of balances, and the man standing in front of him grasps his forelock. But two figures behind him (a man and a woman) have missed their chance, and the woman turns away in tears. Another fragmentary relief (on the choir enclosure) shows a figure turning on a wheel—Ixion, so rarely depicted even on Greek vases that he is seldom recognized here. Outside once more, seat yourself for a moment on the throne of Attila (thus guaranteeing your return to Torcello) and then enjoy, not just the food and drink provided by the Locanda Cipriani nearby, but the view across their garden to Santa Fosca with its octagonal portico.

If you search for genuine solitude in the lagoon today, best to seek out the well-named island of San Francesco del Deserto, a twenty minute ride by *sandalo* from Burano, where an active community of Franciscans serves a church associated with a visit by Saint Francis of Assisi on his way back from the Orient. A pine tree is said to have grown from the staff he planted in the ground. Cypress trees, well-tended flower borders, and benches close to the shore invite the visitor to rest and ponder the island's felicitous motto: *O beata solitudo, O sola beatitudo!*

HELEN F. NORTH
Classicist

RECOMMENDED READING
Robert Browning, "A Toccata of Galuppi's" (poem).

SAN LAZZARO DEGLI ARMENI

 #20 from Riva degli Schiavoni

Monastery
Open 3pm–5pm daily

Home of Mechitarists (the Armenian Catholics), San Lazzaro has the third largest Armenian manuscript library in world, a marvelous collection of Kütahya 18th-century pottery, and a charming garden. Byron used to row across the lagoon and helped the monks produce the first Armenian/English dictionary. You can take the *vaporetto* from Venice or hire a rowboat from the Lido.

JOHN CARSWELL
Curator and art historian

Editors' Note: There is a plaque to Byron on the island, and in the church a Byron Room with his portrait and some of his books.

NORTHWEST
ITALY

NORTHWEST ITALY

SWITZERLAND

Lago
Maggiore

Aosta

Varallo

VALLE D'AOSTA

FRANCE

Po

Rivoli
Stupinigi

Torino

PIEDMONT

LIGURIA

MONACO

PIEDMONT & VALLE D'AOSTA

RIVOLI
13 km west of Turin

Castello di Rivoli
Begun 1715, Filippo Juvarra

Located on the outskirts of Torino, the Castello di Rivoli dates from the 18th century, but was never fully completed. Used at one time as a residence, then for a number of other functions, and bombed in the last century, it now houses a museum of contemporary art with outstanding changing exhibits. As interesting as the art are the architectural spaces and interiors, partly preserved and partly left in a semi-deteriorated state.

LESLIE RAINER
Conservator

STUPINIGI
10 km southwest of Turin

La Palazzina di Caccia
1729, Filippo Juvarra
Piazza Principe Amedeo 7, ☎ 011 35 81 220

Think of this hunting lodge, built for Vittorio Amedeo II, not as a log cabin in the woods but as the Italian version of Versailles. This huge villa is set among vast gardens both formal and park-like. The star-shaped plan builds up elementally to the domed Great Hall, atop which proudly stands a bronze stag (lest you miss the point). As a bonus, it also houses a museum displaying 17th- and 18th-century furniture and furnishings.

ROBERT KAHN
Architect

Editor's Note: La Palazzina's bronze stag is the work of Torinese sculptor Francesco Ladetto. It was hoisted into place in 1766.

VARALLO
103 km northwest of Milan

Sacro Monte
Founded 15th century
Hilltop above Varallo

The Italian Renaissance initiated a period of massive change in the economic, political and artistic life throughout Europe, one that during the 16th and 17th centuries began to be defined on religious grounds, primarily as a reaction against the Reformation. The true believers in the doctrines of the Catholic Church (including new religious orders, such as the Jesuits) wanted to expand the Church's influence within Italy and throughout the world, whether the populace could understand the Latin mass or not. Thus the simple vision of Renaissance architects and artists—interpreting their culture through a new understanding of antique Roman forms and the new science of perspective—was modified to produce mannerist or baroque works, including churches with sinuous interior spaces adorned with sensuous depictions of the sainted heroes and heroines of the Church. In order to keep people visually engaged during the service, the scriptures were made 'realistic' by introducing vivid and surreal pictures of passion into the sacred precincts.

In northern Italy, several religious complexes were established in the late 15th and early 16th centuries, to depict various scenes from the New Testament three-dimensionally. Located on hilltops near small towns, these sites were called Sacri Monti (sacred mountains) and enabled the faithful to perform pilgrimages from urban churches to park-like settings where the Stations of the Cross were made manifest. One of the most ambitious and best-preserved of these sanctuaries is above Varallo, a small town in the foothills of the Alps. The complex, comprised of 45 chapels that illustrate events in the life of Christ, is a rich composite of baroque architecture, life-sized sculpture, and painted frescoes. Although the statuary has become somewhat dusty and forlorn, the visceral effect of these scenes (the suffering Christ, sneering Roman guards) is still powerful today.

Other Sacri Monti worth seeing are the Santuario di Crea near Casale Monferrato (23 chapels dedicated to the Rosary) and the Sacro Monte in Orta San Giulio (twenty chapels dedicated to San Francesco). The interesting town of Orta has several good small hotels sited on the lake, Lago d'Orta, as well as a beautiful view of the Isola di San Giulio, with its Romanesque basilica.

ROBERT EVANS
Architect

Even the most hard-boiled Italian Marxist will look at you kindly, pausing a moment out of respect, if you tell them you're going to Sacro Monte—one of the Catholic retreats northwest of Milan that display life-sized dioramas of the Stations of the Cross. Here is a faux-Renaissance town built in the Renaissance, and if you're one of those that thinks the Renaissance was the root of Western advertising then this is the place for you!

These incredible buildings date to the 16th century, and each contains as many as fifty characters fleshed out with exquisite realism, including bucking horses—all out of painted plaster. Life-sized Neapolitan creches; agonized faces worthy of the great sculptors; amazing *trompe-l'oeil*. Some figures look a little down at the heels but I for one am astonished that these painted life-size plasters have survived centuries of Alpine winters. They make wax museums look like mannequin shops.

Admittedly, I had to struggle with my secular human-ist intentions. But you should, too, if you go to Italian churches just to look at the art. Here, part of the struggle is the walk from the mountain railroad station of Varallo (though cabs are also available). You feel more empathetic after a twenty, thirty minute climb on foot. But the surprise of this Arcadian park with its sublime buildings in the rarefied alpine air is that it will make you feel like taking up a pennant that says, "Go Jesus!"

PIER CONSAGRA
Artist

RECOMMENDED READING
David Freedberg, *The Power of Images: Studies in the History of Theory and Response*, University of Chicago Press, 1991.

Bernardo Vittone Tour

The Piedmont in northwestern Italy is a region of gently rolling hills, bounded by the Alps, the Lake District, and the foothills of the Italian Riviera. An area of great culinary and vinicultural distinction (home of the *tartufi bianco* and the *nebbiolo* grape), its major city, Torino, served as the capital for the Dukes of Savoy from the 16th through 19th centuries. During the latter part of the 17th century, the Savoy gave refuge to one of Italy's most creative architects, Guarino Guarini. A world-famous scholar and mathematician, Guarini expanded upon Borromini's baroque conception of space, purifying its elliptical amplitudes into large, geometrically-rigorous structures that remain among the most unique spaces ever constructed. The cupolas for San Lorenzo and the Capella della Santa Sindone in the Duomo of Torino are his only major domes still extant: spaces in which ethereal light, not the stone structure, seems material.

However, it is Guarini's followers, designing small churches in the countryside near Torino, whom I find most intriguing. Bernardo Vittone produced dozens of ecclesiastical buildings that remain intact (although the interiors are frequently difficult to visit). Designed for poor farming parishes, they were constructed of inexpensive materials (using brick, not stone, structural walls; plaster, not marble, decorations). But their feats of structural vaulting and effects of mysterious lighting are unique in all of Italy. Vittone's first experiments, Santuario di Vallinotto near Carignano and San Luigi

Gonzaga near Corteranzo, combined Borromini's plans with Guarini's open vaulted structures in tiny chapels in the countryside. Graduating to larger, more urban projects in the 1740s, he created churches with central plans (such as Santa Croce in Villanova Mondovì, Santa Chiara in Bra), where the pendentives that translate the circular dome structure onto the piers of the square church have been carved away, allowing light to pour through the juncture between the heavenly and human worlds. In his later work (such as Santa Maria di Piazza in Torino), the buildings negate the Renaissance's ideal central plan, elaborating on Guarini's studies that linked a series of discrete volumes into a unique whole. (Another example of the spacial experimentation of the era is Alfieri's remarkable Parrochiale in Carmignano, where the nave consists of a semicircular vault: an interiorized version of Bernini's Piazza San Pietro!) Vittone's creation of magically light-filled space is, perhaps, best represented by San Michele in Borgo d'Ale, where stucco cherubim and seraphim float back-lit in front of pastel-colored plaster.

As the Duchy of Savoy once straddled both sides of the Alps, its cuisine is closer to classical French than Italian. That said, in honor of Vittone's work, one should dine in one of the many fine restaurants in the Piedmont's hill towns, surrounded by vineyards. Near Barolo, Il Giardino da Felicin in Monforte d'Alba has outstanding home-made specialties, and, on a clear day, an astounding view of the Alps from the Riviera to Mont Blanc. Nearby, in Alba, gourmands should visit the Fiera Nazionale del Tartufo in early Fall, where one may fondle, sniff, and purchase a panoply of erotic white truffle nodules. At the Cannon d'Oro in Cocconato, one may dine on the odoriferous little tubers for a price. They are shaved thinly over a simple dish of pasta, and priced by the weight of your order. Just remember to say "*Basta,*" or you may find that your simple meal has become the most expensive of your entire stay.

ROBERT EVANS
Architect

LIGURIA

GENOA / GENOVA

Via Garibaldi and Piazza Fontane Marose
16th century palazzi

This street of magnificent palazzi of the late Renaissance is the spirit of the 16th-century Genova. Designed by Italian and northern Flemish architects, the street and its buildings reflect the wealth and prosperity Genova achieved through trade and its seafaring economy—one palazzo is richer than the last. This culminates at the Piazza Fontane Marose, lined with palazzi, many of whose façades are painted with illusionist faux architectural elements. The museums are well worth the visit, with masterpieces by Dutch and Italian artists. Especially notable is Galleria Nazionale di Palazzo Spinola (Piazza Pellicceria 1).

All of Genova tends to be overlooked. It is a fantastic city, both because of its location on the sea and its rich artistic and architectural heritage.

LESLIE RAINER
Conservator

PORTOFINO

Stroll from San Fruttuoso to Portofino
Take the ferry from Santa Margherita (30 km east of Genoa) to San Fruttuoso

The walk from the village of San Fruttuoso to Portofino is less popular than the well-worn trail that connects the five towns of the Cinque Terre, but it is more spectacular.

The abandoned 12th-century abbey at San Fruttuoso can only be reached by ferry from nearby Santa Margherita. As the ferry entered the small secluded cove and we gazed up at the imposing cliffs ahead, we were reluctant to get off the boat. The path behind the church was difficult to find, and as we watched the boat pull away below, we realized we had no choice but to start the steep climb. After about twenty minutes of ascending a switch-back path beneath a pine forest, the trail leveled off, revealing incredible views of the Tyrrhenian Sea and the Maritime Alps. The trail continued through intimate olive terraces and hilltop orchards, then slowly wound down along narrow stone corridors and the pedestrian alleyways of the urban villas directly above Portofino. When we reached the top of the harborside piazza, the trail culminated in a group of umbrella-covered cafe tables and the tantalizing aroma of *penne all'arrabbiata* welcomed the famished hikers, closing a perfect day.

CHIP SULLIVAN AND ELIZABETH BOULTS
Landscape architect and designer, respectively

PORTOVENERE
14 km south of La Spezia

In May 1999, while living for a month in the Villa Orbiana at the newly-established Liguria Study Center for the Arts and Humanities, which overlooks the Mediterranean and the small town of Bogliasco, I take a break from my work and journey to Portovenere and then hike around the Cinque Terre. I take a local train from Genoa to La Spezia that travels through intensely dark tunnels and suddenly emerges into the blue light surrounding yet another jewel of a village. It is early morning, and at each seaside stop along the Riviera di Levante—including the five lands of Monterosso, Vernazza, Corniglia, Manarola, and Riomaggiore—there is an almost absolute silence full of mist, filtered light, and fresh spring air. Then a *battello* to Portovenere. A simple trip, one already full of distant images and awe, but approaching Portovenere by sea, with La Spezia Naval Base on the right and Lerici on the left side of the bay, is overpowering. The first thing you see in the distance is the medieval church of San Pietro rising from the sea like a dark grey monster.

I check into the Hotel Paradiso on the via Garibaldi,

overlooking the Isola Palmaria, the Apuan Alps, and row upon row of mussel traps with their imposing sticks and colored bottles floating in the Gulf below, and jaunt down to the harbor to arrange a tour of the outer three islands: Palmaria (the largest, with its reddish-green Grotta Azzurra and the Grotta Vulcanica which is surrounded by hundreds of screaming seagulls); Tino (with the frightening remains of a German World War II bunker alongside the Romanesque Abbey of San Venerio); and Tinetto (whose rugged beach is split between nude sunbathers and a military zone hovering above). These islands as well as Byron's Bay off the tip of San Pietro are best explored by *traghetto* (in my case captained by Arrigo, a longtime local resident and fisherman in his late eighties who remembers fishing from the window of his palazzo before Mussolini built a road that made it difficult to cast into the sea). The fantastic, striated and whirling marble of all three islands shows the scars of extensive excavations of an earlier time.

Back on land I enter the medieval city through its portal with the White Madonna overhead and walk up the ancient (now commercially lined) via Capellini, up to the church of San Lorenzo, the Castello Doria, and a wondrous view of San Pietro from the vast town cemetery built into the cliffs. Walking back down the promontory and near the Piazza Eugenio Montale with the poet's famous tribute to this city carved in stone, I discover the Ristorante La Medusa di Canese Manuela, via Capellini 74. I decide to skip the Osteria del Caruggio and Da Iseo (both recommended by guidebooks and friends) for this romantic, cozy place. Good choice: *Gnocchetti alla polpa* (crab); *orata grigliata; vino bianco Cinque Terre 97*.

A man with a sandy voice-box in place of his larynx sits for dinner with his brother. Clearly, more local color. Over a steaming bowl of mussels they are talking about, what, local politics, the weather, their own catch of the day? What are they really talking about? What world do I live in now? I look out the door (of course I'm completely drunk on the regional white wine), and I see the address of the home across the street: 123. Indeed. Everything seems so easy here.

I walk back to San Pietro's. Quiet. No one. Mountains. Sky. Calm sea (peaceful ripples). Golfo dei Poeti. Shelley. Byron. Montale. Me. I look up. Someone is sitting on a rock.

It's late. I walk up to the castle. Cats in every doorstep. Dark blue sky. People fishing in the bay with lighted bobs. A speedboat of fishermen darts into the harbor. Lights. It's about the night, the sea, the old, the dirt, the musty buildings, the fog.

I return to San Pietro's. The figure on the rock is still there. But when I look again, it has vanished. Was it Shelley?

CHESTER BISCARDI
Composer

RECOMMENDED READING
Eugenio Montale, *Cuttlefish Bones:1920–1927,* translated by William Arrowsmith, W. W. Norton & Company, 1992.

Editor's Note: The name Byron's Bay commemorates the poet's famous swim across the Golfo della Spezia from Portovenere to San Terenzo, a distance of four or five miles. An annual swimming competition also celebrates this exploit.

In the journal entry quoted above, Portovenere is entered through the Porta del Carrugio, with its 14th-century portrait of the Madonna Bianca, patron saint of the city, who has a traditional festival every August 17th.

Eugenio Montale won the Nobel Prize for Literature in 1975. The poem "Portovenere," is included in his book Ossi di Seppia *(Cuttlefish Bones).*

LOMBARDY

CASTELSEPRIO
14 km south of Varese

Frescoes
ca. 8th century
Santa Maria Foris Portas
Closed Mondays

This tiny, little-known site was occupied by Celts, then Romans (the name comes from Roman Sibrium), then Lombards, for whom it was an important garrison from the sixth century to the eighth. In the 1940s, the church of Santa Maria Foris Portas was found to preserve under layers of whitewash frescoes dating probably from the eighth century, in a style recalling Byzantium or Alexandria. The fresco cycle in the central of three apses has two horizontal bands adorned with scenes from the Infancy of Christ probably derived from a scroll, represented here on two levels. The upper band illustrates (from left to right) *The Annunciation, The Visitation, The Trial by Water* (an episode from the Apocrypha), *Christ Pantokrator, The Dream of Joseph*, and *The Journey to Bethlehem* (particularly well preserved). The lower band (more damaged) shows (from right to left) *The Nativity, The Adoration of the Magi, The Presentation*, and *The Massacre of the Innocents*. The triumphal arch carries additional frescoes of two angels in flight and medallions containing symbols of the Second Coming.

HELEN F. NORTH
Classicist

CASTIGLIONE OLONA
10 km south of Varese

Baptistery

Saint John the Baptist Fresco Cycle
1435, Masolino da Panicale

This hilly town near Varese preserves many legacies from its great benefactor, Cardinal Branda Castiglione (1350-1443). His most memorable gift was to bring from Florence Masolino da Panicale (who had already painted the marvelous murals of Saint Catherine of Alexandria in the chapel of his titular church in Rome, San Clemente), and commission him to work on the Collegiata and the Baptistery here. Masolino's acknowledged masterpiece is the cycle of scenes from the life of Saint John the Baptist in the Baptistery (1435). *The Banquet of Herod* and *Salome Presenting the Head of the Baptist to Herodias* on the right wall and the *Baptism of Christ* above the altar are breathtaking in their virtuosity. To the right of the altar, Saint John points an accusing finger at the guilty pair and around the corner he sits behind prison bars. The Collegiata across the garden from the Baptistery has six frescoes of the Life of the Virgin on the vault. Down the hill, across from the palace, the Chiesa di Villa also deserves a look, not only inside for its elegant proportions, but outside, where its delicately sculptured doorway is flanked by gigantic statues of Saint Anthony and Saint Christopher.

HELEN F. NORTH
Classicist

COMO

Tempio Voltiano

1927
Giardino Pubblico, viale Marconi
Closed Mondays

This pantheon-like rotunda, set in a waterfront park on Lake Como, houses the Museo Alessandro Volta, and is a tribute to the life and work of the man who invented the first battery and who gave us the "volt." It is a necessary visit for anyone interested in artful science or the beauty found in the thoughtful and creative exploration of an idea.

The "temple" was built during the Fascist era, as part of an exposition of Italian science and technology and in honor of the centenary of Volta's death. Volta's instruments and devices are preciously presented in custommade cabinetry, like a cupboard of wonders and curiosity, or like something from the old Smithsonian Institution in Washington. Each display is numbered according to a guide that is available in English from the feisty old matron at the door.

The materials Volta used in his experiments—wood, metal, glass, wire—create stunning desk-top sculptures and charged compositions of form, texture and sentimentality, in the spirit of Duchamp, Cornell or Rauschenberg.

This monument to electricity is truly an inspiration for artists, craftspeople, and scientists alike.

CHIP SULLIVAN AND ELIZABETH BOULTS
Landscape architect and designer, respectively

Work of Giuseppe Terragni

a. Casa del Fascio, *1931–1936*
   Piazza del Popolo; open after 2pm
b. Asilo Infantile Sant'Elia, *1936–1937*
   Via dei Mille; by appointment only, ☎ 31 25 21 11
c. Casa Giuliani-Frigerio, *1939–1940*
   Vialle Rosseli 34; private house
d. Villa Bianca, *1936–1937*
   Via Garibaldi 15, Seveso

In addition to the villas on the lake, the town contains most of Giuseppe Terragni's *oeuvre*. Most notable among these is the Casa del Fascio which is remarkable for its compactness and overlapping spaces. Who would have thought that a nine-square could be so complicated? For as compact as is the Casa, his Asilo Infantile Sant'Elia (nursery school) is open and airy. The Casa Giuliani-Frigerio is the best of the apartment buildings. In general, Terragni is most remarkable for his ability to specifically mark multiple spatial edges. These projects are no exception. Halfway to Milan from Como is the Villa Bianca in Seveso. The house, now a restaurant, looks as if it were a fragment of a larger building. It has all the modernist ideas of the other buildings compressed into a house.
ROBERT LIVESEY
Architect

Editor's Note: A nursery school in Italian is also rather beautifully called a nido, *meaning nest.*

DESENZANO DEL GARDA
38 km west of Verona

Charming Desenzano is a short train ride from Verona. Located on the southern shore of Lago di Garda and containing the remains of a large, early-imperial Roman villa with many good mosaic floors, the tiny resort of Desenzano offers easy and refreshing access by boat to Sirmione, the peninsular promontory that was the beloved home of the Roman poet Catullus (circa 87–55 BC). The spectacular ruins of an impressive Roman villa once believed to have belonged to Catullus' family are haunting when viewed against the backdrop of a clear sky and the equally limpid lake. Pack a picnic, bring a copy of Catullus (if in English, I recommend Michie's translation), tuck yourself into a secluded niche and travel back two thousand years.

Alfred Lord Tennyson (1809–1892) began his journey to Sirmione from Desenzano and commemorated the voyage in his poem:

Frater Ave Atque Vale

Row us out from Desenzano, to your
Sirmione row!
So they row'd, and there we landed—
"O venusta Sirmio!"
There to me thro' all the groves of olive in the
summer glow,
There beneath the Roman ruin where the
purple flowers grow,
Came that "Ave atque Vale" of the Poet's
hopeless woe,
Tenderest of Roman poets nineteen-hundred
years ago.
"Frater Ave atque Vale" as we wander'd to
and fro
Gazing at the Lydian-laughter of the Garda
Lake below
Sweet Catullus's all-but-island, olive-silvery
Sirmio!

MARGARET A. BRUCIA
Latin teacher

RECOMMENDED READING
The Poems of Catullus, translated by James Michie, Vintage Books, 1969. Currently available from Bristol Classical Press, 1989.
Alfred Lord Tennyson, "Frater Ave Atque Vale" (poem).

LECCO

56 km northeast of Milan

Ferry Boat

15th century, Leonardo da Vinci

Leonardo was fascinated by hydrology and made many sketches of rivers, drainage systems, and canals. He designed a ferry to cross the Adda River at Imbersago in Lecco. The ferry operates on the current in the river and still functions.

FREDERICK STEINER
Professor of planning and landscape architecture

MANTUA / MANTOVA

Palazzo Ducale

Complex of buildings dating from 13th–18th centuries
Piazza Sordello

The ducal palace is a must-see. The *baldacchino* columns on the loggia are a clue to what awaits inside. The court-yard reminds one of the Temple of Apollo at Didyma; the dwarves' quarters are worth bending for.

ROBERT LIVESEY
Architect

Camera degli Sposi

1465–1474, Andrea Mantegna
Castello di San Giorgio

The fortress-like Castello di San Giorgio, one of a complex of several attached buildings which collectively constitute the Palazzo Ducale and the former palace of the Gonzaga, is not an inviting structure—nor was it ever meant to be. You will not be permitted to wander through its many decorated rooms on your own, but instead must wait for a guided tour. But the wait will be worth it when you step into Mantegna's painted masterpiece, the so-called Camera degli Sposi.

The square room is frescoed on all four walls, in the semi-circular lunettes, and on the ceiling vault. Mantegna completed the decoration in 1474, after a working period of almost ten years. During this time Lodovico Gonzaga gave him a monthly allowance, housing, enough food for a household of six, and firewood. As you can see, the relationship between patron and artist has changed considerably since the 15th century—with more autonomy for the artist, but also less material stability.

Look upward, towards the vault. Mantegna has used paint to create the illusion that there is a great circular opening to the sky, known as an oculus. The most famed oculus of antiquity lights the Pantheon in Rome, and this is probably where Mantegna got the idea to render a fictive version here. You can witness how avidly he studied the ruins of Rome if you look at the cityscape of the fresco painted to the right of the entrance door. You will be able easily to recognize the Colosseum, for example, as Mantegna paints the scene with an almost archaeological exactitude.

Peering down at us from the illusionistic oculus appear ladies of the court, a servant woman, a peacock, and several nude angels. All of the figures are rendered *di sotto in su,* which in Italian means "from below, looking up." Note, for example, how we stare right into the genitalia and tushies of the boy angels standing on the oculus rim. Here Mantegna points the way to the painted ceilings of the later baroque period, which seem to dissolve the physical fabric of a building as the figures are swept up in pure atmosphere. But in the Camera degli Sposi all is still grounded, as befits the Renaissance taste for an earthbound naturalism.

BARBARA LYNN-DAVIS
Art historian and writer

Frescoes by Andrea Mantegna are simply breathtaking. Do
not miss.

JOHN C. LEAVEY
Painter

RECOMMENDED READING
Bernard Berenson, *Italian Painters of the Renaissance*, o.p.
Jacob Burckhardt, *The Civilization of the Renaissance in Italy*,
Penguin, 1990.

Casa de Giulio Romano
1538, Giulio Romano
Via Carlo Poma 18
Façade only; interior not open to public

Everyone knows about the Palazzo del Té, which is a wonderful example of mannerism. However, equally dense but
on a smaller scale is Giulio Romano's house. It takes the
eyes a few minutes to adjust to the endless shifts and layers
of the front elevation. Of particular note is the dual compression of the attic and basement and their framing of the
'real' house.

ROBERT LIVESEY
Architect

MILAN / MILANO

Duomo
Piazza del Duomo

Northern Italy is (apart from Venice) sometimes neglected
by travelers, but Milan Cathedral, particularly its sculptures, merits attention.

JAMES FENTON
Writer

Naviglio Grande and Naviglio Pavese
12th–17th centuries, Leonardo da Vinci and others
Ticinese Quarter, south of the Porta Ticinese

The Quartiere Ticinese in Milano is a surprise. This neighborhood of intersecting canals seems more like Amsterdam than Milano. The canals are remnants of the Navigli system in Lombardy. The first of these canals is the Naviglio Grande, built between the 12th and 13th centuries. The second is the Naviglio Pavese, based on a sketch by Leonardo during Sforza's regime during the 15th century, but designed by Giuseppe Meda at the end of the 16th century and built during the 17th century. The canals provide a wonderful place for a walk and they are lined with several terrific restaurants.

FREDERICK STEINER
Professor of planning and landscape architecture

RECOMMENDED READING
Regione Lombardia, Assessorato all'Urbanistica, eds. *Il Recupero Paesistico Dell'Adda di Leonardo*, Milano, 1998. Available in Italian and English.

Pinacoteca di Brera
Palazzo di Brera
Via Brera 28, ☎ 02 72 26 31
Closed Mondays

The Supper at Emmaus
After 1600, Caravaggio
Room XXIX

Caravaggio painted two versions of *The Supper at Emmaus* (and at least one version of Christ's walk to Emmaus, of which only a copy remains, now in Hampton Court.) Of the two *Suppers*, the one in London's National Gallery, with its rich coloration, its plump, beardless Christ, and its famously precarious basket of fruit, is probably the better known. But the later Brera version is not to be overlooked. Here the palette is much subdued and the *chiaroscuro* more pronounced. The florid shadows of the London painting have spread to a pervasive, Rembrandtish murk, from which the characters emerge as spotlit essentials: a hand raised in benediction, eyes widened in surprise. But if the darkness distills the gestures, it also unifies the composition, rendering it uniquely grave and profound. This is a more intimate repast than the earlier *Supper*; its Christ seems sadder and more resigned, and He gives himself away with subtler, more constrained movements. The shadows also envelop the two subsidiary characters, the innkeeper and elderly servant, who, though presumably unaware of the scene unfolding in their presence, are nonetheless drawn into its drama.

The Pinacoteca itself, with roughly forty halls, houses one of Europe's largest art collections. The works displayed are primarily Italian, from the 15th through the 20th centuries; represented are Bellini, Titian, Correggio, Raphael and Modigliani, among many, many others. The museum's three great prizes are Piero della Francesca's portrait of Federico, duke of Montefeltro; Mantegna's *Dead Christ*; and Raphael's *Marriage of the Virgin*. The surrounding neighborhood is lovely for walking; it's filled with elegant mansions and small, chic boutiques.

DAVE KING
Writer

RECOMMENDED READING:
Walter Friedlaender, *Caravaggio Studies*, o.p.

Madonna and Child with Saints

ca. 1472–1474, Piero della Francesca

Piero della Francesca's monumental altarpiece, *Madonna and Child with Saints*, invites contemplation with its enigmatic cluster of still figures. The patron, Federico da Montefeltro, Duke of Urbino, kneels in prayer at right, dressed in shiny armor with gauntlets removed. But perhaps more conspicuous by her absence is the duke's wife Battista Sforza, who died shortly after the birth of her ninth child and only son, Guidobaldo, the Duke's long-awaited heir. John the Baptist (Battista's patron saint) points a narrow finger to her empty spot opposite the Duke. The sleeping Christ child who reclines on the Virgin's lap may also allude to Battista's death. Suspended on a cord under a massive barrel vault, the ostrich egg may symbolize the Virgin birth because ostriches were thought to hatch their eggs by the warmth of sunlight.

KATEY BROWN
Art historian

Editor's Note: Federico married Battista Sforza when she was fourteen. She bore him eight daughters and finally, in 1472, the son and heir Guidobaldo. She died six months later at the age of 26.

Trattoria al Muleto

Corso XXII Marzo 57, &02 70 12 68 14

¶♀ Trattoria al Muleto is a wonderful seafood restaurant in Milano.

FREDERICK STEINER
Professor of planning and landscape architecture

MONZA

14 km northeast of Milan

Autodromo Nazionale di Monza

Via Parco 20052, &039 248 21
3 km north of the center of Monza; for permission to visit the oval track, fax advance request to &039 32 03 24

Set in a centuries-old royal park of great beauty, Monza is the site of the Gran Premio (the Grand Prix of Italy), one of the races which count towards the world driving championship. (Though some might think it's boring to drive around and around the same track hundreds of times, driving at racing speeds is like standing with your back to the wall, dodging from side to side while someone throws knives at you.) Ferraris are made just down the road, and attendance at the Gran Premio is directly proportional to how well they're doing.

Through the years, Monza has been a stage for the drama and tragedy which characterizes racing. In 1961, the German count Wolfgang von Trips crashed his Ferrari, killing himself and eleven spectators—and handing the world championship to his arch rival, the Californian Phil Hill. In 1978, in eerily similar circumstances, Mario Andretti became champion when his teammate Ronnie Peterson was killed.

In the 1950s, an oval track with giant banked curves was added to the course. Over time, the footings settled unevenly and the pavement cracked, becoming too rough for racing. But the banks remain, immense and vine-covered, a sort of Stonehenge of speed.

SAM POSEY
Race car driver, artist, and designer

Editor's Note: The royal park occupies the grounds of what was indeed planned and built as a royal villa, for the Empress Maria Teresa of Austria, starting in 1877.

PAVIA

36 km south of Milan

Pavia is located on the Ticino, the river on whose banks Hannibal skirmished with the Romans in 218 BC, after emerging from the Alps. Dominated today by the University, a successor of a former school of law founded in 1361, Pavia has the flavor of a college town: book shops and youth prevail. The Basilica of San Michele with its octagonal cupola is one of Pavia's important churches, as is San Pietro in Ciel d'Oro, which houses the remains, at two different levels—bunk bed style—of Saint Augustine and Boethius.

MARGARET A. BRUCIA
Latin teacher

NORTHEAST ITALY

NORTHEAST ITALY

Bolzano

TRENTINO-ALTO ADIGE

Trento

Possagno
Masèr
Bassano del
Grappa
Asolo
Casella
Altivole
Fanzolo

Lago di Garda

VENETO

Vicenza

Verona

Lonigo

Padua

LOMBARDY

Mantua

Po

Parma

EMILIA - ROMAGNA

VENETO & TRENTINO-ALTO ADIGE

ASOLO
33 km northeast of Treviso

Villa Cipriani Hotel and Restaurant
Via Canova 298, 31011, ☎ 0423 95 21 66

🍽 This peaceful hill town near Venice and Milano is renowned
🏨 for its arcades and medieval atmosphere. It is also the location of the Villa Cipriani, a renovated 15th-century villa
set in lovely gardens. It is among Italy's most luxurious
small hotels with one of the best restaurants in the Veneto.
However, the reason to stay in Asolo is to be near three of
Italy's most interesting collaborations between architects
and artists: a large farmhouse (Palladio's Villa Barbaro in
Masèr, see p. 174), a funereal monument (Scarpa's Brion-
Vega Tomb in San Vito d'Altivole, see p. 180), and an
addition to a small art gallery (Scarpa's Gipsoteca or
Plaster Cast Gallery within the Casa Canova in Possagno,
see p. 178).
ROBERT EVANS
Architect

BASSANO DEL GRAPPA
15 km west of Asolo

Ponte degli Alpini
Original plan 1569, Andrea Palladio

Buy Bruce Boucher's monograph on Palladio. Start in
Venice or Vicenza, seeing as many as possible of the buildings listed in the back section of this useful book. Visiting
some of the villas around the Veneto can require some
organization and transport. But don't miss out on Palladio's bridge in Bassano, if you want to see an unusual
Italian town. Known as Ponte degli Alpini, the bridge has
been rebuilt, roughly according to Palladio's original plan
of 1569. One looks at the covered wooden bridge, which is

the focus for a lively *passeggiata*. Then one samples the local grappa and grappa-related beverages.
JAMES FENTON
Writer

RECOMMENDED READING
Bruce Boucher, *Andrea Palladio: The Architect in His Time*, Abbeville Press, 1994.

CASELLA D'ASOLO
2.5 km south of Asolo

Trattoria da Mario
Ca'Mario, ☎ 0423 56 40 75

🍽 Delicious food in an unremarkable building in the middle of the Veneto, and near gorgeously-frescoed Palladian villas. Great risotto, grilled meats, and fresh vegetables.
PABLO CONRAD
Writer and editor

FANZOLO
23 km west of Treviso

Villa Emo
ca. 1550, Andrea Palladio

My favorite of the Palladian villas is the hyper-linear Villa Emo. Palladio made a fine art of fashioning a working farm into a showcase for the pretensions of these Venetian gentleman farmers. The long arms stretching to either side of the central pavilion of living rooms housed all the stables, animals, and granaries. One imagines, however, that the smell on hot days, wafting through the *salone*, might have been unbearable. For all the platonic formalism, everything about the villa was utilitarian: the grand entry ramp doubled as a threshing floor, and even the little cupolas at the ends served as pigeon roosts! Although it lacks the grand gardens of its neighbor, I rate this villa highly over the more famous Villa Barbaro nearby.
D. B. MIDDLETON
Architect

LONIGO
21 km southwest of Vicenza

Rocca Pisani
1576, Vicenzo Scamozzi

If you are visiting Vicenza, it is probably to see the works of Palladio. Nearby, in Lonigo, is one of the more interesting footnotes to the tail end of Palladio's career, the Rocca Pisani, built in the 1570s by Palladio's follower and artistic heir, Vincenzo Scamozzi. Here, one can get a sense of what Palladio's villas might have been like when they were first built: sitting at the top of a hill, the Rocca Pisani is still surrounded by fields and barking dogs but hasn't suffered from the tourist invasion that many of Palladio's own villas have. Furthermore, even at the risk of blasphemy, it can be suggested that at least this once, Scamozzi may have outdone Palladio at Palladio's own game.

JOHN MARCIARI
Art historian

MASÈR
9 km east of Asolo

Villa Barbaro
1560–1568, Andrea Palladio
Via Cornuda 2, ☏ 0423 92 30 04
Open Tuesdays, Saturdays, Sundays, 3pm–6pm

Frescoes
1566–1568, Paolo Veronese

Palladio's built works in the countryside north and west of Venice were often inexpensively constructed, poorly maintained farmhouses for the *nouveau riche* of the 16th century—often disappointing compared to the power and graphic clarity of his published *Books*. But the Villa Barbaro has it all: a long *allée* of trees leading toward a symmetrical composition consisting of a central two-storey 'temple' flanked by arcaded wings with oversized sundials.

The interior rooms contain frescoes by Veronese, in which life-sized figures intimately invite you into the Barbaro living quarters where the family's history is portrayed on the walls. The primary residential spaces are on the upper floor facing the hillside to the north, where a grotto carved into the hill completes the arrival process with a big splash (fountains! satyrs! naked nymphs!). A real temple by Palladio, in the form of a small, circular chapel, is sited on the roadway, immediately adjacent to the entrance.

ROBERT EVANS
Architect

Built for the brothers Barbaro, this is less a country getaway than a working farm. Sited squarely with views and access to the fields, rather than atop a hill, this villa marks a significant departure in both use and form from its predecessors. The grand wings were designed not for additional accommodation, but to house animals. Veronese painted the frescoes in every room of the *piano nobile* and the view from this floor to the rear is of a beautiful nymphaeum contrasting the vast openness of the main façade. Is it any wonder that Palladian architecture, arguably the most influential ever, was the model for the antebellum mansions of the American south, signifying the marriage of the gentleman and the farmer?

ROBERT KAHN
Architect

MESTRE
8 km northwest of Venice

Marghera Channels
Located on the mainland next to Mestre

The channels of the industrial area of Marghera, a private or taxi boat trip. An undiscovered experience of the lagoon, to be seen from the waterfront chaos of the city's modern industrial archaeology. Recommended at sunset.

GIANFRANCO MOSSETTO
Merchant banker

PADUA / PADOVA

Cappella degli Scrovegni
Giardini dell'Arena

Frescoes
Early 14th century, Giotto

Cappella degli Scrovegni, often referred to as the Arena Chapel, is situated in the remains of an ancient Roman arena. Inside is one of the great artistic visions of humanity, a cycle of frescoes which portrays the life of Christ in near-symphonic exposition with the chapel's architecture. The paintings are formally composed and highly decorated, yet many scenes reverberate with emotional and expressionistic meaning. This major work, a must-see on any trip to Italy, is an early triumph for Giotto and a great example of the heights to which human expression can strive.
SIMON DINNERSTEIN
Artist

Giotto's fresco cycle was painted circa 1310 for Enrico Scrovegni. Scrovegni commissioned the chapel to expiate the usury of his father, Rinaldo Scrovegni (it was a practice through which he too had profited in earlier years.) After you have decoded the many scenes in the cycles of the lives of Anna and Joachim, the Virgin Mary, and Christ, it is a challenge to see how many references to money and usury you can find. On the lowest level, the seven Virtues and Vices were intended to convey to 14th-century Italians the most basic rules of human behavior.
DAVID G. WILKINS
Art and architectural historian

Editor's Note: Dante devotes a scathing passage in the Inferno (XVII.64ff) to the elder Scrovegni.

One of the most moving of the narrative scenes in the chapel is the *Lamentation*, or mourning over the dead Christ. Christ's body is limp, and the Virgin Mary wraps herself around him as she looks in anguish into his closed eyes. One hand seems to feel for a pulse in his neck, but Giotto's depiction of her creased brow and shadowed mouth tells us she is at the moment of recognizing with finality that her son no longer lives. The angels make explicit her emotions, as ten of them fill the sky with their wailing. Notice the impressionistically painted tails of their robes, which convey a whooshing sense of movement, and were perhaps inspired by the artist's observation of comets in the night sky.

It is just this kind of fascination with the natural world—from the portrayal of grief to the travels of distant stars—that distinguishes the Renaissance artist from his medieval predecessors. Giotto renders a believable, three-dimensional space and fills it with figures we humanly recognize from our own physical world. This is the essential achievement of Renaissance art, and Giotto—as his 16th-century biographer Giorgio Vasari recognized—was one of the first lights of its dawn in Italy.

BARBARA LYNN-DAVIS
Art historian and writer

Oratorio di San Giorgio
Piazza del Santo

Frescoes
1378–1384, Altichiero da Zevio

Frescoes by Altichiero, a *trecento* artist, under-esteemed, of great ability. Obviously everyone sees the Giottos in the Arena Chapel but many walk past the nearby Oratory of San Giorgio . . . a pity.

JOHN C. LEAVEY
Painter

RECOMMENDED READING
Bernard Berenson, *Italian Painters of the Renaissance*, o.p.
Roberto Longhi, *Three Studies*, translated by David Tabbat and David Jacobson, Sheep Meadow Press, 1996.

PORTOGRUARO
66 km northeast of Venice

Antico Spessotto
Via Roma 2, ☏ 0421 710 40

The small town of Portogruaro is a very agreeable old town
that has little to offer besides the pleasant and moderately-
priced hotel, Antico Spessotto in the center of town, and
good restaurants. For fresh fish, go along the river by the
old mill. (I do not eat at any hotel if I can help it.) I recommend Portogruaro, however, as a good base for day trips
by train to Venice and an excellent place to spend the night
before setting out to visit interesting places.
ERNST PULGRAM
Historical linguist

POSSAGNO
9 km north of Asolo

Gipsoteca at Casa di Canova
1957, Carlo Scarpa
Piazza Canova, ☏ 0423 54 43 23
Closed Mondays

Carlo Scarpa (1906-1978) was a modern architect from
Venice who completed few free-standing buildings, and
therefore came to the attention of the world beyond the
Veneto late in his life. He was an acclaimed teacher and
artisan (especially his glassware designed for Venini in the
1930s and 1940s), the majority of whose early work con-
sisted of installations for art exhibits (such as the Venice
Biennale), art museums, and retail stores. One of his first
completed buildings was a small addition to the Gipsoteca,
or Plaster Cast Gallery in Possagno, immediately north of
Asolo. The gallery, designed in the mid-1950s, contains the
overflow of plaster casts from Antonio Canova's adjacent
sculpture museum. Juxtaposed to that barrel-vaulted neoclassical space (albeit a suitable 19th-century setting for

Canova's sensuous neoclassical sculpture), Scarpa created
a single room broken into three distinct volumes and filled
with daylight from surprising sources. High clerestory windows carve away the cubic volumes, allowing the sun to
rake across the white plaster and marble sculptures, revealing their form and voluptuous qualities. The sequence ends
viewing Canova's most famous piece, the *Three Graces*,
against an exterior pool and garden beyond. After visiting
the museum, be sure to circle around back to see the exterior form of this elegant building.

ROBERT EVANS
Architect

Where contemporary architecture successfully meets neoclassical architecture . . . what a phenomenal juxtaposition!
The collection contained in the space is really wonderful. It
includes virtually all of Canova's plaster and terra cotta
models and casts of his life's work. In addition, the house
itself holds tempera drawings and paintings, unfinished
marble statues, and oil paintings. The second floor has all
of Canova's tools, souvenirs from his life, and his death
mask. I was in awe of this space, its contents and history.
The town itself, with fewer than two thousand inhabitants,
is a welcome relief from touring the larger cities in Italy.
My visit was magical.

MELISSA MEYER
Artist

Tempio

1819–1830, Antonio Canova

The Temple was started in 1819 and completed in 1830
(eight years after Canova's passing). I suggest visiting just
as the sun begins to set.

MELISSA MEYER
Artist

SAN VITO D'ALTIVOLE
5.5 km south of Asolo

Brion-Vega Family Tomb
1970, Carlo Scarpa

The experience of entering through the chapel and watching the building reveal itself as you walk through it is quite remarkable. The use of materials, including water and plant life, is very different and creates a definite contrast to the rest of the cemetery. Frank Lloyd Wright's influence on Scarpa is evident, as is Scarpa's influence on contemporary artists including Richard Serra and Sol LeWitt.
MELISSA MEYER
Artist

For a unique architectural experience, one should visit Scarpa's last work, the Brion-Vega Tomb in the cemetery of San Vito d'Altivole, immediately south of Asolo. Commissioned by a wealthy electronics manufacturer to create a unique memorial in his home town, Scarpa spent the last ten years of his life composing a small universe of constructed objects adjacent to the cemetery's traditional tombstones. The complex consists of the tomb of the Brion-Vegas (Giuseppe Vega and Onorina Brion), a separate tomb for their family, a pavilion in a pool, and a chapel—all behind a walled precinct. Scarpa's detailing, with bare concrete forms intermittently decorated with glazed ceramic tiles and precious stones, is often compared to the work of Louis Kahn and Frank Lloyd Wright, but exhibits peculiarly Venetian and Oriental qualities. The chapel is a particularly astonishing architectural feat, where one is constantly aware that every vista, every sequence of spaces, every physical detail has been thoughtfully designed and presented to the visitor as a special gift, just as the chapel itself represents the special gift of life and the metaphysical hope for a life beyond. Shortly after creating this masterpiece, Scarpa himself was buried in a small

niche in the wall between his creation and the town cemetery. A simple marble slab marks the spot, in a place where the women who tend the graves cast the dead flowers that have honored the living.
ROBERT EVANS
Architect

SOLIGHETTO

33.5 km north of Treviso

Locanda da Lino
Via Brandolini 1, ☎ 0438 84 23 77

Set off in the country, about eight miles from Conegliano is a wonderful restaurant, Locanda Da Lino, which is also a hotel or bed-and-breakfast. Enjoy a fantastic lunch with incredible service and try to eat in the garden if the weather cooperates. Also, be sure to check out the paintings on display, an intriguing mix of knowns and unknowns. On the way to the ladies' room, I found a Morandi!
MELISSA MEYER
Artist

TRENTO

97 km northwest of Vicenza

Trento itself is charming. Its palazzi of pink granite stand out against the Alpine setting. Very large sections of the city have been set aside as *isole pedonali*, and it is a delightful place to walk. There is also a splendid Romanesque (and later) cathedral.
CHARLES P. SEGAL
Classicist

Castello del Buonconsiglio
Via Bernardo Clesio 5
Closed Mondays

This is a fascinating monument in a beautiful small Italian city at the foot of the Alps. In its various rebuildings and additions, the Castello offers a panorama through history and art, from late medieval through the Renaissance. There are lovely courtyards, a museum of paintings, and a room of gorgeous 15th-century frescoes of the seasons. The Castello is also fascinating for its glimpses of the struggles for the unification of Italy over the last two hundred years.
CHARLES P. SEGAL
Classicist

TREVISO
30 km north of Venice

Handsome old city; if you are ambitious, go north toward the Dolomites—spectacular and beautiful.
ERNST PULGRAM
Historical linguist

VERONA

The city itself is a work of art. Beautiful buildings, quiet streets (especially welcome after the bustle of Rome), and a winding river to stroll along in the evening. The whole place is romantic—even down to the pink stone sidewalks.
CELIA E. SCHULTZ
Classicist

San Zeno Maggiore
Piazza San Zeno

Bronze Door Panels
11th and 12th centuries (left and right, respectively)
West doors

Verona is for me the most romantic town in Italy. Though it is the second largest city in the Veneto region, the historic

center is intimate and has the feel of a small town. Its
urban fabric is a harmonious composition of various time
periods and styles, from its days as a Roman colony to the
reconstruction period after World War II, from the Gothic
Scaligere tombs to architect Carlo Scarpa's 1956–1964
reorganization of the Castelvecchio Museum. During the
Renaissance, Verona was known as the *urbs picta* (painted
city), for the frescoes that decorated the exteriors of innumerable Renaissance palaces. It is a wonderful surprise to
spot a fading scene on the façade of a palazzo while
strolling through an inconspicuous piazzetta. The Piazza
delle Erbe, which retains the form of the Roman forum
that once occupied the same site, is framed by many of
these painted palaces. When in Verona, I never miss a visit
to the Romanesque Basilica of San Zeno Maggiore. The
48 11th- and 12th-century bronze panels of the west
doors are true masterpieces of medieval art, naive yet
intensely expressive. They represent scenes from the Bible
and the life of San Zeno, including a wonderful interpreta-
tion of the washing of the feet seen from a bird's-eye view.
On the four corners of each panel are tiny masks, all different, that connect one panel to another. And when in
Verona, a pre-dinner glass of Veneto wine in one of the
many *osterie* is a must.

CAMERON ELIZABETH BARRETT
Editor

Chiesa di Sant'Anastasia
Piazza Sant'Anastasia

Saint George and the Princess
1436–1438, Pisanello
Sacristy

In the sacristy of the church of Sant'Anastasia gleams one
of my favorite works of art: *Saint George and the Princess*,
executed in 1436-1438 by Pisanello. Pisanello (whose name
unflatteringly refers to his short stature) came to Verona
from his native Pisa as a young artist-in-training, and his

career eventually took him to Venice, Rome, Ferrara and Mantua. But none of his frescoes survive intact except in Verona, and even this masterpiece in the church of Sant'Anastasia is damaged. Observe how bits of paint have flaked off, and you might compare its surface to the frescoes in the Cappella degli Scrovegni in Padua. While Giotto laid down his pigments quickly on wet plaster to ensure a lasting physical bond between paint and wall, Pisanello worked on dry plaster so that he could proceed with less haste and accomplish greater detail. But the result is a fragile surface, now well-worn through the centuries.

The better-preserved half of the fresco shows the fair San Giorgio by his horse, and the princess on the other side of the animal. Pisanello has made the seemingly odd choice to picture the horse with his behind facing us—not the most attractive view! But this technical feat allows him to demonstrate his virtuosity as an artist. He underscores this by painting the other horse in the picture facing forwards. The two hanged men with broken necks swaying in the left background were studied from life: criminal executions commonly took place outside the walls of Italian towns of the period.

But the figure which ultimately makes this painting a masterpiece is that of the princess. The clarity of her profile and her white, swan's neck tell us she is royal more than any elaborate costume ever could. But Pisanello has dressed her richly nonetheless, wrapping her upswept hair in a crisscross of thick ribbons and draping her body in a heavy blue dress whose folds gather on the ground. She is not the wailing damsel, but rather, stares so intently at Saint George that he seems to anxiously avert his face from her gaze. With her noble, courtly bearing, she quietly steals the scene.

BARBARA LYNN-DAVIS
Art historian and writer

Editor's Note: The fresco was moved to the sacristy after it was detached from the wall of one of the chapels of Sant'Anastasia.

Opera in the Ancient Roman Arena

At Verona, try to see one of the operas given during the summer in the ruins of the ancient Roman Arena; before the overture, the audience of twenty thousand will hold lighted candles, and the effect is magical. Perhaps the best opera to see there is Verdi's *Nabucco*, for when the Israelite slaves sing of their thirst for freedom in the patriotic chorus *Va', pensiero*, the reference was to the contemporary Italian struggle for independence. At the Arena, the Italians in the audience will hum or sing along on this particular chorus, and at the end, someone will invariably call out, *"Viva l'Italia!"*

DAVID G. WILKINS AND ANN THOMAS WILKINS
Art and architectural historian and classicist, respectively

Editor's Note: The performances at Verona's Roman Arena generally sell out. The top ticket price is more than $150, the bottom $20, which may mean standing atop the walls.

Giardino Giusti
16th Century
Via Giardini Giusti 2

A show garden. Famous for its cypresses with a lower formal garden and an upper natural wooded hill. Little is known about the original layout. Garden has a little Renaissance casino, grottoes, rockeries, temples, statues, fountains, endless terraces, and a view Belvedere for a sweeping view of Verona.

JOHN L. WONG
Landscape architect

VICENZA
32.5 km northwest of Padua

Teatro Olimpico
Begun 1580, Andrea Palladio; completed by Vicenzo Scamozzi after Palladio's death
Piazza Matteotti

Visiting this building is like waltzing into a dream . . . Beyond ornate, the interior architecture and ornamentation mimics the architecture of the city; it is so elaborate that it cannot be photographed. Even a video could not do justice to the complex layering in the building and the incredible perspective created by it. The indoor theater has a ceiling painted like the sky. This was Palladio's last work; he died in 1580.

MELISSA MEYER
Artist

Corso Andrea Palladio

Great shopping on the main drag!

MELISSA MEYER
Artist

FRIULI-VENEZIA GIULIA

AQUILEIA
40 km south of Udine

Basilica
Mosaics, 11th century

On the road from Portogruaro to Trieste, turn south at
Cervignano, approximately eight kilometers. The Duomo
has the most marvelous 11th-century mosaics—on the
walls, on the floor, in the crypt. They rate five stars, among
the best in Italy. Visit also the Roman theater and harbor
(what's left of it: formerly on the seashore, now inland due
to silting). Have a picnic on the lawn in front of the
Duomo. Blessedly few, if any, tourists.
ERNST PULGRAM
Historical linguist

CASTELLO DI MIRAMARE
7 km northwest of Trieste

Near Trieste, visit Castello di Miramare, built between
1856–1860, and home of the Archduke Maximilian—
emperor of Mexico!
ERNST PULGRAM
Historical linguist

*Editor's Note: Archduke Maximilian, who built the
Castello di Miramare, was a Habsburg, brother of the
Emperor Franz Joseph of Austria. As a pawn of the French
(under Napoleon III), he became Emperor of Mexico in
1864, and he was shot by Mexican insurgents in 1867.
His young wife, Carlotta, went mad.*

CIVIDALE DEL FRIULI
17 km east of Udine

Tempietto Longobardo
Piazzetta San Biagio

Six Female Figures
ca. 8th–10th centuries

For the most remarkable extant example of Lombard art in Northern Italy you must penetrate Friuli (Roman Forum Iulii) as far as Cividale, about ten miles from Udine. In what was the first Lombard duchy in Italy, look for the church of Santa Maria in Valle, the Tempietto Longobardo, and in its quadrangular nave find the marvel of Lombard stucco-work, a decorative moulding of vine tendrils and interlace, surmounted by a row of six female figures, elongated, elegantly clothed, unidentified, but presumably saints. Their date is uncertain, somewhere between the eighth and tenth centuries; they have a Byzantine look about them.

HELEN F. NORTH
Classicist

Near the Yugoslav border lies a very ancient city once known as Roman Forum Iulii. It's a pleasant town just for hanging around, my favorite occupation when traveling. For a meal, go 18 km south to the village of Cormons and visit Al Cacciatore della Subida (loc. Monte 22, ☎048 16 05 31.)

ERNST PULGRAM
Historical linguist

GRADO

68 km northwest of Trieste

> Grado has been a popular beach resort since the heyday of
> the Habsburgs. Enjoy the shore-walk and Old Town.
> ERNST PULGRAM
> *Historical linguist*

UDINE

70 km northwest of Trieste

> There's not much to see in Udine, but listen to the lan-
> guage; it's Friulian, not Italian. North from Udine lie the
> beautiful Dolomites.
> ERNST PULGRAM
> *Historical linguist*

CENTRAL ITALY

Rimini

SAN MARINO

Urbino   Ancona

Serra di Burano

MARCHE

Perugia

Foligno

UMBRIA

Terni

Tevere

Lago di
Bracciano

Rome

LAZIO   MOLISE

Latina

Terracina

CAMPANIA

ABRUZZO

EMILIA-ROMAGNA & MARCHE

BOLOGNA

In Bologna keep to the porticos which line virtually every street in the historic center. The streets are spokes radiating from the elegant Piazza Maggiore. Follow any of the old ones, via Zamboni, via Santo Stefano, Strada Maggiore, out to the gates that mark the old city walls. The markets off the Piazza Maggiore, behind via Rizzoli, offer a quality of fruit, fish, cheese, and pasta unsurpassed in the world. Enter almost any church and you will find altarpieces by the Carracci and many of their famous pupils and associates—Guido Reni, Domenichino and so on. The closed, but not locked, doors of Bologna lead to beautiful art.

GAIL FEIGENBAUM
Curator

Santa Maria della Vita
Via Clavature 10

The Passion of Christ
1463, Nicolò dell'Arca

When in Bologna, look for the astonishing sculptural project by Nicolò dell'Arca called *The Passion of Christ* (which fell into disrepair but has now been beautifully restored and returned to Santa Maria della Vita.) This 15th-century Tuscan sculptor is not as well known as many of his contemporaries, but in this work he accomplished something unique: a theatrical grouping of seven terra cotta figures, each over life-size, with bright coloration. Each figure responding to the others is wildly expressive, full of emotional contortions and dramatic energy. The modeling is remarkable. The sculptures constitute an artistic and technical tour-de-force of great emotional depth.

There are other sculptures known to be by Nicolò, but none that I know that reach this level. For instance, in the church of San Domenico, his marble angel holding a candelabrum faces its mate carved by Michelangelo.

LAWRENCE FANE
Sculptor

Three Bologna Secrets

ITINERARY

a Sala Anatomica
Via Archiginnasio

b Chiesa Santa Maria
della Vita
Via Clavature 10

c COIN
Via de'Carbonesi 7

Wandering the streets of Bologna, one can't help noticing the preponderance of postcards displaying the three "T"'s for which the city is renowned. They are *torri*, *tortellini*, and *tette*, which if you look closer you'll find displayed as ancient towers, a plate of pasta, and a well-endowed Bolognese female. But after living there for six years, I found much, much more to write home about.

In the center of town are three attractions, very close to one another, which fascinate me time and again. In the Archiginnasio, on the street of the same name, is the *sala anatomica*, a classroom built for medical school anatomy classes in the 17th century. It contains amazing wooden sculptures of human anatomy, layer by layer, in full scale

Practically around the corner, on via Clavature, is the Chiesa Santa Maria della Vita (see p. 194). The church is home to Nicolò dell'Arca's life-size terra cotta sculpture of the late 15th century (to the right of the altar). The detail, the facial expressions, and the integrity of the ensemble make this a most unusual *pietà*. Just a few minutes' walk to via de'Carbonesi 7, is the department store COIN, which ran into some trouble when builders

EMILIA-ROMAGNA & MARCHE

LOMBARDY

Piacenza

EMILIA-
ROMAGNA

Parma

Modena

Maranello

Bologna

Riolo

LIGURIA

Florence

Arno

Siena

TUSCANY

discovered the ruins of an ancient Roman theater as they were breaking ground for the original construction. They actually cleaned up the remains and suspended a glass floor over it so you can visit the ruins and shop simultaneously. Directly alongside COIN is Majani (via Carbonesi 5), which claims to have the best chocolates in Italy. I would most definitely agree.

PETER HARRIS KROSS
Veterinarian

Editor's Note: Majani was founded in 1769, and its most popular concoction is called Fiat Cremino *(nothing to do with the automobile). My conclusion is that this name is a reference to God's famous first words (naturally spoken in Latin):* "Fiat Lux" — "*Let there be light.*" Fiat Cremino *would mean roughly,* "Let there be ice cream."

Basilica di Santo Stefano
Via Santo Stefano 24, ☎051 22 32 56

Santo Stefano is actually at least four different churches (and several chapels and oratories), which represent a wide span of history, beginning with the very ancient. You can wander through the diverse spaces and savor a trip through the history of architecture. There are quiet cloisters where you can enjoy great quiet in the midst of the city bustle. The piazza outside is car-free and splendid. There are many nice little neighborhood stores and restaurants nearby, including Trattoria Leonida (vicolo Alemagna 2, ☎051 23 97 42).

REBECCA J. WEST
Professor of Italian literature and film

Palazzo Magnani (now the bank Credito Romagnolo)
Via Zamboni 20, ☏ 051 33 81 11

The Founding of Rome
1588–1591, Annibale, Agostino, and Lodovico Carracci
Gran Salone

Not really public, as it is a business, but accessible if you
ring the bell and ask, is the Gran Salone, (or Salone
d'Onore), where Annibale, Agostino, and Lodovico
Carracci, the family who charted the course of Italian
baroque art, collaborated on a frieze depicting *The
Founding of Rome*. Here are vivid scenes of the baby twins
Romulus and Remus nursed by the she-wolf in a splendid,
fresh landscape, the abduction of the Sabines, and all the
famous episodes set forth in sparkling colors and unprecedented narrative clarity. These frescoes are punctuated by
antique statues come to life and a charming cast of *putti*,
masks, and satyrs.
GAIL FEIGENBAUM
Curator

RECOMMENDED READING
Donald Posner, *Annibale Carracci: A Study in the Reform of Italian
Painting Around 1590*, o.p.

Ristorante da Silvio
Via San Petronio Vecchio 34/D, ☏ 051 22 65 59

This is a small place where the food appears in front of you
in great quantities and where the atmosphere is relaxed
and friendly. The last time I ate there I counted ten different appetizers on our table, an equal number of desserts,
and, somewhere in between, a pasta and an entree. They
have excellent wines, too.
PETER HARRIS KROSS
Veterinarian

Food Markets
Area around Piazza Maggiore

🎁 Bologna's food markets are sublime! Located in a warren of little streets right off the main square (where San Petronio is to be found), both outside and indoor stands are filled with an overflowing abundance of fruits, vegetables, cheeses and meats. Don't miss the Tamburini's Antica Salsamenteria Bolognese (via Caprarie, ☎051 23 47 26) for a fabulous array of prepared delicacies. Buy a portion of *tortellini al ragù* and some salad and go and sit in the Piazza Santo Stefano nearby to enjoy a great meal in lovely surroundings. Also, walk down the via Zamboni for a stroll in the area of one of the world's oldest universities.
REBECCA J. WEST
Professor of Italian literature and film

MARANELLO
19 km south of Modena

Ferrari S.P.A.
Via Abetone Inferiore 4

When it comes to a physical embodiment of the idea of speed, nothing beats a Ferrari. A red one. A visit to the factory is a pilgrimage to a place where passion is fused with engineering. When the Pope went to Ferrari and blessed the racing cars, it was a redundant act.

Access to the Holy Grail (racing department and interior) is not available unless you are a Ferrari owner. Others can visit the Ferrari Museum nearby (via Dino Ferrari 43, Maranello).

While you're there, buy two because, as Frank Stella points out, one will always be in the shop being worked on.
SAM POSEY
Race car driver, artist, and designer

PARMA
91 km northwest of Bologna

Camera di San Paolo
Via Melloni

Frescoes
ca. 1519, Correggio

The complex iconographic program of Correggio's frescoes, painted circa 1519 for an Abbess of the Convent of
San Paolo, has not been fully explained, but it seems relat-
ed to the Abbess' duel with the local bishop over control
of the convent. Despite this intended political content,
Correggio has been able to create one of the most delightful of Renaissance secular decorations by combining *putti*,
illusionistic sculptures, and garlands that form an arbor.
DAVID G. WILKINS
Art and architectural historian

PIACENZA
60 km southeast of Milan

Museo Civico
Palazzo Farnese, Piazza Cittadella
Closed Mondays

Fegato di Piacenza
Etruscan

Strategically located at the convergence of the via Aemilia
and the Po, ancient Placentia was founded as a colony by
the Romans in the third century BC. Though industrial
buildings ring the city, don't be fooled by the unsightly
approach; within is a rich kernel of a city. The Duomo, a
12th-century Lombard Romanesque church with a porch
supported by *atlantes*, a 14th-century campanile, and frescoes by Guercino could alone be worth the visit. But my
favorite object in Piacenza is contained in the Museo
Civico, located in the Palazzo Farnese: the Fegato di
Piacenza. If you have ever ordered from an Italian menu,

you know *fegato* is liver. The Liver of Piacenza is a small, stylized, bronze, Etruscan liver inscribed with markings that indicate the prophetic properties of a sheep liver. An Etruscan haruspex, like a fortune teller reading tea leaves, would gaze at the still-quivering entrails of a freshly-sacrificed animal and from the liver predict the future.

MARGARET A. BRUCIA
Latin teacher

RAVENNA
76 km east of Bologna

This was once a water city, like Venice, with rivers and canals flowing through the urban center and a nearby port open to the riches of the East. Prosperous and well-defended by water, Ravenna was chosen by the Ostrogothic kings to be capital of the Western Roman Empire in 402 AD, and was enfolded into the Byzantine Empire by 540. But in the centuries of political decline that followed, the waterways and port were lost to silt build-up and land reclamation. The early decline of a once-great capital, however, can mean it is better preserved than cities which go on to modern-day lives, and so in Ravenna mosaic stones laid well over a thousand years ago still astound in all their material and spiritual vividness.

BARBARA LYNN-DAVIS
Art historian and writer

Mausoleo di Galla Placidia
ca. 440 AD
Via Fiandrini

Ravenna was an important Adriatic port in Cisalpine Gaul. Founded by Etruscans and Umbrians, it became a *civitas foederata* in the later Republic and later a *municipium*. Augustus made it a station of the Roman fleet and the sub-urb by the harbor was called Classis (meaning "fleet"). The city became the main residence of Honorius and his sister

Galla Placidia in 404 AD, (or certainly by that time; some scholars fix the date as early as 402 AD). After the fall of the West Roman Empire, Ravenna became the capital of Ostrogothic rule under Theodoric. Reconquered for East Rome by Belisarius, it was made by the Emperor Justinian the seat of the imperial viceroy, the Exarch. Conquered by the Langobards in 751, the city was taken in turn by Pippin the Short in 755, who turned the Exarchate over to the Holy See in Rome. It is also in Ravenna that Dante lived in exile and where he died.

The Mausoleum of Galla Placidia was built circa 440 AD by the sister of Emperor Honorius for her final resting place. It takes the form of a Latin Cross, crowned by a cupola. Here are the oldest mosaics of Ravenna; they show Saint Lawrence, stags drinking from a source, the Good Shepherd, animals and fruits, against a blue background.
URSULA HEIBGES
Classicist

San Vitale
ca. 530–540
Via Fiandrini

San Vitale, built circa 530–540 by Bishop Ecclesius, is a masterpiece of Byzantine architecture. The interior octagon is crowned by a cupola and has seven exedras, the eighth forming the choir with the altar. According to the Byzantine liturgy the upper gallery was reserved for women.
URSULA HEIBGES
Classicist

Sant'Apollinare Nuovo
6th century
Via di Roma

Built in the sixth century under Theodoric (Dietrich von Bern in legend). Greek columns of marble separate the three aisles. The mosaics along the walls show thirteen

pictures of the Passion and Resurrection of Christ, scenes from the life of Christ, saints and prophets, the city and harbor of Classis, a train of 22 virgins preceded by the three kings, and more!
URSULA HEIBGES
Classicist

Mausoleo di Teodorico

6th century
Via delle Industrie 14

Built in the sixth century, the tomb is a round monument covered by a monolithic cupola. The diameter is eleven meters. The lower half of the tomb takes the form of a Greek cross, and the coffin is hewn out of porphyry.
URSULA HEIBGES
Classicist

Sant'Apollinare in Classe

ca. 535–538
Via Romea sud 216
5 km south of Ravenna

This church, built circa 535–538 by Juliannus Argentarius, incorporates remains of the Roman settlement Classis near the harbor of the Roman navy. Three long naves lead up to the apse. The Byzantine mosaics against a green background depict Sant'Apollinaris with a herd of sheep. The walls of the center aisle show offertory processions with participation of the Emperor Justinian and his wife, the Empress Theodora.
URSULA HEIBGES
Classicist

RIOLA
8 km south of Bologna

Parish Center of Riola
Designed 1966, Alvar Aalto

Hidden in a little stream valley in the Apennines near Bologna is the small town of Riola. Somehow, Alvar Aalto was induced to design a small parish center, which was completed in 1978, after his death. It is a gem and is worth the detour. The baptistery is especially evocative; note how the font inside and stream outside relate to each other. The ridges of the roof profile seem to capture the spirit of the mountains girdling the site.

D. B. MIDDLETON
Architect

URBINO

Palazzo Ducale
Completed 1482, original design by Luciano Laurano
Piazza Duca Federico

Urbino is a complex little city in hills that provide lovely vistas. At its center is the Palazzo Ducale, which exalts the Renaissance concept of the enlightened prince and patron. The interior is a museum housing many artworks. The jewel of the palazzo is the ducal library containing wooden book cabinets decorated with extraordinary inlaid wood portraits.

JAMES LATTIS
Historian of astronomy

Editor's Note: Duke Federico of Montefeltro was both soldier and scholar, the latter indicated by the beautiful little library, or studiolo, in the Palazzo Ducale. Federico also built another palace, in nearby Gubbio, which also had a marvelous studiolo. That studiolo was acquired some fifty years ago by the Metropolitan Museum of Art in New York and is now on public display, splendidly restored.

Flagellation and Madonna di Senigallia
Piero della Francesca
Sala delle Udienze, Galleria Nazionale delle Marche

Urbino's incredible Palazzo Ducale dominates the town.
It houses the Galleria Nazionale delle Marche, which contains one of the most interesting of all Renaissance paintings—Piero della Francesca's *Flagellation*, a surprisingly small panel painting—plus Piero's *Madonna di Senigallia* and many beautiful works by other artists. This palace of the 15th-century Duke Federico of Montefeltro is possibly the most elegant and perfect of Italian palazzi. To walk up its stairs is to be drawn up almost effortlessly. The proportions and the materials that make up this structure are of the highest order. They reflect the taste of this remarkable duke.

For people on a Piero pilgrimage as well as for those interested in architecture Urbino is well worth the effort it takes to get there. The town is refreshingly quiet.
ALAN FELTUS
Painter

The Piero della Francesca *Flagellation* is the pride of the collection. Upstairs, don't miss the many works of Federico Barocci, who was from Urbino (little known collection upstairs often closed). The Palazzo Ducale is a most remarkable building, particularly to architectural historians. Afterwards, walk in the town and see Raphael's cast of characters.
JOHN C. LEAVEY
Painter

RECOMMENDED READING
Sir Kenneth Clark, *Piero della Francesca*, o.p.
S.J. Freedberg, *Painting in Italy 1500–1600*, o.p.
Marilyn Lavin, *Piero della Francesca*, Harry N. Abrams, 1992.
Marilyn Lavin, ed., *Piero della Francesca and His Legacy*, National Gallery of Art, 1995.

Editor's Note: Although Raphael was born in Urbino, only a single piece of his art is preserved there, a Madonna *in the Palazzo Ducale.*

TUSCANY / TOSCANA

AREZZO
81 km southeast of Florence

San Francesco
Begun ca. 1322, restored at the turn of the 20th century
Via Cavour, Piazza San Francesco

The Legend of the True Cross
ca. 1453–1464, Piero della Francesca
Call to arrange a viewing, ☎0575 90 04 04, or reserve online
at www.pierodellafrancesca.it
No more than 25 visitors at a time are granted access.

We painters go to Arezzo for the frescoes of Piero della
Francesca in the church of San Francesco: *The Legend of
the True Cross*. These are on display again after years of
restoration and look absolutely beautiful. Piero is a painter
loved by painters for his remarkable composition and his
drama. They are timeless paintings, as modern as any;
powerful paintings.
ALAN FELTUS
Painter

Among the finest works in Italy and not to be missed. On
the right when leaving the church is an excellent restaurant,
🍽 Buca di San Francesco (see p. 213).
JOHN C. LEAVEY
Painter

RECOMMENDED READING
Sir Kenneth Clark, *Piero della Francesca*, o.p.

Santa Maria della Pieve
Corso Italia 7
12th–14th centuries, Giorgio Vasari et al; restored late 19th century

A Romanesque and Gothic jewel. One of the most evoca-
tive and charming churches I have seen.
CLAUDIA CANNIZZARO
Coordinator of the Civitella Ranieri Center

Polyptych

1320, Pietro Lorenzetti

Of course, Piazza Grande is very special, as is the church that backs up to it, Santa Maria della Pieve. Mysterious and ancient in atmosphere. There is one painting here, a beautiful Pietro Lorenzetti polyptych with Madonna and Saints, which wants to be seen.

ALAN FELTUS
Painter

Passeggiata along Corso Italia

Arezzo, birthplace of Petrarch, home of Piero della Francesca's newly restored *The Legend of the True Cross* fresco cycle, was my introduction to Italian life; a high school exchange program brought me to this charming Tuscan city so rich in culture and beauty. The day after I arrived, my hosts proudly toured me around their magnificent city: the Piazza Grande, charmingly asymmetrical and steeply slanting; the Duomo, famous for its 16th-century stained glass; the Romanesque Santa Maria della Pieve with its elegant triple-colonnaded façade; Piero della Francesca's masterpiece in the 14th-century church of San Francesco. Then it was time for the daily ritual of the *passeggiata*: gelato in hand, arms intertwined, we strolled up and down the Corso Italia, the main street of the *centro storico*. *Aretini* (citizens of Arezzo) young and old were doing the same, up the street, turn around, down the street, turn around. They do it every evening, summer or winter, rain or shine. Friends meet up without making an appointment, for they all know that in the late afternoon before dinner, their *amici* will be there, either as part of the mass promenade or in front of some shop along the Corso unofficially designated as their meeting place. On the first Sunday of each month, when one of the most important antique fairs in the country (see p. 213) winds its way along the Corso and through the medieval streets of the

TUSCANY / TOSCANA

Carrara
Colonnata
Barga
Bagni di Lucca
Seravezza
Pietrasanta
Lucca
Poggio a Caiano
Carmignano
Artimino
Viareggio
Pisa
Arno
TUSCANY
Livorno
San Gimignano
Volterra
Abbazia di San Galgano
Grosseto

center, the *passeggiata* crowd multiplies as visitors from all over the world take part.

The ritual of the *passeggiata*, observed in Italian cities both big and small, demonstrates the Italians' love for being in company, their sense of community, and their desire to see and be seen. It is their way of enjoying their city, their friends, the fresh air and a few hours of free time without thoughts of work or other commitments. Walking in circles, without a destination: what could be more delightfully Italian, more civilized? Here's an example of the Italian appreciation of time spent simply enjoying life— the exquisite concept of the *dolce far niente*.

CAMERON ELIZABETH BARRETT
Editor

Duomo
Piazza del Duomo

Magdalen
Piero della Francesca

There is a single-figure fresco, recently cleaned, by Piero della Francesca in the Duomo at the uppermost point of the city. She is Magdalen. She holds a crystal box that is amazing in its simplicity and veracity, and for the bare minimum of color washed onto plaster. (If the painting is unlit, there is a switch on the column opposite.)

ALAN FELTUS
Painter

San Domenico
Piazza San Domenico

Crucifix
1265–1270, Cimabue

From the Duomo, go straight ahead, gently down the hill and to the right to San Domenico. This is another very beautiful church which has an extraordinary Cimabue crucifix.

ALAN FELTUS
Painter

Museo Archeologico Mecenate
Via Margaritone 10, 📞0575 208 82
Closed first and third Mondays of each month

While in Arezzo, visit the Archaeological Museum.
ALAN FELTUS
Painter

Editor's Note: The archaeological museum is a marvelous building with a Roman amphitheater as its front yard. A delightful spot for a picnic.

Antica Osteria L'Agania
Via Mazzini 10, 📞057 253 81
Closed Mondays

🍽 This restaurant is very nice, unpretentious and pleasant, with good food.
ALAN FELTUS
Painter

Buca di San Francesco
Piazza San Francesco 1, 📞0575 232 71

🍽 The restaurant practically touching the church of San Francesco is interesting. It has an atmosphere similar to the church itself, and good food.
ALAN FELTUS
Painter

Antique Markets
Near San Francesco

🎁 The *Fiera Antiquaria* fills the upper end of Arezzo, from the area surrounding San Francesco through Piazza Grande and up to the Duomo and park. It takes place over the weekend that includes the first Sunday of each month, and a trip to this outdoor market combines nicely with the Piero della Francesca pilgrimage.

I find the *Fiera Antiquaria* more enjoyable than Rome's Porta Portese flea market because it is less crowded and almost exclusively antiques. The antiques range from all manner of furniture to paintings, sculpture, jewelry, *presepio* figures, postcards, prints . . . Expensive in general, but good to photograph or just to wander through for fun. Prints are still very affordable: the 17th-, 18th- and 19th-century book plates of animals, plants or anatomy, for example. The silver-plated votives (hearts, figures and parts of the body) average fifteen to forty dollars, depending on the vendor, and aren't as widely available as in the past. I buy hardware, too: old locks, hinges and such things to fit furniture I make for our house.

I also recommend a visit to the studio of a painter named Franco Fedeli, in Piazza Grande within the Logge Vasari. (In the piazza facing the back of the church, his studio is to the right, near the corner of the piazza.) Fedeli has a fine collection of antique mannequins, *presepio* figures and paintings he sells during the Fiera weekends, when his studio transforms into a shop.

Aside from enjoying the abundance of antiques and curios, if you are there on a hot summer day around lunchtime you will see the vendors, many from Naples, eating lunch in grand style on the tables and chairs they hope to sell. Some are stretched out asleep on their antiques as customers stroll by, considering the goods for sale. It's Italian theater.

ALAN FELTUS
Painter

BAGNI DI LUCCA
28 km northeast of Lucca

La Mora
Via Sesto di Moriano 1748, ☎ 0583 40 64 02

🍽 We were in Bagni di Lucca because we'd intended to combine a trip to Lucca with a stopover at the mineral bath. And there was no mineral bath in this *Bagni*; it was a spa that opened at eight and closed at one. We saw signs for a local pool. You know the sign, the line drawing where the boy is diving. A woman in the parking lot was speaking English to her daughter. She was staying with her aunt. How was the pool? "Like paradise," she answered, "with the best view of any pool she's ever seen." The water? "Half mineral water and half . . . It's cold, but wonderful." Restaurants? "There's one called La Mora that my aunt likes very much." "Your aunt? What about you?" "I haven't been there but it's where she takes her friends when they visit and they love it." I expected a quaint mom-and-pop place, not a spacious glass-enclosed dining room surrounded by a breathing forest. I hadn't expected to find an American woman begging for a table because even though she didn't have a reservation she was there to write about it for *Gourmet* magazine. Among our discoveries were the pigeon and a superb local wine, easily as good as the more heralded and expensive *Riservas* from Montalcino. We liked it enough to repeat the experience. And even tried to find the vineyard where this magical dark potion was grown and fermented.

MARK RUDMAN
Poet, essayist, and translator

BARGA
39 km north of Lucca

A hidden jewel of a place that Leonardo admired!

Barga is four hundred meters high and set in the beginning of the Garfagnana mountains, where there are palm trees, a pleasant climate, and few mosquitoes. It is a beautiful and quiet town that becomes very active in the summer with an Opera Festival, Jazz Festival, Art Festival, Town Festival, and my summer workshop in multi-plate color etchings in July. The town, which takes only ten minutes to traverse, is filled with Della Robbias.

In the Renaissance, Barga was the only town in Garfagnana that was under the protection of the Medici of Florence. It was so well-regarded that when Leonardo da Vinci was proposing a new flow of the river Arno, he drew a water route with the walled city of Florence on the extreme right, then—moving left—Prato, Pistoia and Lucca. Above Lucca, on the extreme left, he drew the walled city of Barga. The drawing is now in the Windsor Castle collection.

SWIETLAN NICHOLAS KRACZYNA
Artist and printmaker

Editor's Note: Windsor Castle has a wonderful collection of Leonardo drawings.

CAVRIGLIA
42 km west of Arezzo

Taverna del Lago
Via Borbuio 33, 055 96 10 39

Right outside Cavriglia (in the section called San Cipriano) is a beautiful man-made lake surrounded by hills and woods, with no houses except the Taverna del Lago— home of the best *spaghetti vongole* I ever ate.

EDITH ISAAC-ROSE
Painter and teacher

CHIUSI

21 km southeast of Montepulciano

Osteria La Solita Zuppa
Via Porsenna 21, ☎ 0578 210 06

¶❘¶ This small restaurant was one of my favorite discoveries while working in Tuscany. The town is known mainly for its Etruscan tombs and the Museo Nazionale Etrusco, the latter of which is well worth a visit since its recent renovation. La Solita Zuppa's menu offers delicious and unusual combinations, not only for soups but for all courses. The friendly and helpful owners create a very hospitable atmosphere. Perfect for lunch or dinner if you are in the neighborhood, and worth a detour if you are not.
NANCY A. WINTER
Archaeologist and librarian

COLONNATA

8 km east of Carrara

Marble Quarries
Roman era to the present
For information, ☎ 0585 84 44 03

Drive up into the mountains as far as you can to view the marble quarries and visit artists' studios along the road. One in particular has a railroad car out front, but inside is a treasure of marble works in progress—cutting, sawing, carving. There's also a salesroom where all types of marble—artworks and balls, squares and chips—can be purchased.
NORMA WYNICK GOLDMAN
Classicist

During the course of my career as an artist I have visited the mountainous region of Carrara, just north of Pisa, several times to purchase stone and also to sculpt at the Nicoli Studio. It is possible to drive directly to areas being excavated, and onto the mountain-top town of Colonnata. Locals aver that this little town has been in existence since the ancient Roman era when the quarries were first cut. Generations of quarry workers have lived here for centuries. Quarries are cut right out of the landscape; the scenery changes practically before one's eyes.

Looking down from Colonnata, you can see the city of Carrara and even as far as the Mediterranean. Glancing upward, you can look at the quarries perched precariously on the edge of the mountain peaks. It is a wonder how anyone could work under such harrowing conditions. To watch men move the huge stones is an amazing experience. They navigate the narrow, winding roads upward to fill their flat-bed semi trucks, then drive lickety-split—at what seems to be one hundred miles an hour—down toward the coast. There the marble is cut and prepared to be shipped all around the world.

GWYNN MURRILL
Sculptor

CORTONA
48 km northwest of Perugia

Santa Maria delle Grazie al Calcinaio
Begun 1485, Francesco di Giorgio Martini; completed 1516, after his death
The church is a 15 minute walk from Cortona

Since Etruscan times, the vertiginous hilltop town of Cortona has enjoyed a proud tradition of monumental stone architecture and an artistic reputation that numbers Luca Signorelli, Pietro Berretini (Pietro da Cortona) and Gino Severini among its famous sons. It was at Signorelli's initiative in 1485 that an impressive pilgrimage church was erected on the site of a miraculous apparition of the Madonna, designed by the great Sienese designer and engineer Francesco di Giorgio Martini (1439–1501/2), whose ideas had such a profound influence on Leonardo's intellectual development. Carefully sited on the edge of the steeply ascending hill below the town, this great church, with its Latin-cross plan and centralized east end surmounted by a dome, commands a panoramic view over the Val di Chiana towards Lago Trasimeno. Inside, the sheer austerity of its top-lit space and the smooth, uncluttered walls of white plaster precisely divided, with consummate geometry, into harmonious units by boldly-cut elements in gray *pietra serena*, never fail to shock—especially after one leaves behind the rugged, weathered exterior, where centuries of frost and abrasive winds have largely eaten away an identical system of articulation. After the linear refinements and spatial membranes defining the volumes of Brunelleschi's ethereal Pazzi Chapel in Florence, this powerfully sculptured space at Cortona, enhanced by monumental forms of decoration, already anticipates the sublime language of Michelangelo.

JOHN WILTON-ELY
Art historian

RECOMMENDED READING
Francesco Paolo Fiore and Manfredo Tafuri, eds., *Francesco di Giorgio, architetto*, Electra, Milano, 1993.
Ludwig Heinrich Heydenreich, *Architecture in Italy: 1400–1500*, o.p.

Le Celle

1211, Saint Francis of Assisi, founder
Take road from Porta Colonia

Outside Cortona's Porta Colonia, a gentle road leads to Le Celle (the cells), a monastery and sanctuary founded by Saint Francis of Assisi in 1211. The thirty minute walk away from the city heightens the experience of leaving a secular life and entering the solitude of a spiritual one. One walks alongside blackberries, wild rosemary, fig and almond trees to arrive at a cluster of monks' cells built without architectural design into the side of a mountain. After visiting the church and Saint Francis' cell, one can stroll through well-tended gardens, bridges and a waterfall, all the while admiring the spectacular view of the valley with Cortona on the opposite mountain.

KATEY BROWN
Art historian

LUCCA
25 km northeast of Pisa

Buca di Sant'Antonio
Via della Cervia 1/5, ☎ 0583 558 81

🍴 Eat at Buca di Sant'Antonio.

ROSS ANDERSON
Architect

LUCIGNANO
28 km southwest of Arezzo

A village with extraordinary architecture to the south of Arezzo, Lucignano is especially popular with Italian travelers.

GIANCARLO GIUBILARO
Operations manager of the Civitella Ranieri Center

MAGLIANO IN TOSCANA
47 km southeast of Grosseto

Da Guido
Via Roma 18, ☎ 0564 59 24 47

🍴 Incredible crepe-like ravioli, with either asparagus or mushrooms and *tartuffi*. Homey, warm atmosphere.

CAROL SAPER
Private art dealer

MANCIANO

56 km southeast of Grosseto

Petronio

Statale 74, ☎0564 60 63 45
Closed Thursdays

🍽 Known for grilled Tuscan steak and *gnocci cappa pappa reale*—"the softest in the world."
CAROL SAPER
Private art dealer

MONTEFOLLONICO

60 km southeast of Siena

La Chiusa

Via della Madonnina 88, ☎577 66 96 68

🍽 Having zigzagged through Umbria and Tuscany, following the snake-like Piero trail, one's appetite for artistic stimulation is whetted by another form of art, say, a culinary one. It's then worth the detour on the way to Siena or Montepulciano to stop at nearby Montefollonico for a memorable experience at La Chiusa. Chef Dania Lucherini and husband, sommelier Umberto, serve a tasting menu along with dapples of extraordinary regional wines that raise eating to an art form. In one's lifetime, La Chiusa is not to be missed.
WILLIAM B. CONLON AND JEAN CONLON
Painter and photographers' agent, respectively

ABBAZIA DI MONTE OLIVETO MAGGIORE

35 km southeast of Siena

Life of Saint Benedict

1497–1498, Luca Signorelli; 1505–1508, Sodoma

The abbey, set in a forest of cool cypresses, has a cloister with recently cleaned frescoes by Luca Signorelli and Sodoma which depict scenes from the life of Benedict. Pay

special attention to the small details in the paintings, such as
the animals, which add considerable poignancy to the
scenes. A small shop sells a remarkably wide range of homemade potions and herbal cures for any ailment, among other
items. Plan carefully to arrive during open hours.
NANCY A. WINTER
Archaeologist and librarian

*Editor's Note: The mailing address of the Abbey of Monte
Oliveto Maggiore is the little village of Chiusure, about 35
kilometers from Siena by a complicated route of well-
marked roads.*

MONTEPULCIANO

61 km southeast of Siena

  a. Palazzo Comunale
  b. Palazzo Tarugi, Piazza Grande
  c. Palazzo Cervini, via di Graziano 21
  d. Teatro Poliziano, via del Teatro
  e. Chiesa di Madonna di San Biagio
  f. Casa Cononica

Montepulciano is a classic Tuscan hill town with a splendid mix of Gothic and Renaissance buildings; the Palazzo
Comunale is one of the most remarkable examples of the
transition from one to the other. Antonio da Sangallo the
Elder seems to have had a wrap on the town, having done
at least two of the biggest palaces. The third storey loggia
of the Palazzo Tarugi is not to be missed for its roof garden. The Palazzo Cervini is wonderful for its compressed
scale, rusticated base and vertical layering. However, the
most remarkable interior space has to be the Bibiena-
inspired Teatro Poliziano, done in 1795.

One mile outside Montepulciano, the Chiesa di
Madonna di San Biagio is a marriage of a Greek cross and
a Latin cross. Also by Antonio da Sangallo the Elder, its
fine scale, vertical layering and accommodative quirks
make it one of the best examples of the high Renaissance.

The façade of the adjacent Casa Cononica (Canon House) is again finely-scaled and might be recognized as having been duplicated on the interior courtyard of the Fogg Museum at Harvard University.

ROBERT LIVESEY
Architect

Chiesa di Madonna di San Biagio
Begun 1518, Antonio da Sangallo the Elder; work continued until 1545

The 16th-century pilgrimage church of Madonna di San Biagio, on the hillside just outside the city walls, is one of the most harmonious architectural designs of the High Renaissance. Designed by Antonio da Sangallo the Elder to mark the spot of a miracle, the church was the most extensive building project of the period, second only to Saint Peter's Basilica in Rome. Essentially a Greek cross plan with an impressive dome, San Biagio features two free-standing *campanili* (bell towers) on either side of the façade. Only one was finished, lending a charming, lop-sided appearance. Serene, classical details on the travertine-clad exterior—especially the accentuated apse with balus-trade—and a simple, unadorned interior make this church one of Tuscany's most satisfying architectural experiences. One can't help noticing the stunning landscape from this high point. With a glass of the local *vino nobile*, Montepulciano leaves a lasting impression on the spirit.

KATEY BROWN
Art historian

MONTERCHI
31 km east of Arezzo

Schoolhouse
Via della Reglia

Madonna del Parto
ca. 1445, Piero della Francesca

Near Sansepolcro is the small village of Monterchi, the
birthplace of Piero della Francesca's mother. The famous
Madonna del Parto shows the pregnant Madonna revealed
by angels pulling back a curtain—a rare and unique image
of the Virgin. It is thought that Piero's mother is buried
here and the painting is a memorial to her.
LYNN KEARNEY
Artist and curator

The painting shows a pregnant Madonna, depicted in a
very simple and touching manner. It is in very good condition and was painted right here by Piero almost six hundred
years ago!
SIMON DINNERSTEIN
Artist

In Monterchi is a painting by Piero della Francesca called
Madonna del Parto. She is holding her outer robe open.
BETH VAN HOESEN ADAMS
Artist and printmaker

Editor's Note: Piero della Francesca's Madonna del Parto
*was unknown for centuries and was only rediscovered in
the 19th century. Created when the artist was a young
man, the painting was for many years displayed in the
chapel of the village cemetery. Now it hangs in Monterchi's
old schoolhouse, under lighting conditions described by
one Italian critic as being like those in a* discoteca. *There is
a campaign to have it restored to its rightful place.*

MONTEVARCHI
32 km northwest of Arezzo

Prada Outlet
SS 67, Via Aretina 63, ☎055 978 91 88

Osteria di Rendola
Via Rendola 87, ☎055 970 74 90
Closed Mondays

Montevarchi and San Giovanni Valdarno sort of blend into each other with a short industrial zone between. As they are about 45 minutes by train from Florence and are not hill towns but municipalities on the banks of the Arno, they have a suburban ambiance; I call them the bedroom towns for Florence, which doesn't mean that they have no charm. Montevarchi's contemporary claim to fame is that it is the place where Prada, the famous designer, has a discount outlet that draws travelers from all over the world. Busloads of tourists come every day from Florence, but as the store is on the outskirts of the town, it hasn't upset the ambiance of this quiet suburb.

Thursday is the traditional market day, when the citizens gather to shop and socialize. Italians turn all the mundane chores into a wonderful event. And I can't leave Montevarchi without telling you about a wonderful restaurant called Osteria di Rendola. It is an old *fattoria* (farm house) that has been restored and renovated in the most elegant manner. The food is superb, and when we went there just after it opened we asked the chef and owner where he had learned to cook. He told us that he worked at Le Cirque in New York for a number of years. It is a special dining experience.

EDITH ISAAC-ROSE
Painter and teacher

PIENZA

52 km southeast of Siena

> **a. Piazza Pio II**
> **b. Palazzo Comunale,** Corso Rosselino 59
> **c. Palazzo Piccolomini,** Piazza Pio II

There is no better combination of nature and architecture than the view of the Tuscan hills from the Piazza Pio II. The scale of the piazza, the asymmetrical loggia of the Palazzo Comunale, the cathedral façade and the side entrance to the Palazzo Piccolomini all add to the effect of the 15th-century square. The courtyard, rooms and the stacked loggias of the Palazzo Piccolomini are also well worth a look.

ROBERT LIVESEY
Architect

PIETRASANTA

33 km northwest of Pisa

In the small town of Pietrasanta, I suddenly realized that what I'd taken for clouds in the mountains were in fact outcroppings of the region's distinctive white marble. Pietrasanta teems with summertime stone carvers. A large white Botero sculpture dominates the piazza and pricey stores such as Gucci reflect the town's affluence. I walked down one of the main streets with my companion and we stopped in front of a church. The doors were open, and what drew us close was not the coffin, which stood in the middle of the aisle, but the large macabre painting by Botero that hung on the wall. We continued to Piazza Duomo and, at the recommendation of the contemporary sculptor Gio Pomodoro, had one of our finest meals yet, at Giudea, on via Bersanti.

SUSAN FARRICIELLI
Product designer

Bar Michelangelo
Piazza Duomo

🍴 Michelangelo lived and worked in Pietrasanta while quarrying the marble from the Apennine mountains high above the village. Here is where he found the marble for the *Pietà* and other important masterpieces. If you sit long enough at Bar Michelangelo in the southwest corner of the Piazza Duomo you might hear the *hummm* of pneumatic hammers, and when the hammers stop you'll hear artisans chiselling away at reproductions of Michelangelo's most famous works. If you have enough money, you can even buy one for yourself (the copy of the *David* now in the Piazza Signoria in Florence was carved here in Pietrasanta).

Take a long stroll around the perimeter of the village—you might view copies of the *Venus de Milo*—and if you have time, try to find the medieval wall with the remaining gates which will take you to points east, west and south . . .
MARIANNE WEIL
Sculptor

Editor's Note: There is a good reason Pietrasanta has gates to the east, west, and south, but not north: when the medieval wall was built, there probably was no major access to the north, only mountains.

Pietrasanta and its Neighbors
Viareggio, 12.5 km south of Pietrasanta
Carrara, 20 km north of Pietrasanta

Easily reached by train or *autostrada* from Rome or Florence, the aptly named town of Pietrasanta ("Holy Stone") lies on the flat coastal plain below the Apuan Alps at the south end of the Italian Riviera. Pietrasanta is a recommended excursion for anyone interested in sculpture, in places off the beaten path, or in the way that specialized sub-cultures take root in fertile soil. The marble quarries above the town—which was in Medici territory—were frequently visited by Michelangelo between 1516 and 1519;

his patron Pope Leo X Medici did not want to pay the Genoese for marble from Carrara, just to the north. The Pietrasanta marble was intended for the sculptor's façade of San Lorenzo, Leo X's family church in Florence.

The more famous marble quarries of Carrara still ship stone all over the world, but many bronze foundries were established in Pietrasantra to provide alternative processes to the sculptors who came there. Over time it was Pietrasanta that became the world's most international full-service sculpture center. Today a score of foundries cater to artists from the United States, most European countries, the Far East and South America, and stone is even import-ed from other countries to provide a full range of available colors and types.

Everything sculptural is made in Pietrasanta, from corpulent nude soldiers by Botero to dignified Native Americans by Harry Jackson; from enlargements of palm-sized models by DeKooning to saints and Madonnas for churches around the world, to nymphs and athletes intend-ed to decorate pizzerias and penthouses. Local *bronzisti* or *marmisti* will fill orders or help artists to make almost any-thing: a marble motorcycle, ducks for a dentist's shooting club, or—once upon a more innocent time—a twenty-foot high portrait of Saddam Hussein stretching out his arm to command his troops.

Peering into picturesque courtyards or modern indus-trial buildings will give fascinating glimpses of the range of things being made and the noisy physical labor that goes into sculpture. If you want a personal tour of the inside of a foundry or marble studio, try befriending one of the sculptors who gather after the day's work at the cafes in the square. Hint: marble sculptors tend to be covered with dust and have fat thumbs formed from misstrokes of the mallet; bronze sculptors tend to have wax under their fingernails and—if they do their own pouring—holes burned in their jeans by molten bronze.

The commune of Pietrasanta shares the charms of most medium-sized Italian towns, with an old fort, an imposing cathedral on the main square, shops with splendid things to eat along a pedestrian street, a weekly market, and a fierce competition for parking places. Giving away its special character are more numerous photography shops than you'd expect and a few stores whose windows display bronze and marble tools as if they were Cartier's jewelry. The ex-convent next to the cathedral houses a museum of original plaster models for sculpture donated by the artists who work in the area.

Places to stay in the town itself are not numerous, but the Marina di Pietrasanta, like other beach resorts along the coast, has many. Nearby Viareggio abounds in every kind of lodging, from imposing 19th-century hotels with names like Astor and Principe di Piemonte to small *pensioni* on the back streets. In season they cater to Germans and Scandinavians who come to grill their bodies on rented beach chaises by day and eat grilled fish and pizza in the evening. Viareggio is less chic than the rest of the Riviera, but it remains a port for the astounding private yachts that come into the shipyard for repair, or to disgorge jet setters, industrial magnates and oil-rich Arabs from all around the Mediterranean for shopping the international designer boutiques that line the beachfront promenade. The resort sponsors a famous *carnevale* parade in the spring, featuring huge floats reminiscent of the Macy's Thanksgiving parade in New York, except that here the displays are made of papier-maché and may depict contemporary political figures in biting satire. Off-season Viareggio is the perfect place to go on the lam; no one would ever think of looking for you there.

A visit to the quarries at Carrara is called for, to wonder at the huge blocks of stone being extracted by blasting or running wires, then carried down twisting, narrow roads on seemingly inadequate trucks with squealing brakes. The blocks are brought to the flat area and sliced like bread, then shipped around the world for architectural finishes. Year-round, the mountains are garlanded with white glaciers, looking for all the world like ski runs until you get close enough to see that the glaciers are swathes of discarded marble, the pieces ranging in size from peas to automobiles. Follow the signs for the *cave* (quarries) to enjoy the views, marvel at the process, or buy souvenirs made from marble: ashtrays and chess sets, figurines of David and Venus and, if you look carefully, some quite lovely serving pieces. Or, remembering the weight of your luggage, you might want to select only one perfect sphere or cube of oxblood stone, to anchor the bills from your trip on your desk at home.

VIRGINIA L. BUSH
Art historian

PISA

Don't rush Pisa. I always wish I could organize myself to spend some time out of season and look in a relaxed way at the Duomo, the Museum, the Camposanto and the other important sites.

JAMES FENTON
Writer

Museo dell'Opera del Duomo
Piazza del Duomo

This museum is often overlooked by visitors to this famous place. It has been recently redone and is a very rich small museum of Pisan art and culture from Roman times to the 17th century. The charming courtyard offers spectacular views over the Camposanto and the much-suffering Leaning Tower. There is a collective ticket that includes this museum, and one is often tempted to skip it because there is so much else, but it is very much worth at least an hour's visit.

CHARLES P. SEGAL
Classicist

PITIGLIANO
60 km west of Orvieto

If you are taking a trip around Lago di Bolsena and into
the wonderful surrounding towns (Viterbo, Tuscania,
Montefiascone), don't miss Pitigliano, northwest of the
lake. The town qualifies for the Italian adjectives *suggesti-
vo* and *caratteristico*! It seems to grow out of the tufa spur
on which it sits; for a long while it was one of the main
seats of the Orsini, and there's an imposing Palazzo Orsini
(we ate at a trattoria on the sloping main street near a
marble base which supported a sculpted Orsini bear.) Also,
a church up the street is built into an ancient temple. But
best of all is the old synagogue, recently restored, and
home to an old Sephardic congregation.
KATHERINE A. GEFFCKEN
Classicist

*Editor's Note: This synagogue is of the 17th century and
was reopened to the public in 1964. Pitigliano also has an
annual festival of Jewish film and klezmer music.*

POGGIO A CAIANO
12 km west of Florence

Medici Villa
Rebuilt 1480, Giuliano da Sangallo

Frescoes
Begun 1519, Franciabigio, Andrea del Sarto, and Jacopo Pontormo

Berenson considered this fresco of Pontormo among his best.
JOHN C. LEAVEY
Painter

RECOMMENDED READING
Bernard Berenson, *Italian Painters of the Renaissance*, o.p.
Iris Origo, *Images and Shadows: Part of a Life*, David R. Godine,
1999.

*Editor's Note: Berensen described Pontormo as "led astray
by his awestruck admiration for Michelangelo," but noted*

of this fresco: "What he could do when expressing himself,
*we see in the lunette at Poggio a Caiano, as design, as
colour, as fancy, the freshest, gayest, most appropriate
mural decoration now remaining in Italy."*

ROFELLE
39.5 km north of Sansepolcro

Ristaurante L'Erbhosteria del Castello
Badia Tedalda, ☎ 0575 71 40 17

🍴 This is more than a restaurant; it is an excursion with a
stupendous meal as its epicenter. Your mission is to find
this tiny, very tiny village, Rofelle, and arrive there in
time for lunch on Sunday—the only meal that this third-
generation enterprise serves regularly. (If you have a party
of more than ten and arrange it in advance, they will
open the kitchen on other days of the week). Reservations
are a must.

It is a forty minute to an hour drive from Sansepolcro.
Take SS 258 to Rimini, winding winding winding up into
the heart of the Alpe della Luna. Follow the signs for
Viamággio, and then on to Badia Tedalda, and just as you
enter Badia there is a blue sign indicating Rofelle on your
left. This becomes a dirt road coursing over the ridge and
finally reaching a collection of buildings which includes
the trattoria.

The food is exceptional and known for the fact that
this family effort centers on the herbs and flavors of the
woods and the season. There is no menu; you simply sit
down and listen as dish after dish is explained to you.
Pace yourself. Our meal went something like this: first the
crostini arrived, with wild mushroom and *dragoncello sal-
vatico*, *fave* paste, and fresh ricotta cubes with musty-
flavored purple wildflowers atop. Then the warm antipasti:
wild asparagus, a thin cheese and pear quiche, batter-fried
wildflowers (*clematis vitalba*, or Traveler's Joy), little bun-

dles of yarrow and *millefeuille*. And then the pastas, the risottos, nettle ravioli and the flower and wild herb salads, these followed by veal with porcini, sliced steak with prunes, grilled guinea fowl with truffles and juniper, deep-fried flowers of sambuco and rubina, roast lamb, chicken and sausage, more salad. Desserts we declined, having failed to pace ourselves adequately, so it was just a coffee and a homemade herbal *digestivo*. Twenty dollars per person, including the local wine.

After this a walk is needed, so head up the road to the medieval structures clinging to the walls of the narrowing valley.

GORDON KNOX AND CECILIA GALIENA
Directors of the Civitella Ranieri Center

ABBAZIA DI SAN GALGANO
34 km southwest of Siena

Romanesque church
12th century

Adjacent to the Cistercian-Gothic main structure is a 13th-century Romanesque church without a roof. The views are wonderful, and it was here in 1983 that Tarkovsky filmed the moody final scene of *Nostalghia*.

GIANCARLO GIUBILARO
Operations manager of the Civitella Ranieri Center

SAN GIMIGNANO
37 km northwest of Siena

San Gimignano is best approached by car, as the countryside offers great views. The town can be reached from Siena or Florence and can be covered by foot in an afternoon, including visiting the towers.

JOHN C. LEAVEY
Painter

Collegiata
12th Century
Piazza del Duomo

Frescoes by Barna da Siena, Bartolo di Fredi and Benozzo
Gozzoli. Chapel of Santa Fina by Ghirlandaio.
JOHN C. LEAVEY
Painter

Museo Civico
Palazzo del Popolo, Piazza del Duomo
Closed Mondays

Paintings by Filippino Lippi.
JOHN C. LEAVEY
Painter

Sant'Agostino
Piazza Sant'Agostino

Don't miss the fresco cycle depicting the life of Saint
Augustine, painted by Benozzo Gozzoli in 1465.
JOHN C. LEAVEY
Painter

SAN GIOVANNI VALDARNO
39 km northwest of Arezzo

Museo della Basilica di Santa Maria delle Grazie
Piazza Sasaccio

Annunciation
ca. 1440, Fra Angelico

San Giovanni Valdarno has a singular masterpiece, an
Annunciation by Fra Angelico in a nearby church, which is
a stunning example of his work
EDITH ISAAC-ROSE
Painter and teacher

Editor's Note: There is also an Annunciation, *circa 1472
and attributed to Jacopo del Sellaio, in the church of Santa
Maria delle Grazie.*

SANSEPOLCRO
37 km northeast of Arezzo

Aldous Huxley had it right when he began his essay on "The Best Picture" with the statement that "Borgo San Sepolcro is not very easy to get at." But as Huxley also explained, when one at last arrives, there are "some fine Renaissance palaces with pretty balconies of wrought-iron; a not very interesting church, and finally, the best picture in the world"—Piero della Francesca's *Resurrection*. Also not to be missed are Piero's *Madonna della Misericordia* and some stunning mannerist altarpieces by Pontormo (the *Saint Quentin* in the Museo Civico) and Rosso Fiorentino (the *Deposition* in San Lorenzo).

JOHN MARCIARI
Art historian

RECOMMENDED READING
Aldous Huxley, "The Best Picture" in *Along the Road: Notes and Essays of a Tourist*, Ecco Press, 1989.
John Pope-Hennessy, *The Piero della Francesca Trail*, o.p.

Museo Civico
Palazzo Comunale
Via Aggiunti 65

The Resurrection
ca. 1460, Piero della Francesca

Sansepolcro is the birthplace of Piero della Francesca. In the Palazzo Comunale is Piero's fresco *Resurrection*. I first saw this *Resurrection* and the *Madonna del Parto* of Piero della Francesca with Philip Guston in about 1970, when the *Madonna* was still in the nearby Monterchi cemetery chapel (it's now in a former schoolhouse in Monterchi). Guston first saw the *Resurrection* right after the war, when that room was a hospital room. The Pinacoteca also has Piero's altarpiece, *Madonna della Misericordia*, and a couple of single-figure fresco fragments from other locations. This is a must for those on the Piero pilgrimage.

ALAN FELTUS
Painter

Madonna della Misericordia
1445–1462, Piero della Francesca

In the Palazzo Comunale is the masterpiece of Piero della Francesca, the *Resurrection*, circa 1460; also his *Madonna of the Misericordia*, a polyptych of the Virgin and saints (more than a dozen). This ancient town in itself is a gem and is like walking back into the time of the Renaissance.

LYNN KEARNEY
Artist and curator

San Lorenzo
Via Santa Croce

Deposition
1528, Rosso Fiorentino

In Sansepolcro is a very wonderful, large Rosso Fiorentino Deposition behind the altar of San Lorenzo. This church is a few blocks from the museum, at the end of via Luca Pacioli on via Santa Croce. The church used to be within a school run by nuns, then it closed entirely, but now the front door is open and it is cared for by the commune.

ALAN FELTUS
Painter

In this inactive but non-deconsecrated church you will find a wonderful painting by Rosso Fiorentino. Given the Piero della Francesca fervor that this town rightly stirs, Rosso provides a change.

CLAUDIA CANNIZZARO
Coordinator of the Civitella Ranieri Center

Ristorante Fiorentino
Via Luca Pacioli 60, ☎ 0575 74 03 50

The Albergo Fiorentino has an extraordinary restaurant one floor up. Very good food and wine served by the charming proprietor and his wife. He recites the menu of the day in whatever language you speak. This is one of my favorite places in Italy. If it's closed when you are there, they will recommend another very near, with equally good cooking but a less beautiful dining room.
ALAN FELTUS
Painter

ABBAZIA DI SANT'ANTIMO
48 km southwest of Montepulciano, in hamlet of Castelnuove dell'Abate

This 12th-century Romanesque church is eight kilometers south of Montalcino. Every Sunday the Mass includes a traditional Gregorian chant, performed in authentic style.
GIANCARLO GIUBILARO
Operations manager of the Civitella Ranieri Center

One of the few Romanesque churches in this part of Italy. The interior is built partly of alabaster, so the light in it is beautiful. When I visited, I saw white oxen in the fields nearby. Gregorian chants are part of the service.
JOAN SILBER
Fiction writer

SERAVEZZA

36 km northwest of Pisa

Michelangelo's Road

ca. 1517–1519

The road to Monte Altissimo, from which were quarried the blocks for Michelangelo's sculptures, took three years for him to build and ran through some of the area's roughest terrain. It follows the river Serra, with spectacular waterfalls, numerous swimming holes, and rare flora, and is a relatively easy hike. Sections of the road used to transport blocks down to the seaport are still visible, peeking out from the underbrush, and some of the stones used in construction still bear marks of the wear of wagon wheels. Much of that original road has tumbled down into the ravine along the river, though; in these spots hikers must follow newer paths for a few yards before returning to the original trail. Above, one can see the peak of the mountain and some modern stone quarries; below, the sea. There are places with idyllic pools, and the more adventurous hikers can slide into them through waterfalls or cliff dive from as high as thirty feet.

The town of Seravezza is located at the juncture of two small rivers, the Serra and the Vezza. Facing the mountains (rather than the sea, at a distance of three kilometers) take the lefthand river and follow its path upwards, in the direction of a small *frazione* called Malbacco. After about one kilometer, the road suddenly becomes very steep, and at any point thereafter, going down to the left into the brush will bring you to the remnants of the road, if you're good at spotting traces of old roadways. If not, at several points along the road currently used for cars, you will find trails going off to the left and down into the ravine. I like the one that begins next to a modern cement powerline pole, and there's a space on the other side of the asphalt road where you can park two or three cars. This is a point at which the Michelangelo road almost touches the asphalt road; you'll see that the trail, right at the beginning, is flanked on the ravine side by a stone wall holding it up, which is also the edge of the Michelangelo road.

Alternatively, one can simply ask the locals where the Malbacco swimming hole is; you'll get a variety of answers, all of which are interesting. Bear in mind: the name *paradiso* is used for the largest pool with the highest ledge for jumping.

ANDREW R. WIELAWSKI
Sculptor

RECOMMENDED READING
Irving Stone, *The Agony and the Ecstasy*, New American Library, 1996.

This is an ancient trail that parallels the roadway and stream beside the marble mountain crests. The trail gradually makes its way to the stream, which is ice-blue and as cold. You may be lured into various pockets of beauty and pools of water visible beneath the trail, but follow it to its end. You will pass ruins of old mills and foundations, finally coming to an aquamarine pool surrounded by white marble boulders, rocks, and pebbles. It is fed by a shaft of blue-white water shooting down the mountainside which has carved a gutter in the rock above the pool. It is said this is the pool that caught the marble which was sent down the other side of the mountain. Bring your bathing suit. If you resist swimming, you'll regret it.

PAUL DIPASQUALE
Sculptor

Editor's Note: Friendly locals may advise you not to try diving at Malbacco.

SIENA

Biblioteca Comunale
Via della Sapienza 3
Open weekdays

If it weren't for the crowd of young people congregating outside the door-within-a-door, this impressive library would be hard to find. Walking from Piazza del Campo along via della Sapienza toward Piazza San Domenico, we were first intrigued by the fleeting glimpse we caught of an ornately-frescoed ceiling, as a door swung open from what we assumed was a church. Several days later, we had the courage to enter the dark *vicolo* that leads to the building, and slipped through the small door. It was like stepping into another dimension—we had entered a soaring cathedral of books!

The barrel-vaulted *biblioteca* is laid out like a church dedicated to knowledge: its side-chapels are arches filled with floor-to-ceiling bookcases whose shelves are covered with decorative metal grilles and carved doors. The altar is the circulation desk. The reading room is arranged with large wooden tables and old desk lamps. It is a warm, comfortable oasis in the heart of an ideal city.

The collection itself includes important medieval manuscripts and the letters of Saint Catherine of Siena.

CHIP SULLIVAN AND ELIZABETH BOULTS
Landscape architect and designer, respectively

The Biblioteca Comunale on via della Sapienza houses an intriguing collection of Italian volumes, manuscripts, drawings, examples of Dante and Botticelli, books of hours, Saint Catherine's letters and missals. It is a small treasure filled with rare early manuscripts and exhibits.

JOHN KEARNEY
Sculptor

Museo dell'Opera del Duomo

Piazza del Duomo 8

Gothic Statues

1250–1314, Giovanni Pisano

Maestà

1308–1311, Duccio

Scuplture of Giovanni Pisano, and especially the *Maestà*
by Duccio. The Duomo is a great work inside and out.
Several days in Siena are necessary, and if possible, time
your visit to coincide with The Palio.

JOHN C. LEAVEY
Painter

RECOMMENDED READING
Jacob Burckhardt, *The Civilization of the Renaissance in Italy*,
Penguin, 1990.

*Editor's Note: The Palio is an annual Tuscan festival held
on July 2nd and August 16th, and centered around a bare-
back horserace. The race, which dates to the 13th century,
is held in the campo, and the winner is awarded a* palio,
or banner.

Palazzo Pubblico / Museo Civico

Piazza del Campo 1

Guidoriccio da Fogliano

1330, Simone Martini
Located in the Sala del Mappamondo

Allegories of Good and Bad Government

1338–1340, Ambrogio Lorenzetti
Located in the Sala della Pace

Palazzo Pubblico in the clam-shell piazza. In the Sala del
Mappamondo is the famous fresco by Simone Martini of
Guidoriccio da Fogliano, who was a captain of the Sienese
army, on his way to the siege of Montemassi. (The fresco
was begun and completed in the same year as the siege.)
A most fascinating medieval work showing the caparisoned

horse and rider between two *castelli* complete with walls and moats.

Also in the Palazzo Pubblico are the allegorical frescoes by Ambrogio Lorenzetti (1338–1340), on the theme of the effects of good and bad government. They are early examples of secular painting, showing dancing ladies and genre scenes in and outside the town.

JOHN KEARNEY
Sculptor

Life of the Virgin

1406–1414, Taddeo di Bartolo
Located in the Cappella

The frescoes by Taddeo di Bartolo are unusual because of the inclusion of a map of Rome and figures of ancient rulers and philosophers. The main narrative cycle represents the *Last Days of the Virgin Mary*, when she asked Gabriel to gather the Apostles from all over the world to bid her farewell. Taddeo depicts this event by showing the apostles surging through the air on their way to this final rendezvous.

DAVID G. WILKINS
Art and architectural historian

Baptistery

Entered from bottom of steps behind Duomo

Baptismal Font

1417–1430, Jacopo della Quercia, Lorenzo Ghiberti, and Donatello

This marble Renaissance font was designed by Ghiberti and decorated with gilded bronze reliefs and figures by Ghiberti, Donatello, and Jacopo della Quercia in the 1420s. Donatello's relief of the *Feast of Herod* is the clear champion in what must have been a Renaissance competition; its illusion of deep space is a tour-de-force, but more important is the manner in which the relief's explosive composition and undulating Salome capture the human horror and fascination of this biblical tale.

DAVID G. WILKINS
Art and architectural historian

SOVANA
60 km west of Orvieto

Hellenistic Etruscan Tombs and Santi Pietro e Paolo

Here's a little-visited site that preserves the quality of a small Etruscan community. Sovana was an outlying satellite of Statonia, one of a cluster in the near neighborhood. The rock-cut tombs are of very curious architecture and iconography. The Romanesque Church of Santi Pietro e Paolo is unrestored and boasts some remarkable capitals, as well as a fine original plan.

L. RICHARDSON JR.
Classicist

RECOMMENDED READING
Ranuccio Bianchi Bandinelli, *Sovana, topografia ed arte*, Rinascimento del libro, Firenze, 1929.

TREQUANDA
23 km northwest of Montepulciano

This medieval village, well worth a detour, is a favorite with Italian travelers.

GIANCARLO GIUBILARO
Operations manager of the Civitella Ranieri Center

VIAREGGIO

21 km northwest of Pisa

Carnevale

Late January to late February; varies relative to Easter

The Carnevale at Viareggio that occurs annually during Mardi Gras is known for its politically critical and incredibly creative floats and parades. With oversized representations of public figures (larger than the surrounding turn-of-the-century seaside buildings of the town) and vocal commentary from both onlookers and organizers, Viareggio's festival can be described, with no exaggeration, as Felliniesque.

LESLIE RAINER
Conservator

VOLTERRA

56 km northwest of Siena

Volterra is my favorite medieval city. Once an imposing Etruscan community, the towered, fortified town rises on a precipitous hill. Volterra is a veritable gem. A walk along the remains of the Etruscan walls reveals lovely surprise views of the valley where the Etruscans buried their dead in precious alabaster urns. The smaller medieval city's walls also offer beautiful vistas, and culminate in the Etruscan city gate guarded by three enigmatic heads. Above the walls, near the Porta San Felice, is a small chapel, the Oratorio di San Felice (1707), which commemorates by means of eloquent frescoes the miraculous survival of a woman who had fallen from the wall near this spot. The Etruscan Collection of the Museo Etrusco Guarnacci is a must! It houses the hundreds of alabaster cinerary urns from nearby cemeteries and the famous Ombra della Sera; the elongated bronze figure of a pious youth. Truffles and wild boar are delicacies on the menu at the Pozzi degli Etruschi. Not to be missed is the picture gallery's small eclectic collection and its masterpiece: Rosso Fiorentino's *Deposition*. It alone is worth the trip to Volterra.

HELEN NAGY
Art historian

Pinacoteca e Museo Civico
Via dei Sarti 1

Deposition
1521, Rosso Fiorentino

Drive to Volterra, a wonderful hill city, to see Rosso Fiorentino's *Deposition* in the Pinacoteca e Museo Civico, and compare it with Pontormo's masterpiece at Santa Felicita in Florence. These two paintings are worth the trip to Italy.

RICHARD L. FEIGEN
Art dealer

UMBRIA

ASSISI
26 km east of Perugia

Basilica di San Francesco
Begun 1228 (lower church), consecrated 1253 (upper church)
Piazza di San Francesco
Call as times vary; ☎ 075 81 90 01

Assisi is a very beautiful hill town made famous by Saint Francis and Saint Clare. It is a Roman spiritual city built over in medieval times and for the most part not changed since. The major attraction, the Basilica di San Francesco, is made up of two churches, one above the other (with the chapel around the tomb of Francis functioning as a smaller third level beneath the altar of the lower church.)

Construction began two years after the death of Saint Francis. This is Italy's first Gothic church, with the earliest stained glass in Italy, among the oldest surviving anywhere. It is almost totally frescoed, floor to ceiling, by the best of the early Renaissance painters: Cimabue, Giotto, Pietro Lorenzetti, Simone Martini. Also represented are equally wonderful lesser-known painters, like the Maestro di San Francesco, whose frescoes are in the nave of the lower church, and the Maestro delle Vele, who painted the ceiling vault over the altar of the lower church. In fact, you will find the attribution of some of the painting varies; the most uncertain are the 28 large frescoes depicting the life of Saint Francis in the upper church—though books and post-cards originating in Assisi claim these are Giottos. The Giottos in the lower church are undisputed, and in my mind the attribution has little to do with their importance. They are incredible paintings, inviting repeated visits and quiet contemplation.

Some days there is insufficient light to see one chapel, but elsewhere the light is fine. The Simone Martini chapel is usually unlit, but when it has its lights on it reveals another series of amazing paintings. The whole basilica is like that, in fact.

These two churches, the lower dark and Byzantine, like something from Eisenstein's *Ivan the Terrible*, and the upper all light and air and harmony, together have a quality that transforms the visitor. Whether there's a spiritual factor or purely an aesthetic experience is something we all have to determine for ourselves.

ALAN FELTUS
Painter

Basilica di Santa Chiara
Piazza Santa Chiara

Crypt
19th century

Descend into the crypt of the church. There, beneath a painted starry sky you will find the withered body of Santa Chiara (Saint Clare), dressed in an immaculate habit and clutching a bouquet of fresh flowers in her mummified hands. The story of how she saw Saint Francis give up his wordly goods (and clothing) in the main piazza of Assisi and was forever devoted to him is one for a romance novel. She cut off her golden hair, which can be found in a glass box elsewhere in the church, and founded her own order, the Sorelle Povere di Santa Chiara, or Poor Clares. As you gaze upon her, know that this delicate figure is the patron saint of television. One Christmas Eve she was too ill to attend Mass, and saw the whole service in a vision. I wonder if she knows what she started . . .

PAMELA KEECH
Artist, curator, and historian

Editor's Note: In 1958, Pius XII officially designated Santa Chiara the patron saint of television.

San Damiano
South of the Porta Nuova

Every summer I come to Assisi, and the view on the plain as I drive from Santa Maria degli Angeli—the town shimmering on the side of Mount Subasio like some mirage—makes me gasp each time I see it. Everyone knows about the double Basilica and the story of Saint Francis as Giotto painted it on the walls of the upper Basilica, but not everyone knows about San Damiano, the tiny church outside the walls where Santa Chiara spent her life amid the fields. (The church is a short distance south of the Porta Nuova, near the church of Santa Chiara.) The first time I saw it, there was a group of young monks playing soccer, having a wonderful time as they picked up their robes to kick the ball. Going back into the city, walk over to Piazza San Rufino where the only cybercafe (one computer) sits in the corner of the piazza and you can sit there looking at one of the most beautiful of Romanesque façades.

Then walk through the town, and go out the back (the northwest corner of Assisi) through Porta San Giacomo, between the centuries-old cypresses lining the road to the cemetery. Go into the cemetery, as it gives you a wonderful insight into the Italian reverence for family and death. Outside the cemetery, keep walking around the back of Assisi, and you will see the remarkable pink stone quarry that gives Assisi its special glow. Go have a drink or dinner at the Hotel Giotto's wonderful terrace (via Fontebella 41, ☎075 81 22 09), and sit and look at the Umbrian plain as the sun sets and the golden pinks of the sunset color the houses and a sense of peace and tranquility washes over you.

EDITH ISAAC-ROSE
Painter and teacher

BEVAGNA
10 km west of Foligno

From its charming access, affording a view of a large
public pool for washing clothes, to its two 12th-century
Romanesque churches, San Michele Arcangelo and San
Silvestro (one of which contains a decaying saint, visible
through glass, behind the main altar), to its Roman bath
mosaics, this little Umbrian hill town is a gem. You might
even see a modern mosaicist at work in a shop near the
baths. Known for rope production in the Middle Ages,
Bevagna hosts a medieval craft fair in late June.
MARGARET A. BRUCIA
Latin teacher

Mercato delle Gaite
10-day festival towards the end of June
For information, ☎ 0742 36 18 47

Walking into Bevagna during its Mercato delle Gaite is
like walking into a living, breathing medieval performance
piece. Bevagna is a small charming medieval (12th-centu-
ry) town not far from Assisi, and its Mercato delle Gaite
is a wonderful (and scrupulously researched by the Bevag-
nites) festival of medieval life. The visitor can listen to
medieval folk songs, eat medieval food, learn how brass
pots, string, cakes and cloth were made, and see
impromptu medieval folk plays. What's unusual here is
the accent on art and *l'artigianato*. The booth I liked best
at Bevagna's festival was the reconstruction of a silk
store, with all the blind, butting worms busy spinning
silk or getting ready to. (Slow crawling into position,
slow munching of leaves.) The different worms corre-
spond to different colors, from white to off-white,
cream, and pale yellow. Bevagna's citizens, dressed up in
historically faithful costumes, are our performers.

Bevagna, with its intimately graceful medieval piazza,
gems of Romanesque churches, octagonal fountain,

Palazzo dei Consoli, and medieval arched corners every-
where, makes the perfect backdrop for the *Festa*.
JANE OLIENSIS
Cultural historian

Roman Mosaics in Terme di Mevania

2nd century AD
Via Porta Guelfa 4, ☎ 0742 36 03 06
Ring custodian at #2 if closed.

The whimsical Roman mosaic from Bevagna's second-
century AD Roman baths, the Terme di Mevania, should
not be missed. Who but the Romans (those stoics) would
want to bathe with alarming sea-monsters seemingly
about to nibble their toes? In the water, those sea-creatures
would move!
JANE OLIENSIS
Cultural historian

BURANO

11 km northeast of Gubbio
Drive north from Gubbio on S 219 to S 452 (known as "La Contessa"),
going east until left turn to Burano

For an excursion outside Gubbio, make your way north.
Burano is a ridge of mountains between Umbria and
Marche, and one of the most remote, magical landscapes
of the region. Legend has it that the region got its name
from an influx of people fleeing Venice long ago, perhaps to
escape the plague. In fact, there are several small settlements
in the area that bear names beginning with "Ca'." Along
this road is da Baffone, a wonderful family style restaurant
which serves typical homemade Umbrian cuisine, including
several excellent *antipasti* and pasta dishes made with local
truffles. The atmosphere is far from elegant, but the food
and company are excellent and offer a glimpse of a part of
Umbria which has so far escaped gentrification.
CAREN CANIER
Painter

Editor's Note: Though we can find no documentary histor-
ical evidence to corroborate the notion that Burano was
founded by people fleeing Venice, there is no question that
memory of the past in oral tradition often contains at least
a kernel of historical truth. The Serra di Burano and the
Fiume Burano ("ridge" and "river," respectively) near
Gubbio are in the hills only about 120 miles south of
Venice, and it is certainly true that the usual strategy in
times of plague was to "head for the hills." (One familiar
example is the exodus from Florence during the Black
Death in the 14th century, which provided the background
for Boccaccio's Decamerone.*) So the legend could be true,*
but the evidence to substantiate it from place names is pre-
carious. There is, to be sure, an island named Burano near
Venice, but Burano was not a unique name elsewhere in
the area; for example, there is another Burano on Lake
Como. As for places named "Ca'," that is indeed a term
used in Venice. There is a Ca' Rafaello very near Serra di
Burano, but there are also literally dozens of other towns
all over northern Italy whose names begin that way—even
a Ca' di Giulietta near Bologna. Most likely, the legend in
the Gubbio area arose from a relatively recent imaginative
attempt to account for already existing names.

CASTIGLIONE DEL LAGO

45 km south of Arezzo

Rocca del Leone
Construction began 1247, Frederick II
For information, ✆ 075 96 52 484

The beautiful, pentagonal castle perched here above Lago
Trasimeno is my favorite in Italy. It was created by
Frederick II, Italy's first Renaissance man, who traveled
throughout Europe with his own private zoo and was a
philosopher, naturalist, architect, and patron of the arts,
especially poetry—not to mention Emperor of the Holy
Roman Empire. The castle is like Frederick's famous obser-

vatory in Puglia, Castel del Monte: sculptural as the Guggenheim Museum in New York is sculptural. It has unified, organic form, and its pentagon is somehow a formal expression of the beautiful lake of which it affords so many breathtaking views. I visited with some English tourists, and as we climbed here and there (towers, battlements, ramparts) and dawdled and gazed, one of them said, "You can feel it's got an aesthetic. It's not just being a castle." Yes, that's it. A playground for grown-ups, and a wonderful place to come with children.

Very pleasant, too, are the Castiglione beaches. I especially recommend the Lido Arezzo, with its bar, paddle boats, striped beach umbrellas and formal amateur volley-ball tournaments, for a delightful experience of an Italian beach.

JANE OLIENSIS
Cultural historian

Editor's Note: The Puglia observatory was also a glorified fortification and residence, in an ideal spot for one of Frederick's favorite pursuits, hunting (on which subject he had a small monograph). It commands a 360-degree view of the horizon.

CITTÀ DI CASTELLO
17 km southeast of Sansepolcro

Centro delle Tradizioni Popolari
Villa Cappelletti, ☏075 855 21 19

If you are on the E 45, exit at the Città di Castello *sud* exit. Take a left at the T and continue on towards the city. About a kilometer or two after the T, as you come to a rise, you will see a parked locomotive on your left in front of a large villa. Stop and go in. The center is closed at lunch time. Entrance is free, although a five thousand lira tip to the 'guide' is nice and well-appreciated if he has shown you around.

This museum is the brainchild of the formidable Livio Dalla Ragione, a local hero in every sense of the word and a passionate supporter of the intelligence, elegance and 'art' of everyday objects. Signor Dalla Ragione persuaded the city fathers of Città di Castello to obtain this rambling villa and surrounding sheds, barns, and workshops from the departing Marchese Cappelletti. He then turned it into a museum of 'popular traditions.' The building is pretty much the way it was when the last of the Cappelletti and their many *mezzadri*—sharecroppers—pulled up stakes and left in the early 1970s. Since then, Livio Dalla Ragione has scoured the local hills and towns with an eye for the unusual, the interesting or elegantly detailed tool, household item, bit of furniture or piece of linen. He has taken his finds and added them to the farm's existing collection of furniture, bottles, clothes, shoes, forks, shovels, etc. that line the walls and rooms of this wonderfully eccentric museum.

In the workshops on the ground floor you will find walls with racks of spiky metal cow bras, ingeniously and humorously designed to dissuade young calves from nursing, or a forge with stacks of metal-pounding and -handling tools and a bellows the size of a Fiat *cinquecento*, olive oil and wine presses and their associated cantinas, bottles and filters. Upstairs was the living area for the *contadini*. In the large, smoke-tinted communal kitchen and dining room you will find hand-painted bowls, vases and pitchers, an odd assortment of mousetraps, pots, pans and cooking tools. In the bedroom the walls still have the occasional print of the Madonna or an important saint, sagging beds, piles of linen and closets full of clothes with patches on the patches. There is even a tin tobacco box filled with hand-carved buttons. It feels like a moment frozen in time, as though the *contadini* will return at sunset for their evening meal; sort of a Pompeii, but for a way of life that is only decades—not centuries—over the horizon.

GORDON KNOX AND CECILIA GALIENA
Directors of the Civitella Ranieri Center

DERUTA

18.5 km south of Perugia

Maioliche

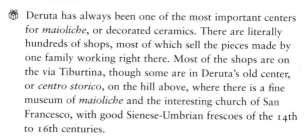

Deruta has always been one of the most important centers for *maioliche*, or decorated ceramics. There are literally hundreds of shops, most of which sell the pieces made by one family working right there. Most of the shops are on the via Tiburtina, though some are in Deruta's old center, or *centro storico*, on the hill above, where there is a fine museum of *maioliche* and the interesting church of San Francesco, with good Sienese-Umbrian frescoes of the 14th to 16th centuries.

Of all the shops in upper and lower Deruta, many as good as any other, there is one that makes copies of antique tiles from the Deruta area. This shop is Veschini (via Tiberina 159). The tiles are of two sorts: thick, hand-cut squares or commercially-made thinner tiles compatible with normal bathroom tiles. The same images occur on both, but selection varies depending on when you visit. There tend to be many beautiful ones most of the time. One tile is a good gift, or many can be bought to place in walls, as we have done.

Maioliche di Pierluigi Monotti (via Tiberina Sud 276), makes copies of antique ex-votos and other large tiles from antique originals. When some years ago many ex-voto plaques were stolen from the church Madonna dei Bagni (see p, 256), this shop was given the job of reproducing the missing ex-votos from photographs. They continue to make ex-votos for townspeople whose prayers to this particular Madonna have been answered. The shop sells beautiful copies of many of the antique ones on the walls of the *santuario*.

M'Art di Nulli, Maria Teresa (via Tiberina 132), also has copies of ex-voto plaques like those in the church of the Madonna dei Bagni.

Flli. Marcucci (via Tiberina 204), has extraordinary pitchers, plates, and platters copied from antique examples in museum collections.

ALAN FELTUS
Painter

Madonna dei Bagni
16th century until present
2.5 km south of Deruta, immediately east of SS 3

I highly recommend going to the church called Madonna dei Bagni. The church is behind a gate, and the walls are covered with ex-votos in majolica that span several centuries, all devoted to the miraculous Madonna. The story is that a farmer whose wife was very sick was walking to the pharmacy to get her some medicine when he found a fragment of a plate with the Madonna and Child painted on it. He placed the fragment in the crotch of a tree and said a prayer for his wife's recovery. When he returned home, he discovered she was well. The fragment, in its piece of tree, is enshrined behind the altar in this church. And the ex-voto images that cover the walls all contain an image of the Madonna in the tree with the baby Jesus in her arms, plus a depiction of one or another illness, accident, or war injury suffered by those who were eventually cured by this Madonna. The ex-votos date from the 16th century to today; the injuries include the Bosnian war, motorcycle accidents, lightning, and so on.

ALAN FELTUS
Painter

FOLIGNO
18 km south of Assisi

Monastero Santa Anna
Via dei Monasteri 46

Foligno is a relatively unvisited town because it doesn't have any monuments of great fame, but it always reminds me of Rome from my earliest memories, when Rome was quieter, with fewer cars. Lying in the valley, Foligno is defined by the winding Topino, much as Rome is defined by the Tiber. The town is small, and it's easy to walk the *centro storico* in a few minutes.

I discovered the Monastero Santa Anna quite by chance. To find it, you can ask for Standa (Standa is a small department store chain in Italy, and this one is located in a nondescript contemporary building.) Walk a few steps down the small street whose entrance faces the façade of Standa, and turn into a courtyard on the left side. Ring the bell of the little convent and explain to the voice that answers that you want to see the frescoes. A nun will guide you through. Once within the inner doors, you will leave behind all traces of the present (so evident in Standa's mid-20th-century architecture, a stone's throw from where you stand.)

Inside, the feelings of tranquility and beauty are very special. The experience of being in a small Renaissance convent, still home to a handful of nuns, and with several rooms of wonderful 14th- and 15th-century frescoes, is well worth the detour from places better known.

The frescoes are rewarding on their own, but another quite different revelation awaits. The nun will show you a miracle: a handprint burned into the back of an *armadio*, or wardrobe, by a beloved deceased sister who wanted her community to know she returned to visit. This is one fine example of the many, many hidden treasures in Umbria.

ALAN FELTUS
Painter

GUBBIO

41 km northeast of Perugia

Gubbio remains undervisited partly because it doesn't have train access. But for those driving, I recommend Gubbio, a very beautiful medieval hill town with ancient Umbrian and Roman origins. There are fine examples of Renaissance architecture, such as the Palazzo dei Consoli, which is worth seeing for its own merits and for the view over the rooftops. There are also some interesting churches and charming streets.

ALAN FELTUS
Painter

Gubbio Stroll

In Gubbio, Piazza Grande, Palazzo dei Consoli and Palazzo Ducale are magnificent architectural sites not to be missed. Via Galeotti, above Piazza Grande, with its medieval bridges and passageways, is also a must. My favorite neighborhood, however, is the Quartiere di "Sammartino," or San Martino, which lies in the northern section of the walled city, around the church of the same name. Here the ancient Roman grid of the rest of the city breaks down and its medieval character truly prevails.

Instead of parking in the main visitors' lot (Piazza 40 Martiri), park in a smaller lot diagonally across from the Roman theater, inside the city walls behind Piazza Bosone. From there you can enter the city through a pedestrian passageway or through the Bar Bosone, where you might stop for a snack. Either way, the passage and contrast between outside and inside the city walls warms the spirit as Gubbio envelops you with its richly textured stonework and tight spaces. Turn left onto via Cavour and walk towards Piazza Bruno, where the church of San Martino is located.

You will pass Pompeo, one of the finest butcher shops in the region. It's often mobbed, but worth the wait to purchase fresh, locally-raised meats from one of the nicest merchant families in Gubbio. Try the *prosciutto nostrale*, the *bresaola*, or any of the fresh meats displayed.

Walk through Piazza Bruno, bearing right to discover a bridge over the little Camignano River. (There's a wonderful *forno* and *pasticceria* by the bridge, and the aroma of baking fills the air.) If you follow via del Camignano, a passageway that hugs the river, you will find yourself in a charming medieval neighborhood of bridges, alleys and hidden gardens behind stone walls. The river is almost always dry in summer, but suggestive all the same. If you head uphill, you will eventually wind your way up to via dei Consoli, the main drag, where Piazza Grande is located. On the way up is my favorite ceramics shop, Leo Grilli Arte, a two-storey shop chock-full of pottery more tasteful than many of the more tourist-oriented shops on via dei Consoli, (although Grilli now has a second outlet location among them). Along via Baldassini, the street just below Piazza Grande, are many fine antique shops and the home of Sant'Ubaldo, patron saint of Gubbio. You can also glimpse some of the huge vaults beneath Piazza Grande and Palazzo dei Consoli.

On the other, northernmost side of Piazza Bruno, wander through winding medieval streets and alleys and end up at via Capitano del Popolo, with its stunning Palazzo del Capitano del Popolo and the northern gate to the city, Porta Castello. The road outside this gate leads to a turn-off for the Basilica of Sant'Ubaldo, which is at the top of Monte Ingino (too far to walk for most), and looks out over all of Gubbio and its environs. The several bars and restaurants up there are a refreshing escape from the heat of summer. (Sant'Ubaldo can also be reached by funicular from the south side of town. I find the funicular terrifying, but my husband and sons love it.) If you don't turn off for Sant'Ubaldo, the road leads through a spectacular mountain pass to Scheggia and towards Monte Cucco, in the Apennines, a center for mountaineering activities in the summer.

CAREN CANIER
Painter

Mastri Librai Eugubini
Via dei Consoli 48

The finest contemporary bookbinding I've seen anywhere
is found in Gubbio. The shop is called Mastri Librai
Eugubini, on the left a short distance past the Palazzo dei
Consoli, and it's easy to miss, being very small. The work
is leather, marbleized paper, or both, and the most tasteful
you'll see. Goods range from small address books and
agendas to photo albums, the grandest of which are amazingly large books that come with their own boxes. They
have several sizes of blank handmade paper books as well.
All the work is done in the basement and in another location at via Gabrielli 24, and if you need a really beautiful
gift, this is one of the best places I know.
ALAN FELTUS
Painter

LERCHI
5 km northwest of Città di Castello; 17 km southeast of Sansepolcro

Associazione Archeologia Arborea
For information, ✆ 075 855 38 67

San Lorenzo, the deconsecrated parish church on the hill
over Lerchi, is just north of Città di Castello, on SS 221,
the way to Monterchi and the *Madonna del Parto*. Once
you leave Città di Castello going toward Arezzo, you pass
through Lerchi, and just after the central section of this tiny
town the buildings open up and you will see on your left a
sign pointing up to San Lorenzo. Take that road, continuing straight, past the farm and up a very steep dirt road,
following the signs until you reach the ridge and the houses.
Park and walk in; shoo the geese away and ask for Livio.

The Association for Arboreal Archaeology is a labor
of love as well as a concrete step towards the preservation
of the Upper Tiber Valley's wealth of fruits and vegetables.
Isabella and Livio Dalla Ragione have spent the last ten

years sneaking into abandoned monastery orchards, overgrown parish gardens or back yards of collapsed farm
houses to collect the seeds of the multitude of endangered
fruit trees, medicinal plants and vegetables that were so
carefully cultivated for myriad uses over the past centuries.
The vision and effort of this father-and-daughter team of
devoted plant lovers has resulted in a nursery of some five
hundred garden plants and fruit trees that would otherwise
be facing extinction. There are scores of types of apple
trees alone; each producing a specialized fruit, those good
for winter storage, sweet for early summer eating, small
and sour for cooking or jam-making, and bearing a variety
of names which range from spring-rose to donkey's ass.
The nursery is on the breathtakingly beautiful hillside that
also hosts the vineyard producing Livio's delicate rosé.

The association offers these rescued plants for 'adop-
tion.' For a one-time fee of 150,000 lire you can become
an associate member and the lifetime 'guardian' of a van-
ishing apple, pear, cherry or fig tree, or a small but powerful herb, perhaps one that can be added to a pasta sauce to
add zing and enhance your liver. The stipulations are simple: adopt a plant and make an effort to return annually to
the hillside to nurture your charge and collect the fruit,
leaving always one fruit for the moon, one for the soil and
one for the plant. If you are lucky you will be invited to
join Livio for a meal, perhaps a simple pasta with an artichoke and rose petal sauce accompanied with baked eggplant and *panzanella*.

GORDON KNOX AND CECILIA GALIENA
Directors of the Civitella Ranieri Center

RECOMMENDED READING
Isabella and Livio Dalla Ragione, *Archeologia Arborea: diario di
due cercatori di piante*. Ali&no, 1997.

NICCONE

35 km northwest of Perugia

La Chiusa

2 km from Niccone on SS de Niccone, ☎075 941 07 74
www.lachiusa.com or lachiusa@netmedia.net

Dada and Claudio Rener run this small organic farm with
rooms to rent and a wonderful kitchen. It is quiet, relaxed
and delicious. Organic homemade food; everything from
the bread to the *tiramisu* is made on the farm and mostly
with products raised or grown there. An excellent home
base for forays into the upper Tiber valley, or you can just
go for dinner. Call ahead.

GORDON KNOX AND CECILIA GALIENA
Directors of the Civitella Ranieri Center

NORCIA

45 km northeast of Spoleto

As any traveler knows, exposure to great cultural artifacts
can stun as well as stimulate the beholder. I spent five years
in Rome, living in a dingy palace that once housed Michelangelo, and a modest five minute walk to masterpieces of
Borromini, Bernini, Caravaggio and Michelangelo himself
left me in a daze: too much of a great thing. I did the only
thing a kid from California could do; I tried to find a trout
stream. I wanted to distance myself from all things that
called for assessment.

High in the Abruzzi I found the Sangro River, then the
Volturno, the Ninfa and the Velino, but I learned that it is
impossible to escape the distraction of high culture in Italy,
no matter how remote the site. Then I heard about the
Nera River. Surely no cultural threat could exist near so
bleak a town as Terni, and I set out with high hopes of
finding nature devoid of culture.

The trout in the Nera are an isolated strain of the
Fario. They have a golden blush to their bodies and are

dappled with red and black spots. I became possessed by them and made weekly pilgrimages to the Valnerina through the spring and summer and lured friends to come along whenever I could. One of them, Bill (William Overton) Smith, the composer and jazz clarinetist, actually caught a trout.

For the first dozen or so visits to the river, I took no notice of my surroundings. Other fishermen will know that the mesmerizing effect of a fly bobbing toward a likely trout will obliterate all other awarenesses. I would glance up occasionally and see a castle here, a monastery there, but they were spotty and did not worry me much.

I recall, in particular, one long day on the river with George D'Almeida, the painter, and Paul Getty, the naturalist. We decided to find lodging in a town at the end of the Cascia valley, and twenty dusty, winding kilometers later, we found our hotel in the dark. After a mountain of lentils and wild boar sausages, we fell into beds decorated by wolf skins.

The following morning we awoke to the splendid sight of Norcia. Norcia was born as a Roman garrison (Nursia) and is circled by a 13th-century wall that echoes its origins. The generous main square is anchored by the Church of San Benedetto and the Palazzo Comunale on one side and by the Castellina on the opposite side. Each building is a gem set off by the contrasting styles of the others.

The shock of stumbling onto Norcia while expecting a dull rustic town confirmed my notion of Italy—that its greatness was inescapable, and I was bound to encounter it at every turn. I resolved to enjoy, not confront, Italy's great presences. At the same time, I began to make sculptures of rivers and waterfalls, so weird a subject that they could not be compared to any art of the past. A great relief!

Above Norcia is the Piano Grande, a mountain meadow covering about ten square miles, which blooms into an astonishing range of color and texture. Follow the signs to Castelluccio.

It is easier now to reach Norcia through tunnels and paved roads and I'm sure the wolf skins are long gone. No doubt there are more fishermen than there were in my day, but I like to think the trout are still there.

JACK ZAJAC
Painter and sculptor

Editor's Note: Norcia, birthplace of Saint Benedict, is famous for truffles.

ORVIETO

Duomo
Piazza Duomo

Last Judgment Cycle
1499–1504, Luca Signorelli
Cappella San Brizio/Cappella Nuova

This great and unusual series of paintings—intense, pulsing, colorful—is a visionary work, traditional yet filled with modernist, even avant-garde leanings; some viewers may be reminded of Mexican surrealism. Signorelli's images surround the viewer with the coming of the Apocalypse and depictions of the doomsday moon and sun. Notable for their draftsmanship and their strong figural compositions, the Orvieto paintings are said to have influenced Michelangelo's Sistine frescoes. Don't miss Jonathan B. Riess' writing on this subject, especially *The Renaissance Antichrist*, in which he contends that the painting represents a not-too-veiled anti-semitic program. Placing the painting in the context of the religious and cultural turmoil of the time (in particular, Savonarola), the author makes a strong case for his view of the painting's underlying themes and symbolism. It's a dense and thought-provoking account, which left this artist with many questions. A powerful and provocative work of art, Signorelli's frescoes are the visual equivalent of a great symphony or novel.

The Cathedral also has a wonderful and intense relief of Lorenzo Maitani on the front façade.

SIMON DINNERSTEIN
Artist

RECOMMENDED READING
Jonathan B. Riess, *The Renaissance Antichrist: Luca Signorelli's Orvieto Frescoes*. Princeton University Press, 1995.
Jonathan B. Riess, *Luca Signorelli: The San Brizio Chapel*, Orvieto. George Braziller, 1995.

Pozzo di San Patrizio

1527–1537, Antonio da Sangallo the Younger
Viale San Gallo

If you would like some vigorous exercise in a very unusual place, visit the Pozzo di San Patrizio. When I first visited Orvieto I did not know what *pozzo* meant, just saw the sign and, out of curiosity, went in. Begun in 1527 and completed ten years later, this is a very large and deep well built in a double helix with two stairways, one going down and one up, each wide enough for a donkey carrying water buckets. It was constructed to supply the city with water in case it came under siege. The stairway descends 203 feet to the bottom of the well and the climb out is 248 steps. Perhaps *pozzo* climbing will become the next health craze, and we will be on the cutting edge.

PAMELA KEECH
Artist, curator, and historian

Saint Patrick's well, built between 1527 and 1537 and designed by Antonio da Sangallo, is a precursor of the genome project! An incredible double-helix stairway lets you descend about two hundred feet, look up and ascend without ever retracing your steps. This allowed donkeys to avoid head-on collisions when carrying water up to the surface.

ROSS ANDERSON
Architect

Antica Trattoria dell'Orso
Via della Misericordia 18–20, ☎ 076 334 16 42

🍽 Located in an unpromising little street off the Piazza della
Repubblica and named after a trained bear that once frequented the neighborhood, this is arguably the oldest
restaurant in Orvieto, a city of considerable if unheralded
artistic interest. Don't ask the owners—the ursine Gabriele
(who learned his English in New Jersey) or the cherubic
Ciro—for a menu, but simply say, "*Abbiamo fiducia in
Voi,*" and let yourself be charmed by all that follows, in
conversation and in cuisine.
JOHN VARRIANO
Art historian

PISSIGNANO
39 km southeast of Assisi

Fonti del Clitunno
Off the Via Flaminia near Pissignano

In front of the Castello di Pissignano is a small natural
park with a little lake and an island. The beautiful springs
are a perfect stop in the shade between Foligno and
Spoleto.
CLAUDIA CANNIZZARO
Coordinator of the Civitella Ranieri Center

The road from Perugia to Spoleto or vice versa affords
several rewarding detours. The most famous and important
of these is of course Assisi, but about half way between
Foligno and Spoleto is the diminutive but thoroughly
delightful Tempietto del Clitunno, now known as the church
of San Salvatore. In contrast to the crowds of tourists and
pilgrims that overwhelm Assisi, this wonderful and largely
forgotten building in a small park-like setting offers an oasis
of quietude enhanced by the plashing spring above which it
rises and after which it is named. Constructed of *spolia* in
the late 4th or early 5th century, according to most scholars,

this most classicizing of Early Christian monuments is a small temple in the Ionic order on a podium approached by flights of stairs to either side. The façade contains four spirally fluted columns *in antis*, a beautifully inscribed frieze, and a pediment decorated most simply but elegantly in mosaic, with an image of the cross in the center surrounded by voluted eucharistic vines.

JOHN F. KENFIELD
Art historian

Editor's Note: The springs, usually called the Fountains of Clitumnus in English, were already a tourist attraction in antiquity. Pliny wrote a letter with an appreciative description of them, and Caligula is known to have visited them.

SAN PRESTO
14 km north of Assisi

Ristorante Il Pino
Frazione San Presto 100, ☎ 075 80 21 02
Reservations advised for lunch; closed for dinner unless arrangements made in advance; closed Tuesdays.
To get there from Assisi, exit from the Porta Perlici and take the state road, SS 444, toward Gualdo Tadino. It's on the left, about 10 km from Assisi

🍽 If you are in the Assisi area with a car and have the time for a beautiful scenic drive and a delicious lunch, then make a reservation at Ristorante Il Pino in the hamlet of San Presto, north of Assisi. Several years ago I had a most memorable meal in this moderately priced country restaurant. I was in the company of three Italians, and we've all been talking about it since then, vowing to return for the specialities of *tagliatelle con funghi porcini*, *fagottini con tarfufi* and *pollo alla cacciatora*. Dish after delicious dish arrived at the table, and all for a very modest sum.

MARTIE HOLMER
Artist

SPELLO
11.5 km southeast of Assisi

Visitors to Umbria usually spend a day visiting the beautiful city of Assisi and a few hours in the traditional Umbrian village, Spello. The typical way to reach Spello from Assisi is to travel eleven kilometers down the SS 75 toward Foligno and exit at Spello. What most tourists don't realize is that a far more beautiful (though at thirty kilometers, somewhat longer) route awaits those up for a bit of adventure.

Most tourists end their visits to Assisi with a stop at San Francesco's hermitage. But the winding road that continues beyond the hermitage to the peak of Monte Subasio, through the regional park of the same name, offers spectacular vistas reminiscent of what Saint Francis himself must have turned to for inspiration. Passing the hermitage on your right, continue up the steeply curving road to the table-top summit of Mount Subasio. Stop for a welcome bit of cool, mountain air; enjoy the 360-degree panoramic views and watch the paragliders take off.

Continue on the same road as it descends the other side of the mountain. Heading down, don't let the winding dirt road intimidate you; shortly after the summit, asphalt paving returns. Stop for a *gelatto* in the beautifully restored (and undiscovered) village of Collepino before reaching Spello.

SASKIA REILLY
Author and journalist

Santa Maria Maggiore
Via Consolare

Cappella Baglioni Fresco Cycle
Signed and dated 1501, Pinturicchio

The hill town of Spello is about twelve kilometers southeast of Assisi but figuratively, if not literally, in its shadow—as are Perugia, Spoleto, and Gubbio in the awareness of all but a few of even the most sophisticated travelers in Umbria. Yet Spello contains several ancient Augustan Roman architectural outcroppings and bastions, including two magnificent gates in a splendid state of preservation the last time we saw them. Though that was before the earthquakes of 1997, I have been told that the town was not badly damaged by the event.

When we lived in Umbria in the 1970s, however, what mostly drew us to this almost untouched little perched village was an absolute jewel of Renaissance painting. The three frescoed walls of a small chapel by Pinturicchio in the church of Santa Maria Maggiore depict the *Annunciation*, the *Nativity*, and the *Preaching in the Temple* restaged in the costumes and landscape of the painter's contemporary Umbria. These are three rich little wall-sized worlds of human drama enacted amid fruit-, flower-, and animal-bedecked panoramas of verdant mountain foothills and valleys not far removed from those one has just driven through from the Superstrada connecting Perugia to Foligno. There are also, on either side of the high altar of this church, frescoes by Pinturicchio's master, Perugino, and up the street in another church, Sant'Andrea, another single Pinturicchio, but it is this chapel which is the gem of the visit.

There is an excellent restaurant, Il Molino (Piazza Matteotti 6/7, ☎ 0742 65 13 05), between the two churches.
JAMES MCGARRELL
Painter

Don't miss the frescoes by Pinturicchio.
CLAUDIA CANNIZZARO
Coordinator of the Civitella Ranieri Center

TODI
40 km south of Perugia

Duomo
Piazza del Popolo

The Duomo in Todi has an incredible collection of capitals
on its inside columns. Each is a variation of the Corinthian
theme—each a different kind of leaf, some twisting one
way in the wind, some another. The church itself is light
and airy.

ALAN FELTUS
Painter

Santa Maria della Consolazione
ca. 1509–1607
Outside the city walls

One of the blockbusters of High Renaissance architecture,
this grandiloquent church crowns a rise in the road on
the western outskirts of the picturesque Umbrian town of
Todi. Its elegant centralized groundplan is a simplified
reduction of Bramante's earliest designs for Saint Peter's
in Rome, although its provincial detailing belies the traditional attribution to Bramante himself. In light of the later
transformation of Saint Peter's, the Consolazione, like the
contemporary church of San Biagio in Montepulciano,
preserves the nobility and self-confidence of Italian ecclesiastical architecture before Catholicism was humbled by
the 1527 Sack of Rome and the onset of the Reformation.

JOHN VARRIANO
Art historian

LAZIO

BAGNAIA
5 km east of Viterbo

Villa Lante
Begun 1566, Vignola
☎ 0761 28 80 08
Closed Mondays

Growing up in a small town in upstate New York, my perception of a garden was the back yard of someone's house. The most familiar garden was the vegetable garden, often tended by a little old lady, and I have depressing memories of being browbeaten into weeding under the pretense that it was family activity. Not exactly my idea of fun. Ironically, I was to become a landscape architect later in my life, but at this point I hadn't developed a high regard for the "garden." This was all to change.

While in Rome on my honeymoon, I was taken to see the Villa Lante. This was my epiphany, and I was fortunate to have this particular garden as my first experience, because it is the finest example of the Renaissance garden. Here was revealed a new perception of the garden, without the little old lady. Here I encountered a work of art equal to any sculpture or painting, an environment that expressed subtle and elegant ideas through plants and stone. Embedded in the design of the Villa Lante were history, form, sequence, metaphor, humor and more.

Starting at the lower terrace, I entered the water parterre, an emulation of a medieval cloister garden. A peripheral path and two cross paths brought me to the center of the garden, which features a fountain, Fontana del Quadrato, with an elegant late 16th-century sculpture, the *Quattro Mori*, or *Four Moors*, by Taddeo Landini. The simplicity of this initial statement set the stage for the remaining experience. The design unfolded as I walked up

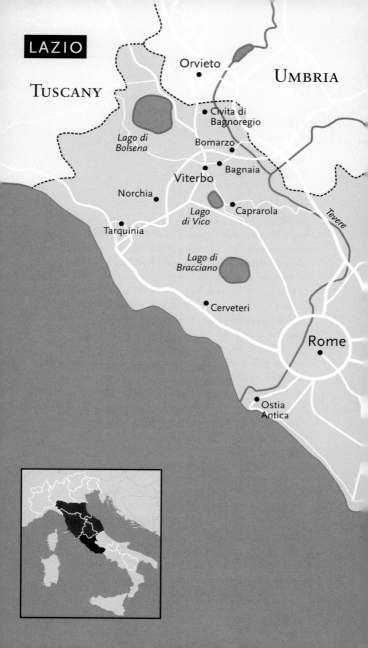

the hill through a sequence of paths and terraces, each depicting a specific period of garden history.

Vignola, the landscape architect of the Villa Lante, was a master of metaphor. The first terrace is devoted to Neptune, the god of the sea, with sculptures and a linear stone form with a long pool carved out of the center. This pool served as a table for the feasts that were held on the terrace, and the guests were encouraged to float plates of food up and down the table. The table, itself a beautiful form, lent humor to the experience, and one can picture ancient diners pushing plates of food up and down the table, laughing as they do so.

From this terrace, you traverse a cascade of steps flanking a baroque water channel; water is used to unify and animate the composition. Terminating the experience is the grotto, symbolic of the primal source of life. In other words, the end is the beginning.

M. PAUL FRIEDBERG
Landscape architect

BOMARZO
18 km northeast of Viterbo

Parco dei Mostri
ca. 1552–1585
Daily until dusk; call to confirm hours, ☎ 0761 92 40 29

In Bomarzo, the gardens of the 16th-century Villa Orsini are filled with sculptures featuring weird animals and masks. A real change from all the classical art.

BETH VAN HOESEN ADAMS
Artist and printmaker

Filled with monsters and oddities by the mad Count Orsini, and now overgrown, the garden is a wonderful walk in the park. The leaning house is the most disruptive to one's senses.

ROBERT LIVESEY
Architect

This town near Rome is home to what is often called the Park of the Monsters, a sprawling garden of strange, oversized sculptures. Commissioned by Prince Vicino Orsini in the mid-16th century, the park contains an elephant carrying both a house and soldier, a building shaped like a monstrous head with a gaping mouth, a gigantic turtle, astonishing carvings of mermaids, and a multitude of other fanciful sculptures in stone. A trip to Bomarzo is what we would now call an interactive experience. You can climb on parts of the sculptures, enter the great mouth, look out the windows of the leaning building, and feel the strange sensation of seeing a tilted landscape.

Local legend attributes the carvings to Turkish prisoners of war, but they were probably made by Italian craftsmen. Either way, it is a bizarre but marvelous place to visit.
LAWRENCE FANE
Sculptor

At Bomarzo, the experience is bizarre. This is not about form and elegance. I've been given many conflicting reasons for the design of Bomarzo, but the answers are relatively unimportant in light of the experience of unusual landscape. It is reminiscent of the Mos Eisely cantina in *Star Wars*. Massive rock outcroppings have been sculpted into grotesque, sub-human and non-human forms. Monsters of all descriptions come at you from all directions and angles, with little logic but with great impact. A patina of moss covers much of the stone, rendering the monsters part of the landscape and making them even more eerie. The garden must be seen to be experienced; to describe it further would be like describing, rather than having, a supernatural experience.

If gardens are your religion, then this is your mecca.
M. PAUL FRIEDBERG
Landscape architect

Romantic, secluded, and slightly overripe, the so-called
Parco dei Mostri at Bomarzo is more likely to enchant
than frighten you. Some have seen learned literary references in the garden's design, others a distraught husband's
tender homage to his deceased wife. Whatever purposes
Vicino Orsini had in mind when he commissioned the
boschetto, constructed during the second half of the 16th
century, it is an overwhelming sense of nostalgia that per-
meates the place today. Such is perfectly appropriate
because the vast installation, with its allusions to ancient
earthquakes and long-past devastations, was meant to look
old from the very beginning. Thus, feigned architectural
fragments, cut from the natural rock, seem recycled like
ancient *spolia* (translated literally, booty or spoils.
Architectural historians use this term to refer to parts of
ancient buildings, such as columns or decorative fragments,
that were reused by later builders—for example, early
Christians in their churches or Islamic architects in their
mosques.) A building, part carved from the natural rock,
part constructed, tilts as if toppled by some upheaval. Four
hundred years of aging have only added to the patina of
the place. You won't run from the giants or the hellmouth.
You'll take your photo near them and, in quiet reflection,
marvel at the wit, sophistication, and artfulness of wealthy
society in the twilight of the Renaissance. Pair this sojourn
with a visit to the nearby Villa Lante (see p. 271), with its
classic order, and you will have a perfect exposition of the
two sides of Renaissance landscape art—and a perfect day.

MICHAEL MARLAIS
Art historian

RECOMMENDED READING
Claudia Lazzaro, *The Italian Renaissance Garden: From the
Conventions of Planting, Design and Ornaments to the Grand
Gardens of Sixteenth Century Central Italy*, o.p.
Margaretta Darnall and Mark Weil, "Il Sacro Bosco di Bomarzo"
in *Journal of Garden History*, iv (1984), pp. 1–91.
Esther Gordon Dotson, "Shapes of Earth and Time in European
Gardens" in *Art Journal*, xlii (1982), pp. 210–216.

Editor's Note: Vicino himself refers to the Parco dei Mostri as the Sacro Bosco. Bosco *means a grove;* boschetto *a small grove.*

CAPRAROLA
62 km northeast of Rome

Palazzo Farnese
Begun 1559, Jacopo Barocci di Vignola
Closed Mondays

There is little left to imagine about the relationship between the Palazzo Farnese and the town. However, the scale of the palace on the inside is completely different. The two-storey circular courtyard façade is a surprise, but the one storey "town" elevation recessed above it is the real culmination of the axial town street. The circular stair is remarkable for its balustrade, shape and frescoes. After visiting the palace, the garden pavilion cut into the hill is not to be missed. From the Hermes columns, to the separation of the natural and the man-made, to the baroque water feature, the pavilion has all the human-scaled refinement missing in the large-scale house.
ROBERT LIVESEY
Architect

Zi Franco
Via Borgo Vecchio 107, ☎0761 645 25
Closed Sundays and Mondays

After enjoying the Renaissance splendors of the Villa Farnese, including its whisper gallery and its gardens with water cascade (featured in the 1999 film version of *A Midsummer Night's Dream*), stroll down the hill to Zi Franco for a scrumptious five-course, modestly-priced lunch that will have you asking the chef to come out of the kitchen for a bow. Be sure to sit on the far side next to the window; the dining room is cantilevered over a valley.
MARGARET A. BRUCIA
Latin teacher

CERVETERI
45 km northwest of Rome

See the Etruscan ruins. They are bold in their simplicity and are visually satisfying. The tufa stone resonates along the via dei Monti Ceriti. I especially like the Tomba della Casetta.

D.B. MIDDLETON
Architect

Carved out of the soft, volcanic tufa stone, the mysterious Etruscan tombs in Cerveteri are worth an extended visit. This city of the dead literally recreates the homes of the deceased, complete with built-in furniture, chairs, even beds with pillows! All suitable for the eternal life of the netherworld. The domestic scale of these tombs is unsettling, one feels like a welcome guest in this strange world of ghosts.

ALEXANDER GORLIN
Architect

CIVITA DI BAGNOREGIO
20 minute walk from Bagnoregio, 27 km north of Viterbo

This city on a mountaintop has extraordinary vistas, both spectral and mystical. The sides of the mountain have eroded so the city's perch is unusually dramatic, and the tiny village of only thirty inhabitants is definitely secret. A foot-bridge provides the only approach—and the sense that you are walking to Shangri-La! A mind-blowing experience. . .

SIMON DINNERSTEIN
Artist

ABBAZIA DI FOSSANOVA
35 km east of Latina

The 12th-century Cistercian abbey is well worth a visit. The starkness of the stone and the simplicity of the massing—one of the finest examples of Italian Romanesque period architecture. Note the backside of the monastery between the cloister and the fortress.

D. B. MIDDLETON
Architect

GENZANO DI ROMA
30 km southeast of Rome

Ristorante Da Ivano
Piazza 4 Novembre 3, ☎06 93 97 420

🍴 Don't be fooled by the décor, which might be described as "Vulgarian Hunting Lodge." The food is fresh, delicious, and moderately priced, and should tempt visitors to the Alban hills from as far away as Rome.

Cacciagione (game) is the house specialty; my favorites, in season, are the *pappardelle con cinghiale* (boar) and the *cervo arrosto* (roast stag). Fresh vegetables are served in abundance, and the meal is well set-off by the local *vino sfuso* (literally, wine in bulk). Customers are occasionally treated to a visit to the 16th-century cantina excavated under the restaurant, far below the modern street. There Ivano will let you sample a sweet sparkling wine he stores in the cellar, then finish you off with an *amaro*.

GREGORY S. BUCHER
Classicist

LICENZA
20 km northeast of Tivoli

Villa d'Orazio
1st century BC
Closed Mondays

When we arrive at Horace's villa outside Tivoli, a bright-eyed eleven-year-old with a beret that says WHISKY O COCA? asks, "Where's the villa?" "This," the archaeologist says, "is Horace's bedroom." And she points to what once was a garden, as if to say that this is what his shutters looked on. My eyes are drawn to the surrounding hills, my ears to the rill of the waterfall. I had imagined Horace living a Robert Frost-like existence, in the Augustan equivalent of a Vermont farmhouse (say eight rooms) looking out over his land in the hazy heat, but I never thought he could walk to a waterfall, or that when he wanted to invite his girlfriends like Tyndareus to stay the night they would have also been anticipating a steam bath and some "quiet time" meditating by his indoor fishtank, waking to look out at his *paradisum* which would have put Alexander Pope's English garden to shame. This was more like the Roman equivalent of Jack Nicholson's house.

I am sad that Thomas Creech, who did a wonderful translation of Ode 1.17 (1684), one of many pearls to be found in Kenneth Haynes' and D.S. Carne-Ross's *Horace in English*, hanged himself in an apothecary's garret when a love affair was over. Especially the line that on this estate you would not "hear the Evening Wolves grin round the fold." The power of wishes. This is one of the great stanzas of Horace in English, tender yet tormented.

> *No lurking Venom swells the harmless mold,*
> *The Kids are safe, the tender lambs*
> *Lie bleating by their Dams,*
> *Nor hear the Evening Wolves grin round the fold.*

MARK RUDMAN
Poet, essayist, and translator

RECOMMENDED READING
Horace, *Horace in English*, Kenneth Haynes & D.S. Carne-Ross, eds., Penguin Classics, 1996.

MONTE CIRCEO

Monte Circeo Excursion

a. Monte Circeo is 45 km southeast of Latina
b. Terracina is 20 km east of Monte Circeo
c. Sperlonga is 16 km southeast of Terracina
d. Gaeta is 18 km southeast of Sperlonga

Travel by automobile south from Rome on via Cristoforo Colombo, through the 1960 Olympic Village of EUR. Continue on through Aprilia and Latina to Monte Circeo, which is about one hundred kilometers. There you will find yourself in an absorbing setting overlooking the Tyrrhenian Sea and countryside. Pack a picnic or try the terrific seafood and superior local wine in Terracina, Sperlonga or Gaeta. In Terracina, see the Piazza del Municipio and view the Temple of Jupiter Anxur. In Sperlonga, visit Tiberius' cave (Grotta Di Tiberio). Gaeta is a nice town with a Duomo and a beach. For the northbound return to Rome, take the shore route to enjoy the beaches and swim in the sea in season. (In 1961, the season began in February.)

WAYNE TAYLOR
Artist, architect, and professor

Editor's Note: EUR (pronounced eh-OOR and written without periods) stands for Esposizione Universale di Roma, a kind of World's Fair that was planned for the twentieth anniversary of the Fascist Era in 1942 (when they actually had World War II instead.) Some buildings at EUR were adapted for the 1960 Olympics, but these mostly took place at the Foro Italico, at the extreme opposite end of Rome.

NORCHIA

23 km southwest of Viterbo

Necropolis
6th–2nd centuries BC

The meeting of landscape and architecture with a little walking thrown in. . . Drive on the via Cassia near Tarquinia, then approach on foot through a field. The tufaceous Necropolis of Norchia is a cut in the earth, unlike the typical Etruscan elevated sites. (They always found the best locations for life or death.) Invisible from above, the descent past vertical carved walls with porticos, dados and false façades allows you to fall back in time to where the spirit of the serene *Etrusci* remains fresh and palpable. Eat, drink, and try to figure out where their Mona Lisa smiles came from.

ROSS ANDERSON
Architect

OSTIA ANTICA

Viale Romagnoli 717, ☏06 565 00 22

Better cared for than Pompeii, this ancient port city of Rome is an exciting place with many *insulae*, baths, warehouses, sanctuaries, temples, *thermopolia* (cook-shops), and a fine museum. But the real treasure is the underground Mithraeum with its original statue of Mithras killing the bull. Dozens of the city's structures still have painted wall decoration. The entire town can be seen and appreciated in one day with easy rail access from Rome's Ostiense rail station. The visitor gets a real feel for life in an ancient Roman city and how well organized it all was.

ANTON RAJER
Conservator

PALESTRINA
40 km east of Rome

Museo Archeologico Nazionale Prenestino
Palazzo Colonna Barberini
Via Carberini

Nile Mosaic
Late 2nd–1st centuries BC

Some miracle saved the Nile Mosaic when Allied bombard-
ments during World War II removed the face of Monte
Ginestro, whose slopes were largely stripped of modern
Palestrina town. The town, twenty-four miles east of
Rome, was conquered in the early fourth century BC, but
never lived comfortably in the Roman orbit. The mosaic is
one of the largest extant mosaics of the Hellenistic period
and was probably created by artists from Alexandria, many
of whom were working at Rome in the second and first
centuries BC.

The Allied bombings revealed a multi-terraced sanctuary of Fortuna Primigenia, whom the Romans also called
"Fortuna Praenestina." ("Praeneste" was the ancient
town's name.) It was originally installed in the floor of an
apsidal room, and its slight incline allowed water from the
pipes at the base of the apse to run slowly and glisteningly
down its length. At the top of the mosaic appears the
(imagined) source of the Nile, with real and legendary animals helpfully labeled in Greek, and hunters in pursuit.
The artists bring the spectator's gaze down along winding
loops of the flooded Nile to scenes of Nilotic life near the
more developed and familiar delta: animals and hunters
appear again, along with small figures of natives, fishes of
various kinds, leisure architecture which shelters merry-
makers, temples with imposing royal/divine statues, and
public structures where soldiers and civic officials gather.

Egyptian/Egyptianizing art was very popular during
the last century of the Roman Republic, most especially

after Julius Caesar and Mark Antony dallied in Alexandria with Cleopatra and Octavian engineered his conquest of the wealthy country. The visitor to Fortuna's sanctuary at Praeneste could see in this mosaic a kind of charming handbook of the zoology, botany, and anthropology of the mysterious land of Egypt—a land whose fertility was crucial, when the mosaic was executed, to the provisioning of Rome's populace.

In more recent times, some gifted individuals have been linked to Palestrina. One who particularly engages my interest is Margherita Colonna, orphan offspring of the powerful, aggressive, and contentious Colonna family. For several medieval generations, the family had holdings centered on the town. (The Palazzo Colonna Barberini, which houses the museum, is named for successive family owners.) During the 13th century, Margherita, later venerated as Beata Margherita Colonna, chose not to marry and instead established a community of laywomen in Palestrina. As the church attempted to shore up the failing fortunes (monetary and spiritual) of some Roman parishes, Margherita and her community of women were invited to replace the Benedictines of San Silvestro in Capite. (I make a pilgrimage to this odd and wonderful little parish church on post office square every time I'm in Rome.) Subsequently the women were credited with spiritual activity and excellence of a hands-on kind which markedly enlivened the faithful in the surrounding community. (For more information about Margherita Colonna, refer to Brentano's book listed below.)

I should add that Palestrina was the birthplace, in 1525, of Giovanni Pierluigi da Palestrina (most commonly known as "Palestrina"), one of the greats of church music composition.

Palestrina makes a marvelous day-trip from Rome and can easily be combined with stops in Tivoli and Subiaco.

LINDA W. RUTLAND GILLISON
Classicist

RECOMMENDED READING
Paul MacKendrick, *The Mute Stones Speak: The Story of
Archeology in Italy*. W.W. Norton & Company, 1984.
Robert Brentano, *Rome Before Avignon: A Social History of
Thirteenth Century Rome*, University of California Press, 1991.

ABBAZIA DI SAN BENEDETTO
ABBAZIA DI SANTA SCOLASTICA
3 km east of Subiaco, 75 km east of Rome

As long ago as 1981, I traveled on a spring day to Subiaco,
on a kind of pilgrimage to the birthplace of the Benedictine
Order and, in a sense, of western monasticism. As our
group was not intent on a grueling pilgrimage despite the
Chaucerian appropriateness of the season, we drove to the
town and then up into the mountains. The winding road
makes its way up a rocky gorge, and precipitous drop-offs
threaten with distressing regularity. Below, at the canyon's
base, flows the Aniene River—the Anio in Latin—which
was source for two of ancient Rome's aqueducts: the Anio
Vetus and the Anio Novus.

En route up the gorge, we passed the ruins of Nero's
wild luxury villa called Sublaqueum—named for its position "under the lake." Intended, in a typical Roman mock-
ery of limits and definitions, to represent a seaside villa
(Villa Maritima) in the mountains, it benefitted from a set
of artificial lakes created by the damming of the Anio. The
modern name, Subiaco, is derived from the villa's name.
Nero was a terrific builder and lover of luxury. Like
Tiberius, he was unpopular with some segments of the
city's population, and when lightning struck his dining
table at Sublaqueum, some people hopefully interpreted the
event as a sign of his impending doom (Tacitus' *Annales*
14.22). Rome was to live with him for another eight years.

More famous and longer-lived are two other foundations in the neighborhood of Subiaco—the monasteries of
San Benedetto and Santa Scolastica. During the sixth century, Benedetto (or Benedict), scion of a rich family of

Nursia and student at Rome, left the city and his family and submerged himself in spiritual retreat. For three years, he stayed alone in a mountain cave, after which he began to collect groups of men whose communities would give rise to the Benedictine Order. It is possible to visit, walking up from Subiaco town, first the monastery named for Benedetto's sister, Scolastica (or Scholastica). (Nuns never lived at this convent, despite its name.) When I visited there with students in 1996, the superb guide who was a required accompaniment to our bus and driver arranged for an Italian-speaking Benedictine to lead us through the convent. Since this would clearly create some linguistic complications—the guide and I had to translate the monk's words for the students—I was puzzled. The conclusion of the visit, though, answered all of my questions in the most satisfactory of ways. We entered the convent chapel and the monk, who, it turned out, was also the venerable organist of the community, treated us to a unique concert. The surprise performance opened with Bach's "Toccata and Fugue in D Minor" (at full, beam-shaking volume) and moved on to conclude with his "Ave Maria." The experience took our collective breath away. I can't guarantee you'll succeed, but I strongly advise you to inquire after this community organist when you visit Santa Scolastica. He may, if he's still there, just be tickled that you've asked, and you will love the music. That I can guarantee.

The only other of Benedetto's dozen original monasteries to survive is San Benedetto, the very place where he made that first retreat. The lower church of this foundation includes the Holy Grotto—Benedetto's shelter (circa fifth-sixth centuries). There is also a very early depiction of Saint Francis, which may even have been done during the saint's life. When we visited, a spirited ancient Benedictine named Father Gianni (or Johnny—he hails from Australia) guided us around the convent. His knowledge and love of the place and of Benedetto were patent, and his sense of humor enlivened everything he said. Like other Benedictines, he has been in the same community, to which he made his original commitment, for his entire religious life.

The walk to both monasteries is not for the faint-hearted. You will need more than twenty minutes to climb to Santa Scolastica and another fifteen or so—mostly mountain roads—to San Benedetto. That makes for a real pilgrimage, and if the weather is clement and you are in the mood, it's an experience to be treasured.

Subiaco's valley lies in the Monti Simbruini—a wild and beautiful area which will offer an excellent break from whatever you may be doing in Rome. Bring a picnic and press on (by car, now) to the Altipiani (the high plains) di Arcinazzo, where Italians vacation, play soccer and *bocce*, and ski in season, and you can drive boulder-bordered winding roads through fields dotted with wildflowers in spring. It's remote and ruggedly beautiful—the real, most non-Roman Italy—and a special pleasure.

LINDA W. RUTLAND GILLISON
Classicist

RECOMMENDED READING
Cornelius Tacitus, *The Annales of Tacitus*, reprinted by Cambridge University Press, 1993. Originally published in the 2nd century AD.

Editor's Note: The dates for the various components of the Benedictine monuments near Subiaco are very fluid and variously reported because the buildings underwent construction and renovation for centuries (major construction, circa 12th century).

The reason Saint Francis' image is thought to have been made during his lifetime is that he doesn't have his halo yet.

Located in a rugged, isolated spot ten miles off the via Tiburtina, this monastic retreat cleaves to the mountainside not far from the site of one of Nero's villas. In section, the architecture creeps horizontally along the rock edge of the hillside, then shifts suddenly to the perpendicular within the nave. There it descends to the sacred cave of

San Benedetto (Benedict) himself, the carved rock forming an articulated surface within the edifice. Nestling and settling from centuries of use, this is a location of quiet tranquility and contemplation, replete with layers of early Christian history.

FREDERICK BIEHLE
Architect

Editor's Note: Though the nearby villa of Nero is now only a ruin, it serves as a reminder that the village of Subiaco had its origin in one of this emperor's typically grandiose hydraulic projects.

In 1464, the German printers Sweynheim and Pannartz established Italy's first printing press here, less than ten years after Gutenberg.

SERMONETA
76 km southeast of Rome

Castello Caetani
13th century

South of Rome, in the foothills of the Apennines, is the charming, quite medieval, walled city of Sermoneta with its 13th-century church (subsequently much altered) and Caetani castle, where the doorkeeper still closes the gate at night. The view from the castle ramparts, particularly in a rainstorm, is an unforgettable experience: the Apennines on the right and the plains of Latium on the left, leading to the sea. The juxtaposition of the grey stone used in the city's buildings with the lush green of the surrounding fields leaves a permanent impression. The castle keep has murals, vestiges of previous inhabitants and great vaulted rooms. A small synagogue is testimony to what was once a vibrant Judaic community. In the summer, temporary exhibitions enliven this sleepy town from the Middle Ages.

ANTON RAJER
Conservator

SPERLONGA
55 km southeast of Latina

Grotta di Tiberio
1 km south of Sperlonga

Just a few miles' drive south of Rome, you can visit a cave where Rome's second emperor was almost killed by a rock collapse. It happened in 26 AD, when Tiberius and his entourage were stopping en route to Capri at a coastal villa called Spelunca because of its most exquisite feature: a cave decorated with statue groupings focused on the wanderings of Ulysses (as the Romans called Odysseus). The modern name, Sperlonga, is a corruption of that Latin designation.

The Romans knew how to site a villa, and modern-day Italians have agreed on the pleasantness of the area. You can find Sperlonga on the web, with advertisements for hotels of various kinds. There is a most agreeable beach, very popular with Italians and perhaps becoming more so with foreigners as well. When I was last there, several years ago, the bathers seemed to be mostly Italians: the topless women walking on the beach alarmed the thirteen-year-old male member of our group, who fled. Within sight of the beach is the famous *spelunca*, which fronts on a group of the seaside fish-raising pools which were so popular with Rome's wealthiest citizens.

Ancient Romans loved the natural setting of a cool cave for relaxation, when they could get it. If not, they often constructed grottoes which mimicked natural caverns. Here at Sperlonga, the cave is a natural but developed one (a nymphaeum), and research has indicated how it was decorated for imperial entertainments. Sculptural fragments from massive to minuscule have been discovered in the cave, and three attempts at reconstruction have been displayed at various times, the most recent in Munich (winter of 1999–2000). The most striking is the immense group of Ulysses, three companions, and the drunken Cyclops

Polyphemus: Ulysses and two friends tote a huge log of a pike, the sharp end of which they are on the point of plunging into the Cyclops' single eye. Other groups represent the monster Scylla, the theft of the Palladium—one of the Greeks' numerous attempts at conjuring the fall of Troy—and, disputedly, the recovery of the body of Achilles after the death of this greatest of Greek heroes. Pools which front the cave and extend back into its interior would have reflected the light of the sun onto the cavern's walls and ceiling during the afternoon; in the evenings, the interiors would have been torch-lit. There would have been music and other entertainments: dancers, philosophical discussion, poetic recitals, and the like.

On the occasion which brought the site into historical record, Tiberius and his guests were enjoying dinner, probably on a late afternoon or evening. Tiberius was in disgusted flight from Rome, after relations between him and the Senate had become increasingly tense. In the midst of the entertainment, guests had to flee a rock fall, but Tiberius himself was caught in the cave. The historian Tacitus records (*Annales* 4.59) the event's ominous effect on Tiberius' reign, when Sejanus—a social climber and schemer of the most dangerous ilk—saved Tiberius' life at serious risk to himself. To quote the historian: "Sejanus, on hands and knees, and mirroring in his expression his physical stress and his anxiety for Tiberius, threw himself between the emperor and the falling rocks. He was found in such an attitude by the soldiers who hurried to their assistance." The consequences for Tiberius and Rome were dire, as the historian assures readers that "from that time on, [Sejanus] was even more influential with Tiberius and, however disastrous the actions to which he urged the emperor, since he had seemed heedless of his own safety, he was heard with trust." (Tacitus hated both Tiberius and Sejanus, who he felt was the *eminence grise* of a bleak reign.)

At Sperlonga, you will not be allowed to enter the cave, lest you experience the same fright that Tiberius

did—and in a far more litigious age. But visit in any case:
the entire situation is charming on a sunny afternoon in
spring or summer. You'll love the beach.
LINDA W. RUTLAND GILLISON
Classicist

RECOMMENDED READING
Bernard Andreae, "L'accecamento di Polifemo" in *Forma Urbis*, iv,
12 (December, 1999).
Paul MacKendrick, *The Mute Stones Speak: The Story of
Archeology in Italy*, W.W. Norton & Company, 1984.
Alexander Gordon McKay, *Houses, Villas and Palaces in the
Roman World*, Johns Hopkins University Press, 1998.
Cornelius Tacitus, *The Annales of Tacitus*, reprinted by Cambridge
University Press, 1993. Originally published in the 2nd century AD.

Museo Archeologica Nazionale
1 km south of Sperlonga, at the Grotta di Tiberio

A fabulous museum in Sperlonga, on the Tyrrhenian coast,
south of Rome, near Terracina. This is where the Grotta di
Tiberio was rediscovered in 1957—a great cave opening on
the sea with huge ancient marble sculpture representing
myths of Ulysses, including the wreck of Ulysses' ship.
They were found in the grotto but are now mostly housed
in the museum dedicated to the late Hellenistic art of the
first century BC. They were most likely carved by the same
family of sculptors who did the Laocoön in the Vatican.
The site is fantastic with the legends associated with
Tiberius. They are continuing to excavate the site. The
small museum is a treasure.
LYNN KEARNEY
Artist and curator

TARQUINIA
90 km northwest of Rome

Necropolis
Etruscan wall paintings, 6th–2nd centuries BC
Located 1.5 km southeast of town

Etruscan tomb paintings combine narrative and abstract imagery. I love their direct and fresh beauty. Tarquinia is an easy day trip west of Rome. There is a cluster of underground rooms for whole family burials. The paintings are fragile and can be visited on a limited basis. Additional tombs may be viewed when a *permesso* is secured through advance planning. Also in Tarquinia is the Museo Nazionale Tarquiniense, with Etruscan sarcophagi and additional information.
ANDREA CALLARD
Artist

Museo Nazionale Tarquiniense
Piazza Cavour
Closed Mondays

Tomba del Triclinio Frescoes
4th century BC

Volumes have been written on the Etruscans, but the recent conservation and reinstallation of the five painted tombs in the Museo Nazionale Tarquiniense breathes new life into ancient tomb decoration, including the spectacular Tomb of the Triclinium. This extraordinary display comes after misguided mural detachment projects were carried out after World War II. Now, after languishing in storage for decades, the murals are again on display in all their full painted glory.
ANTON RAJER
Conservator

Editor's Note: Right after the war, thin painted surface layers were painstakingly peeled from the walls and ceilings of

*five tombs and reassembled in the museum with air condi-
tioning, special lighting and controls, and shiny linoleum
floors. Going into these tombs was a strange experience—
sort of like being inside a kind of oversized gingerbread
house. When the museum underwent a later renovation, the
murals were once again inaccessible to the public.*

TERRACINA
39 km southeast of Latina

Museo Archeologico
Piazza Municipio

Temple of Jupiter Anxurus / Tempio di Giove Anxur
1st century BC
3 km above town, 40 minute walk

Terracina itself is a wonderful site of an ancient Roman
city. Its most famous monument, the Temple of Jupiter
Anxurus, was perched on high ground in a defensive position, surrounded by ancient walls. The Temple of Rome
and Augustus once stood in Terracina's Piazza Municipio;
now, a Cathedral stands there and the Appia Antiqua runs
lengthwise through the Piazza. A small museum, Museo
Archeologico, covers the ancient and medieval periods
of the city's history. The climb by foot or car up to the
Temple of Jupiter Anxurus is long and worth it. There are
dozens of sights to see in this small, ancient city.
LYNN KEARNEY
Artist and curator

Sanctuary of Monte Sant'Angelo

Located on the coast, south of Rome, the complex at
the Sanctuary of Monte Sant'Angelo on top of the hill
overlooking the modern town consists of several pagan
temples, a cryptoporticus, and a medieval tower: fascinating, and with great views of the sea.
ARTHUR LEVERING
Composer

TIVOLI
33 km east of Rome

Hadrian's Villa / Villa Adriana
Hadrian, 2nd century AD
Via Tiburtina
6 km southwest of Tivoli

Parents of young children touring Italy will often be frustrated by the lack of child-friendly sites, though not by the warm reception children receive from the Italians themselves. Hadrian's Villa (only six kilometers from Tivoli) provides a spacious retreat for families. The large site is ideal for exploration by children and their parents, especially as a day trip from the confines of Rome.
PHILIP FREEMAN
Classicist

With the power of Empire behind him, scholars wonder why Hadrian chose to build his villa on a flat plain. But take a picnic lunch to his lake, spread it out on the ruins of his banquet table, and see how the water, the statues and the expanse of plain make it an ideal thinking and dreaming space, well-suited to this private man. His courtiers preferred the surrounding hills, as did the Cardinals of Rome. Go up into these hills and visit the 16th-century Villa d'Este. Its water fantasia gardens were the Disneyland of the day and the summer palace of the Cardinals. Think of Franz Liszt composing music here. Follow the water that trickles from the mouths of beasts and the breasts of goddesses; it moves faster and faster until it ends in furious jets on the lowest terrace. As daylight fades, eat dinner at the Temple of Vesta. The quiet restaurant here, with the moon framing the Corinthian columns, makes the past seem unreal. And yet compelling enough that I made a series of paintings in these places—places half-seen and half-understood.
CAROLE ROBB
Painter

Editor's Note: The restaurant at the Temple of Vesta is the Antico Ristorante Sibilia (Piazza della Cittadella), whose walls are covered with inscriptions recording visits from royalty and other guests such as Goethe and D'Annunzio.

Villa Gregoriana
Piazza Massimo

Temple of Sibilla
2nd–1st centuries BC
Piazza della Cittadella

This park provides paths and overlooks to the spectacular three hundred foot falls. The temple of Sibilla stands prominently on the rim of the cliff, overlooking the falls and caves. Under-used and minimally maintained, this site provides the visitor with an authentic feel for the mass of humanity that has walked and lived here before.

The lower falls of Tivoli, also accessible here, have been painted and drawn for centuries. I was told this was one source for clay bricks for Hadrian's Villa, visible from the top of the cliff.

PAUL DIPASQUALE
Sculptor

Flea Market
Near Villa Gregoriana
Last Sunday of every month

In Tivoli, just two streets from Villa Gregoriana, is the city center flea market. It is very authentic, not touristy, and a terrific place to find very old books, furniture, war relics, coins, and more.

The city center and the Villa Gregoriana are only four blocks from the train station.

PAUL DIPASQUALE
Sculptor

VITERBO
46 km south of Orvieto

Bagni di Viterbo
4 km west of town center

On a Sunday afternoon, the spa town of Viterbo provides the perfect escape from Rome. It's an easy drive of just over an hour; the destination is an unmarked field immediately on the west side of the airport. In the far end of this field is a very large natural hot mineral water pool with an exotic aqua-colored sediment, excellent for coating the body.

There are no facilities, so plan on bringing towels and bathing suits. Park on the side of the road as others do, lock your valuables in the car, and hike into the field. If you arrive late in the afternoon, you can watch the sun set as you soak, then stop in one of the local villages for dinner on your trip back into Rome.

WAYNE RUGA
Social architect

Il Richiastro
Via della Marrocca 16/18, ☎ 0761 22 36 09
Hours are 12pm–3pm and 8pm–11pm; closed Mondays, Tuesdays and Wednesdays

🍽 Viterbo is about an hour and a half from Rome to the northwest. The restaurant Il Richiastro is a valuable detour. The recipes are from the Middle Ages, with excellent vegetarian selections. Call ahead, and be aware that locating this restaurant can be a challenge; it is between via Orologio Vecchio and via Mazzini.

ANDREA CALLARD
Artist

SOUTHERN ITALY

SOUTHERN ITALY

Pescara

L'Aquila

Fossacesia

Alba
Fucens

ABRUZZO

Avezzano

MOLISE

Pietrabbondante

Campobasso

Isernia

LAZIO

Saepinum

Sepino

Benevento

Caserta

CAMPANIA

Naples

La Solfatara

Cumae

Ercolano

Pompeii

*Lago
d'Averno*

Torre
Annunziata

Ravello

Salerno

Bacoli

Ischia

Sorrento

Amalfi

Vietri
sul Mare

Capri

Paestum

Foggia

PUGLIA

Andria

Bari

Castel del Monte

Venosa

Rionero in
Vulture

Potenza

Matera

BASILICATA

Padula

Maratea

CALABRIA

ABRUZZO & MOLISE

Editor's Note: Abruzzo is one example of a word for which several different spellings (one or two B's) and styles (with or without the article), in any combination, seem to be considered acceptable. In English you can say, "Abruzzo," "Abbruzzi," "the Abruzzo," or "the Abbruzzi." Italian adds the complication of different articles for singular or plural, so you can say "l'Abruzzo," "gli Abruzzi," "l'Abbruzzo," or "gli Abbruzzi." Please don't ask me to explain it.

ALBA FUCENS
8 km north of Avezzano, near village of Albe

Archaeological sites fascinate people not only because of their remains, but also because of the panoramic positions in which they often appear. One of these sites is Alba Fucens, alt. circa three thousand feet. (It is easily reached from the A 24, the highway that connects Rome to Pescara on the Adriatic coast.) Alba Fucens was founded as a Roman colony in 304 BC after the local population, the Aequi, had been defeated by the Romans. Of the Roman colony remain the regular layout of the city, the Forum with basilica, a temple for Hercules, theater and amphitheater, parts of the city walls and houses from the republican and imperial ages. On one of the surrounding hilltops stood a temple for Apollo, later transformed into the church of Saint Peter and rebuilt after a terrible earthquake dramatically damaged the whole area in 1915. Inside the church is an extraordinary pulpit from the medieval age, beautifully restored. From there a panoramic view allows the visitor to see to the now-drained Fucino lake near Avezzano, the stage for a grandiose mock naval battle when the emperor Claudius tried to drain the lake for the first time. On another hilltop are the ruins of old Albe, destroyed by the earthquake of 1915. The modern village is now on the opposite side of the ancient site. Meanwhile, to the north, Mount Velino, alt. 8,159 feet, rises up as a guard, a perfect introduction to the natural beauty of the Abruzzo region. It is now a natural reserve that can be visited via spectacular trails. When in Alba Fucens, take the time to sit down and wonder and eat a snack at the bar near the entrance of the excavations.

JAN GADEYNE
Archaeologist and ancient art historian

FOSSACESIA

45 km southeast of Pescara

San Giovanni in Venere

11th–13th centuries

High on a cliff looking over the Adriatic stands the abbey San Giovanni in Venere, whose Romanesque foundations are built on a Temple to Venus. If you are driving along the Adriatic through Fossacesia Marina, it's worth the detour up the winding road to reach the abbey. In addition to an interesting carved *portale*, if you descend the stairway to the crypt you'll find remarkably bright frescoes. The abbey is nicely situated near several restaurants and a seasonal country bar—much less frantic than the resort town below. Be sure to take a walk along the right-hand side of the abbey to see a magnificent vista of the Adriatic and the coast.

MARTIE HOLMER
Artist

PIETRABBONDANTE

26 km northeast of Isernia

Samnite Village

Pre-Roman

Roughly thirty-five miles from Saepinum is Pietrabbondante, originally an ancient Samnite sanctuary with temples and a theater of the Roman age, spectacularly located on a steep slope overlooking an endless valley. Here the Samnites, the most powerful population of southern Italy before it was conquered by the Romans, met to sacrifice the weaponry that they had conquered from their enemies. The site knew its major moment of glory during the third and second centuries BC. Last time I saw the site, the weather was terrible, which gave the whole area a dazzling and dramatic aura. For an overview of the Samnite population, go to the recently reorganized museum in Benevento and the National Archaeological Museum in Naples. I also highly recommend the (rather rugged) ride from modern Sepino to Cerreto Sannita for its spectacular nature.

JAN GADEYNE
Archaeologist and ancient art historian

SAEPINUM

3.5 km north of Sepino; 45 km northwest of Benevento

Saepinum is exactly what a real ancient site should offer: not only archaeological remains, but also the original landscape around it. The small town has everything a Roman town had: city walls, a *decumanus maximus* and a *cardo maximus*, a theater, a forum with basilica, temple, baths, institutional and industrial buildings, houses, funerary monuments, etc. But above all, it still breathes the air of two thousand years ago: the air of the countryside, with its farmhouses located around it, and the sheep that occasionally still pass through the ancient town center. Don't forget that the region in which this little town is located was the crossroads of the *transumanza*, whereby endless flocks of sheep were brought from the mountains to the lowlands and vice versa, according to the time of the year. We can assume that Saepinum started as a station on one of these itineraries. Amusing are the inscriptions on the west gate that describe a controversy between locals and shepherds regarding the passing of sheep through the city. The tension apparently got so high that during the time of Marcus Aurelius (161–180 AD) local administrators wrote to the imperial administration in Rome for the final word.

JAN GADEYNE
Archaeologist and ancient art historian

CAMPANIA

CAMPI FLEGREI

Lago d'Averno
20 km west of Naples

Solfatara
14 km west of Naples

The Campi Flegrei, or the fiery fields of Naples' hinterland, are among the most geologically active sites in recorded history. Lago d'Averno was once the northern terminus of a covered canal, lined with colonnades, that stretched all the way to the Golfo di Pozzuoli and is attributed to the Emperor Nero. None of that remains, and only a few buildings ring the wooded shoreline of this volcanic crater, once commonly believed to be the mouth of hell. Sulfuric fumes rising from the magma reservoir beneath the lakebed asphyxiated birds flying overhead. The sight of these unfortunate creatures, dropping out of the sky to the lake below, was rumored to have inspired Dante's *Inferno*, and Virgil explicitly referred to this spot as the entrance to the underworld.

The same magma chamber is responsible for the activity of the nearby Solfatara volcano. Modern-day visitors who have difficulty associating the now-placid lake with its dire reputation need not go far to see the choking yellow steam, over two hundred degrees Celsius, that gave Lago d'Averno its name. At Solfatara, two *sudatoria* (saunas) dating back to ancient times are still called Purgatory and Hell; the latter, of course, is hotter. A host of geological spectacles await discovery there: from boiling mud pots to egg-yolk yellow formations of crystallized sulfur and belching gas vents. Explore without fear, since University of Naples scientists daily monitor gas concentrations and seismic activity.

The lake lies at the base of Mount Nuovo, a lava

dome which rose abruptly to its current elevation of
approximately 450 feet as the result of a failed eruption
in 1538; lava pushed up the land but never ruptured the
earth's crust. Researchers believe the hill was formed over
the course of a day or two, a sudden feature of the dramatically changing landscape of the Campi Flegrei.
ANDREW PATRICK
Geologist and teacher

*Editor's Note: The phenomenon of asphyxiated birds,
reported by the Roman poet Lucretius (*On the Nature of
Things, *Book VI, lines 738 ff) and by other ancient
authors, is said to be the etymology of *Avernus, *from the
Greek word* aornos, *meaning "birdless." Virgil specifically
uses the term* Avernus *to refer to the entrance of the underworld, via the cave of the Sibyl at Cumae (*Aeneid, *Book
VI, line 126: "facilis descensus Averno").*

Piscina Mirabile
South of the village of Bácoli, 26 km southwest of Naples

The few available photos of this ancient Roman edifice
never capture the awe we experience when we walk
through this giant cistern. The columned subterranean
behemoth fulfills our expectations of classic, rational
Roman engineering, with the added insistence of beauty
and timelessness. The aisles, the columns, the arches, the
gently sloping floor; the high clerestory windows with gentle, filtered sunlight. It is a temple; it is a church; it is a
modern industrial space. It is hard and formal; it is soft and
surreal. It is immense, yet it readily sparks the imagination.

To check this out, ask the old lady up the street for
the keys (via Creco 10).
MICHAEL GRUBER
Architect

CAPRI

Villa Iovis
1st century AD
East of town center, 1 hour walk along via Tiberio

A delightful alternative to shopping in Capri is a hike along well-marked paths to a crest of the island, where you can see the material remains of a villa that belonged to the reclusive Tiberius, Augustus' stepson and successor. There are wonderful views down to the sea, more than one thousand feet below, and tradition has it that Tiberius often had enemies pitched over the edge. Take a picnic and eat in the ruins of his *triclinium* (dining room), then stop at the church of Santo Stefano to see a recycled *opus sectile* floor that once decorated the villa. Now it adorns the altar area, providing yet another example of the Christian reuse of antiquity.
DAVID G. WILKINS AND ANN THOMAS WILKINS
Art and architectural historian and classicist, respectively

On a clear day from this vantage point, one has what is perhaps the most beautiful view in all of Italy: the bay of Naples with Vesuvius looming in the background. Take a picnic to enjoy in the ruins of the emperor Tiberius' villa.
ARTHUR LEVERING
Composer

Excursion to Capri

ITINERARY:

a Blue Grotto/Grotta
Azzurra

b San Michele
Anacapri

c Villa Iovis
(see p. 305)

A good way to reach the palace of
Tiberius on Capri is by walking from the
town of Anacapri. (It's also possible to
walk from the town of Capri, on the other
side of the island.) You reach Capri by
boat from Naples, the easiest, fastest way
being a pleasant trip of a half-hour on the
hydrofoil which skims over the top of the
water. After a tour of the Blue Grotto, you
can reach Anacapri easily from the harbor
town (Marina Grande) by the funicular
which runs all day and costs very little.
In Anacapri, tour San Michele, the villa
of the Swedish physician Alex Munthe
(author of the classic *The Story of San
Michele*, originally published in 1930);
the villa is built on the remains of one of
several villas of Tiberius. But to reach
the main royal palace at the summit, you
must walk to the very top of the island's
northeastern end. A gently sloped walking
path, lined first with gardens of
bougainvillea and other cultivated flowers,
and then with open fields of wildflowers,
exotic birds and butterflies, leads the visitor to the top in only half to three quarters of an hour of walking, and the hike
is well worth the effort. Augustus had
resided on Capri, but the palace, called
Villa Iovis (Villa of Jupiter, king of the
gods), was built and made famous by
Tiberius, and it probably continued as
a resort of subsequent emperors.

Today a small church sits at the summit, and it, along with a caretaker's cottage where tickets for touring the site can be purchased, are the only roofed structures on the palace grounds, but the layout of the palace on at least five levels is apparent in the remains. From the arrangement of walls, one can imagine the variety of rooms: dining halls, bedrooms, reception rooms, and baths as well as huge cisterns for holding water, since there are no wells atop the rocky summit.

The beautiful walls are of *opus incertum*, a popular style of wall construction. Stones of various size were set into concrete in haphazard, *incertum*, fashion, and the walls were then plastered over and painted with various styles of painting. Since none remains on the walls, this painting must be imagined. Originally, there might have been panels of color with painted cornice moldings above and dado moldings below—this is known as the First Style of mural painting. (The architectural *trompe-l'oeil* decoration is the Second Style, and the paintings of mythological or genre scenes are in the Third Style. The Fourth Style combines all of the previous styles.) Today only the *opus incertum* stone walls are left, but the size and variety of the rooms at many levels testify to the opulence of the palace of Tiberius, the son of Livia, stepson of Augustus and second of the Roman emperors.

NORMA WYNICK GOLDMAN
Classicist

RECOMMENDED READING
Alex Munthe, *The Story of San Michele*, o.p.

Casa Malaparte
Begun 1938, Adalberto Libera
Punta Masullo

Having arrived at the port in Capri by way of the ferry from Naples, Sorrento, or Salerno, hire a boatman to take you by water to visit the most famous house on the island: it's the most exciting way to approach the rocky crag which accommodates the house that the writer Curzio Malaparte envisioned and Adalberto Libera designed. It is a place of unique beauty where clear planning choices determine a perfect—not imitative—synthesis of nature and architecture. The reddish color of the plaster contrasts with the gray of the rock and green of the pines.

Outside, a brick stairway leads to a terrace with no railing, with only a curving white screen interrupting the view to the horizon. Inside, an entrance and service zone, and a large living room with a stone floor and four picture windows which frame views over both sides of the island. At the end, the bedroom from which one sees only sea and sky.

Some say that Malaparte, when he found the spot for his house, sent an aerial photo to Libera, and the designer used a key to inscribe on it a rough sketch of the plan. Others believe the outline derives from the steps of a church the writer visited in Sicily and proposed as the model. Whatever the inspiration for the design, the result is the fruit of this collaborative invention between two visionaries: a minimalist work—*ante litteram*—simple and complex and poetic.

LUIGI CENTOLA
Architect

CASERTA
27 km north of Naples

Palazzo Reale
Begun 1752, Luigi Vanvitelli
Via Douhet 2
Closed Mondays

The Palazzo Reale, designed by Vanvitelli, is somewhat unremarkable, but the garden is outstanding for its huge scale and wonderful features. The cascade is almost three kilometers long and is graced with a number of wonderful fountains. The town roads cutting through at a lower level remind one of the crosstown streets in Central Park. The ruined loggia in the English garden is impressive for its size and light-filled spaces.
ROBERT LIVESEY
Architect

CUMAE
25 km west of Naples

Cave of the Sibyl
6th–5th centuries BC

This evocative site is not hard to get to but little visited. It's excavated to a balance of the visible and the hidden. The area is ringed wth thermal vents, odd Felliniesque spas that have been used since the time of the Greeks. Their legends feel alive, the tumult of modern Naples and the depth of its history blending into a kind of timeless magic realism.
SUSAN KLEINBERG
Artist

For those who have read Robert Graves' *I, Claudius*, this is the oracle to which the terrified Claudius journeys at the beginning of the novel. Although there is no historical evidence that the future emperor ever visited the Sibyl, her lair at the end of a long, dark corridor carved out of solid rock still retains the power to evoke a little *frisson*, if not actual terror.

ARTHUR LEVERING
Composer

RECOMMENDED READING
Robert Graves, *I Claudius*, Vintage Books, 1989.
Robert Graves, *Claudius the God and His Wife Messalina*, Vintage Books, 1989.

The seat of the Sibyl of Cumae—who appears in the *Aeneid* and was painted by Michelangelo on the walls of the Sistine Chapel—is entered through a powerful perspectival space of slanted walls where a "crag has been dug into a cave; a hundred broad ways lead to that place, a hundred gates; as many voices rush from these—the Sibyl's replies". . . to all who dared visit her. (*Aeneid*). The procession is more scary than the hall leading to the Wizard of Oz in the Emerald City!

ALEXANDER GORLIN
Architect

RECOMMENDED READING
Virgil, *The Aeneid*, Penguin Classics, 1991.

ERCOLANO
11 km southeast of Naples

Herculaneum
1st century BC

Thermae
Insula VI

In the *caldarium* of the Baths, the lava that destroyed the town was removed from the interior, but excavations stopped at the doorway. Time is thus reversed, one can experience the sense of horror at the very moment that the flow from Vesuvius was about to engulf the body in molten mud, thereafter becoming one of the empty mummy cases that captured the frozen time of death.

ALEXANDER GORLIN
Architect

ISCHIA
Bay of Naples

Cava Scura
Take footpath from Sant'Angelo

Ferries leave regularly from Pozzuoli Harbor to the Phlegraean Islands, the largest of which is Ischia. On the boat journey, gaze across the Golfo di Pozzuoli and imagine the Roman navy stretching from shore to shore, a chain of ships for Caligula to gallop across in a show of his fleet's—and therefore his empire's—greatness.

The bay is a part of the Phlegraean Caldera, an enormous volcanic crater, and Ischia dots its outermost edge. The island is best known for its restorative thermal baths, a reputation which dates back to the days of the Roman Empire. Volcanically heated mineral water is reputed to cure everything from rheumatism and arthritic conditions to mental dysfunction, for both its ancient and modern visitors. The water, at times eighty to ninety degrees Celsius, is channeled into various pools where its temperature is either maintained or cooled; in other chambers, steam pours from the rock, creating natural saunas.

The oldest of these bath complexes, on the southern shore of the island, is Cava Scura. A footpath from the fishing village of Sant'Angelo winds through a steep-sided valley and leads to the baths. Cava Scura consists of a series of rooms carved into the side of the mountain; the baths, stone depressions, are named for individual deities. The baths of Cava Scura are far more secluded, and charming, than their glamorous counterparts in the Gardens of Poseidon—an expensive and well-manicured resort complex set in a formal garden. But beware: in certain of the island baths, the water contains high concentrations of radioactive minerals, obliging those convinced of its healing qualities to persuade a doctor to agree; check in advance to determine which baths require a doctor's written approval.

ANDREW PATRICK
Geologist and teacher

Editor's Note: The episode of Caligula riding across the bay in a display of naval might is told by Suetonius in his Lives of the Twelve Caesars *(Cal. 19). In this instance, the emperor outdid the famous Persian king Xerxes, who bridged the Hellespont with ships for the invasion of Greece. Caligula (37–41 AD) was also the loony emperor who appointed his horse to a high government office in Rome.*

NAPLES / NAPOLI

The entire city of Naples is an underappreciated gem. The reluctance of tourists to visit is understandable in light of its reputation for lawlessness, but on a recent visit I noticed many positive changes. Buildings were being cleaned and restored, streets repaired, and there seemed to be a new sense of civic pride in the air. Neapolitans have much to be proud of: not only their artistic and historical heritage, but also their well-deserved reputation for kindness and hospitality.

SUSAN E. WOOD
Art historian

Duomo
Via del Duomo

Basilica di Santa Restituta
North aisle of Duomo

Baptistery of San Giovanni
5th century AD
End of right aisle of Santa Restituta

Attached to the northern side aisle of the Duomo is Santa Restituta, Naples' oldest surviving basilica. Within Santa Restituta lies the baptistery of San Giovanni with its splendid and iconographically unusual mosaics of the second half of the fifth century AD. Though seldom visited, this early Christian monument, along with the Museo Archeologico and the Museo di Capodimonte, is one of the artistic glories of Naples and well worth a visit.

JOHN F. KENFIELD
Art historian

Stroll through Spaccanapoli

From via del Duomo past Piazza San Domenico, Piazza Dante, and Port'Alba, to the Archaeological Museum

One of our most enriching walks is through this characteristic quarter. No comparable stroll yields a richer mix of churches, palazzi, alleyways and shops that bespeak the essential character of old Naples.

Stepping from the broad and sunlit via del Duomo, one enters the shaded, narrow via San Biagio dei Librai, a remarkably straight street reflecting the ancient Roman *decumanus inferior* whose path it follows, and which, as "Spaccanapoli" intimates, virtually splits the city in half. Almost immediately, at number 81, the uniqueness of the district is demonstrated by the Ospedale delle Bambole, a cluttered shop of antique dolls and doll parts. A few paces farther is the cross street via San Gregorio Armeno. Clustered around the church of that name are a number of artisans' shops that market *pastori*, the small sculptures so essential to the traditional Neapolitan *presepe*, or Christmas nativity scene. The figures and the scenic elements and accessories—including miniature baskets of fruit and fish and tiny furniture—range from unglazed terra cotta to more expensive, exquisitely painted and sculpted characters clothed in rich fabric. In recent years the shops have introduced new characters, including images of contemporary Italian politicians.

The dark, narrow street widens at the Piazza San Domenico, a pleasant, open space with a number of bars with outdoor tables. The focus of the piazza is a spectacular *guglia*, one of the several ornate baroque obelisks unique to Naples. The Church of San Domenico Maggiore (see p. 316) is rich in painting and sculpture and merits a visit; however, a few steps to the north will bring the visitor to the Cappella di Sansevero, a tiny gem that contains an amazing tour de force—Giuseppe Sammartino's marble sculpture of the dead Christ draped in transparent fabric.

At this point the street changes its name to via Benedetto Croce and leads to another open Piazza with yet another *guglia*, as well as two major churches, Santa Chiara and Gesù Nuovo. Each of these is beautifully decorated, but the Cloister of Santa Chiara, adorned with majolica tiles and terra cottas, is truly unique.

A few paces farther lies the via Roma; then we leave the old *decumanus* and turn north to enter the crescent-shaped Piazza Dante. This large open area edged by the curved façade of Luigi Vanvitelli's *Hemicycle* features several bars and typical restaurants facing the central monument to the poet. At the far end of the piazza is the unique Port'Alba, an arched gateway through which one enters a stretch of booksellers' establishments. These shops trade in new and old books and prints, and their bins crowd the narrow passage.

The booksellers' row ends as it intersects the elegant Santa Maria di Constantinopoli. This broad, tree-shaded avenue leads to the Museo Nazionale Archeologico, the city's renowned repository of ancient art which includes the Farnese sculptures and the frescoes and mosaics found at Pompeii and Herculaneum. The via Santa Maria di Constantinopoli is of particular interest as a thoroughfare lined with elegant antique and bookshops, as well as the venerable and well-stocked Giossi art supply store (via Constantinopoli 25, ☎ 081 564 05 49), which has been a source of materials for the students of the adjacent Accademia di Belle Arti for several generations.

JAMES J. HENNESSEY AND PAMELA POTTER HENNESSEY
Professor of painting and art historian, respectively

Editor's Note: Guglia *is a very old Italian word originally meaning "needle;" it's derived from the Latin* acu. *(The current Italian word for needle is* ago, *much closer to the Latin original.) The term* guglia *came to be used for a particular kind of needle, namely pointed church spires, obelisks (as here), and pyramids. There is an important Italian cinema prize—sort of like the Oscar—called the Premio "Guglio di Napoli."*

Museo Archeologico Nazionale

Piazza Museo Nazionale 19, ☎081 44 01 66

Hey, that's a big phallus! This wonderful museum contains a huge store of frescoes, mosaics, statues, and household goods from Pompeii, Herculaneum, and other places buried by the eruption of Vesuvius (including many items from the Villa of the Papiri). It also features an extraordinary collection of erotic art, mainly from Pompeii, which opened to the public in April of 2000, after being accessible only to scholars for more than a century.

ARTHUR LEVERING
Composer

Museo Nazionale di Capodimonte

Parco di Capodimonte
Closed Mondays

The Museo Nazionale di Capodimonte (Parco di Capodimonte) is worth a tour; hopefully it isn't as dilapidated as in the 1980s. All the Italian "big boys" of painting are there: Michelangelo, Titian, Masaccio, Carracci, Raphael, and Bellini.

D.B. MIDDLETON
Architect

Castel Sant'Elmo

1329–1343, rebuilt by Pedro Luis Escrivà in the 16th century
Via Tito Angelina, ☎081 57 84 030
Open 9am–2pm; closed Sundays. Take the Montesanto funicular to the top of the Vomero hill

Originally carved into the top of the Vomero hill to be a military fortification and a prison, this building is the closest you will come to being inside of Piranesi's fantastic and surreal Carceri etchings. The lower levels are sculpted, and you ascend gradually into built form. The spaces are wild and eccentric, long conical holes open out at odd angles to bring in light, two staircases will intersect at a window.

The geometrics are both rigorous and organic, as if Le Corbusier collaborated with a rodent. Not yet a tourist destination, you'll have it to yourself.

DAVID WINTER
Sculptor

Presepi

The nativity crèche figures of Naples are world-famous and are manufactured by artisans who sell their wares in shops located near the Istituto Universitario Orientale de Napoli, which is on via Partenope. The artisans' shops are found on various little side streets. Figures are of plaster and clothed in textiles and fur; especially notable are the shepherds, or *pastori*.

DAVID KONSTAN
Classicist

San Domenico Maggiore
Piazza San Domenico Maggiore

Cappella Sansevero
18th century
Via de Sanctis 19

Recently cleaned, restored, and magnificently lit, this wonderful ensemble of 18th-century architecture and sculpture is well worth a visit, and not nearly as well-known as it deserves to be, beyond art-historical circles. The iconography is mysterious (perhaps intentionally so), and the crypt contains a creepy surprise. But whether or not you can decipher the alleged hidden Free-Masonic messages, you can easily appreciate the beauty and virtuosity of the marble statues, particularly Sammartino's poignant *Dead Christ* (1735).

SUSAN E. WOOD
Art historian

Santa Chiara
Via Benedetto Croce

Il Chiostro Maiolicato
mid—18th century

When I first saw Dom. Antonio Vaccaro's 18th-century cloister of Santa Chiara, it was under adverse conditions. The venerable Angevin church had suffered a direct hit in the bombing of Naples in World War II and was a shambles, and during the restoration of its original Gothic shell, the cloister and gardens had been preempted by the builders' workforce. The vines were down, the fountains dry, and heaps of charred wood and sherds of baroque plaster were everywhere; dust lay thick over everything. But it could not destroy or diminish the glorious quality of the place, and since then, whenever I have been in Naples, I have returned to see it, linger among its arbors and alcoves, and drink in again the magical serenity it embodies and imparts in the heart of the frenzy of Neapolitan life.

The gardeners, all of whom always seem to be very old and gnomelike but endlessly at work, have trained vines in a lush roof over the walks, most of them on arbors supported by stout octagonal columns covered with bright majolica tiles decorated with thick garlands of green foliage tied with yellow ribbons that are wound in spirals around them. Between the columns are long baroque benches also completely covered with tiles, their backs showing landscapes populated with lively scenes, now of Campanian life, now of fantastic cars in allegories of the elements, none of which is exactly self-explanatory. But it hardly matters. At intervals there are large ancient marble fountains set in majolica basins or places to assemble in small groups, or sit and meditate. And combined with these there are rustic walks and a lofty Gothic arcade of great delicacy, a singularly happy blend of centuries and styles, the vision and project of Maria Amalia, the Saxon queen of Charles III, realized in the hands of Vaccaro.

Although it is unique, it is quintessentially Neapolitan, and this effect is strengthened by the lushness of the gardens, a thick tangle of ancient vines and giant cypresses combined with fruit trees and flowers.

Don't miss it; you will never forget it.

L. RICHARDSON JR.
Classicist

RECOMMENDED READING
Roberto Pane, *Il Chiostro di Santa Chiara in Napoli*, L'Arte tipografica, Napoli, 1954.

Pizza

One word: Pizza! You can't go wrong at any pizzeria with an authentic wood-fire oven. Alas, however, due to the pollution of the Bay of Naples, it is wise to avoid the *pizza frutta di mare* (sigh!).

SUSAN E. WOOD
Art historian

PADULA
65 km southwest of Potenza

La Certosa di San Lorenzo
Under ongoing construction since the 14th century

This is the only charterhouse I know of that preserves the late 18th-century feeling of such complexes, with their individual apartments and gardens. It also boasts a grand exterior staircase in its own—comparable to the one at Blois—and a Rococo library that is unrestored and exquisite.

L. RICHARDSON JR.
Classicist

PAESTUM

41 km southeast of Salerno

Greek Temples
6th–4th centuries BC

Southeast of Salerno, below Naples is a rare Magna Grecia group, Paestum. Paestum has some of the world's best preserved Greek architectural monuments anywhere (including Greece). Once this was a thriving Greek colony, founded circa 600 BC; later came the Romans. There you'll find a 36-columned Doric temple, a basilica from the sixth century BC, a Roman forum and amphitheater, and a museum. The area is strewn with wildflowers on a tranquil plain and is worth the trip, though it is well off the beaten path.
JOHN KEARNEY
Sculptor

The temples at Paestum are among the best-preserved extant Greek temples. They sit in a verdant valley with vistas to the hills beyond. The so-called temples of Hera II and Hera I (Basilica) have massive peripteral limestone columns and parts of the *cella* colonnades intact. These days, birds nest among the exposed capitals and architraves, lending a lyrical ambiance to the sacred site. The lighting at Paestum is warm and brilliant. It's truly a sanctuary. The nearby museum has excellent examples of carved metopes and painted stelae, including the Tomb of the Diver.
SUSAN SILBERBERG-PEIRCE
Photographer and historian

Those big fat columns! That silent stone standing magnificently by the seashore. Someone observed, however, that when built, the temples would have had solid *cella* walls and been surrounded by other buildings, rendering the transparency and visual layering seen today a phenomenon of the ruins, not the intent of the architects. But still so poetic.
D.B. MIDDLETON
Architect

In Paestum, we walked along the shore where Doric Temples were still standing in serene majesty. The basic structure of running base and fluted columns with pediment were well preserved. The color of the stones was a pale red ochre in the sunlight, and we couldn't help wondering what these stones could tell.
ROBERT BERKELEY GREEN
Artist and teacher

La Pergola
Village of Capaccio Scalo, 3 km from Paestum
Via Nazionale 1, ☏ 0828 72 33 77

🍽 Paestum is a moving and beautiful archaelogical site with three optimally preserved Greek temples. La Pergola, on via Nazionale in the nearby town of Capaccio Scalo, is the site of my most memorable Italian meal—expensive but worth it.
ANDREA CALLARD
Artist

Food Vendors

🍽 Along the coast road, north of Paestum, are food vendors from whom one can purchase fresh *mozzarella di bufalo*, prosciutto, and bread. These, together with a bottle of local Italian wine, can be taken into the site of Paestum for a wonderful picnic among the ruins. It's a truly relaxing way to spend an afternoon.
SUSAN SILBERBERG-PEIRCE
Photographer and historian

Gifts

🎁 Not far from the site are vendors who sell terra cotta replicas of metopes and other reproductions such as the head of Medusa. These make lovely gifts and souvenirs.
SUSAN SILBERBERG-PEIRCE
Photographer and historian

POMPEII

24 km southeast of Naples

A tour of the grounds reveals, among other things, houses that were quite generous in proportion. The Villa of the Mysteries contains brilliant reds and soulful blacks in the frescoes and is not to be missed. The Forum is a great lesson in miniature of the more famous Forum Romanum in Rome. The *frigidarium* in the Terme di Donne is especially interesting for its conical section and skylight. The *caldarium*, on a sunny day, has a soft, evocative light reminding me of Le Corbusier's Ronchamp chapel. And there's the House of the Tragic Poet, the plan of which inspired Corbu for his Maison Laroche in the 1920s.

D. B. MIDDLETON
Architect

Garden of the Fugitives

Via Noceria

Set in the dazzling ruins of Pompeii is a stark reminder of human tragedy—the Garden of the Fugitives. In 79 AD, the eruption of nearby Vesuvius sent dark gray clouds billowing up into the sky; within twenty hours, the city was buried in eight to nine feet of volcanic ash. The ash has solidified over the centuries, protecting the site from the elements and preserving much of the ancient city. However, archaeologists were puzzled when, during the earliest excavations of Pompeii, they encountered pockets of air below the hardened ash. Eventually they realized these cavities corresponded to human forms; the bodies had long ago decomposed but the ash had held their shapes. By filling the cavities, scientists have been able to make perfect casts of individuals, a technique which has continued since its first use in the mid-19th century and which was applied to the figures in the Garden of the Fugitives, discovered in 1966. Today, visitors to the site are faced with the ghostly forms of a small band of adults and children struck down

at the foot of a wall, beyond which lay the sea and escape.
ANDREW PATRICK
Geologist and teacher

Editor's Note: There are a grim thirteen in the Garden of the Fugitives, seven adults and six children.

Villa dei Misteri
Outside the main site on the viale della Villa dei Misteri

The well-preserved Villa of the Mysteries lies outside the city walls of Pompeii, on the road to Herculaneum. When Mount Vesuvius erupted in 79 AD, this country house, like all of Pompeii, was covered with fallout—ash and small pumice stones called *lapilli*. The villa takes its name from an interior room in the residential portion of the house with wall paintings unique to the villa and unlike any others in Pompeii. The walls of this rectangular room are completely covered with mural paintings of scenes that are generally referred to as Dionysiac and therefore part of the mysteries of this secret cult. They are thought to represent the initiation of a young woman into the mysterious world of sexual pain and pleasure in preparation for marriage.

In scenes read like a scroll from left to right, 29 life-size figures appear in the paintings, beginning with a portly *matrona*, perhaps the owner of the house, standing in profile while a young Cupid reads from a scroll to a seated young initiate. The figures are painted against a reddish, cinnabar-colored background, interrupted by black vertical stripes between or behind episodes. The actors in this ritual drama are half-mythological and half-real. The mythological ones include elderly Silenus figures, satyrs, an adult Dionysus reclining across the lap of Ariadne, a goddess with raised whip for flagellation, and several Cupids. The real figures may be images of locals: the *matrona*, the initiate, a priestess and her attendants, a female undraping an upright object, (possibly a phallus or Mount Vesuvius), the initiate or other female being alternately terrified and comforted, dancing in ecstasy, calmly being groomed as a bride, and finally appearing as the *Domina* or matron herself.

The villa dates from the mid-first century BC, but it was repeatedly enlarged and renovated; following the earthquake of 62 AD, it seems to have been in the process of reconstruction when Vesuvius erupted. It may always have been the country house of vine-growers, for there are work and storage rooms along the original farmyard front of the building, and the original wide entryway on the eastern side (not the present one on the west side) was flanked by sheds and outhouses. One of the workrooms contains the original wine press, excavated and on display, with channels and pits and access to a courtyard around which must have been storage rooms to accommodate jars for fermenting the crushed grapes. This part of the villa also contains kitchens and a series of small bathing rooms. There is a room with ovens and one with a square peristyle with four columns. Other small rooms were probably bedrooms.

In the western part of the house are the residential and social rooms including several *triclinia* or rooms for dining, now devoid of the three couches that gave the dining room its name: *tri* (three) and *clin* (recline). Some of the smaller rooms may have been bedrooms. The famous room with the Dionysiac paintings is to the right of the room with Egyptian-style paintings and the Tuscan-columned atrium. Some rooms were decorated in the so-called Second Style of mural painting: the use of architectural features, with columns, arches, lintels, doorways, etc., all painted on flat surfaces but representing three-dimensional architecture through *trompe l'oeil*. There are rooms with painted walls of beautiful solid black panels decorated with wreath swags.

You will not enter the Villa of the Mysteries today by its original wide central entrance on the farmyard side, but by a narrow modern opening on the opposite side where a rounded apsidal room with large windows opened onto the sea. Here the owners and their guests could view the water, although today, of course, the sea is farther removed from

the villa. There were hanging gardens on each side of this
seafront viewing room, which sits atop a *cryptoporticus*
running the entire length of the house. It seems that the
owners were in the process of building a series of larger
bathrooms within the villa when the eruption of Vesuvius
in 79 AD buried the entire structure in ash fallout.
Preserved in amazingly good condition are the paintings in
the special room that today gives its name to the villa, a
room probably reserved for the women of the household
and their guests, containing what has been called
"A Roman Bridal Drama."

NORMA WYNICK GOLDMAN
Classicist

RECOMMENDED READING
L. Richardson Jr., *Pompeii: An Architectural History*, Johns
Hopkins University Press, 1997.

Motel Villa dei Misteri

Via Villa dei Misteri 11, ☎081 861 35 93

The best hotel convenient to Pompeii is located just outside
the ancient walls on the road below the Villa of the Mysteries. As you emerge from the train station, it's a short
walk up the hill to the left. Consisting of a four-storey
structure with balconied rooms overlooking its lovely
swimming pool, this is a modestly-priced delight for those
visiting the ancient city site. The sunken circular pool is
surrounded by modern copies of female statues in classical
attire, and the beautiful setting is matched by the careful
attention of the friendly staff. Across from the residential
part of the hotel, on the other side of the pool, is a large
rectangular dining room where delicious lunches and suppers are served. Continental breakfast, included in the
price of the room, appears on the tables in the residential
part of the motel from 7am-9am. You can even purchase
some of the delicious honey or preserves that the hostess
has in jars for sale, so as to take a sweet memory of your
stay with you when you leave. A good night's sleep, and

you are ready to tour Pompeii. The entry is just a short walk down the hill. Return by five to enjoy a swim and a nap before supper at eight.

NORMA WYNICK GOLDMAN
Classicist

RAVELLO
26 km west of Salerno

Ravello is breathtaking. From above, we looked down under the clouds. Patches of mist rose from the sea, and we watched them abut the side of the mountain, then lift and float overhead. Enrico Caruso came to Ravello to rest from his busy schedule. The town became a favorite for many celebrities, including movie stars. It is an idyllic spot.

ROBERT BERKELEY GREEN
Artist and teacher

SORRENTO
54 km southeast of Naples

Russo Zi'ntonio
Via de Maio 11, 081 87 81 623

🍴 Russo Zi'ntonio has an excellent menu.

D. B. MIDDLETON
Architect

TORRE ANNUNZIATA
19 km southeast of Naples

Villa Oplontis
1st century AD
0.5 km from train station

Thought to be a small palace once belonging to Empress Poppaea because of a lead pipe bearing her name, the Villa of Oplontis at Torre Annunziata is a spacious structure consisting of a series of rooms, most of them decorated in the Second Style of mural painting—architectural features—and the Third Style—figures from mythology and genre scenes. The rooms extend in two asymmetrical wings behind a central deep portico with garden features in front, although the area behind the house has not yet been excavated, and further gardens may appear in the future. One of the most famous of the Second Style architectural painted rooms is the one with a series of columns forming a portico, painted on a completely flat wall. A formal garden along the area to the left, facing the villa, has been excavated by the team working with botanist-archaeologist Wilhelmina Jashemski. She has worked out a system of carefully exploring the holes left from the decay of the roots of ancient trees, shrubs, and flowers to allow cement to be poured into the cavities. The shape of the root then can be identified to indicate the kind of tree, bush or plant that originally decorated the garden.

The entire villa is easily accessible from the train stop at Torre Annunziata, between Pompeii and Herculaneum on the Circumvesuviano, the train that goes from Naples to Sorrento. Just walk down the hill of the main street and on the left, about twenty feet below street level, is the villa, cut out from the ash fallout (*lapilli*). The interior rooms are not laid out with strict axial symmetry, but with a formal atrium a bit off center, surrounded by *triclinia* (dining rooms) and bedrooms. A large peristyle with double colonnades completes the area on the left, while a second atrium with surrounding rooms opens on the right. The porticoed entrance faces away from the sea, and one can imagine a loggia or viewing area on the other side, still under the present city, which in antiquity faced the sea. Part of the right side of the villa still lies under the modern street, and in the solid wall beneath the street one can see the layers of pumice, about twenty feet deep, that covered the city when Vesuvius erupted. The use of the villa after the death of Poppaea (she was the second wife of Nero, but Suetonius says that she was killed by him), if indeed she ever owned and lived in it, is speculative. Certainly it could have belonged to the Caesars, although it has been suggested that it could have been a spa with adjacent residences. These would lie under the present modern town, but few other sites at Torre Annunziata have been excavated.

NORMA WYNICK GOLDMAN
Classicist

On August 24, 79 AD, according to Pliny the Younger, Vesuvius erupted, eventually burying not only those well-known towns of Pompeii and Herculaneum, but also this large suburban villa located about three miles from Pompeii. Its supposed ownership by Poppaea (the wife of Nero) or her family is based on the discovery of an amphora (in the latrines of the villa) with the inscription "Secundo Poppaeae"—that is, "To Secundus (slave or freedman?) of Poppaea". The buildings are decorated with strange and wonderful frescoes, many similar in style to those of the Villa of the Mysteries in Pompeii.

ARTHUR LEVERING
Composer

VIETRI SUL MARE
5 km west of Salerno

Ceramiche Artistiche Solimene SHC Vicenzo Solimene
Paolo Soleri
Via Madonna degli Angeli 7

At the beginning of the Amalfi coast, along the road between Salerno and Vietri sul Mare, there is an unusual, daring building, one of the first works of the young Paolo Soleri: the Solimene workshop of ceramic art. Inspired by the genius of Wright and with a profound understanding of local production techniques and materials, Soleri, who worked for some years with the *Vietresi* ceramicists, has brought the sequence of operations into a spatial effect that relates them to each other.

The elongated spiral accomodates all phases of the

craftsmen's work, from greenware to decoration and firing. In the center is the gallery where finished products are displayed, unchanged for more than fifty years: plates, glasses, pitchers, lamps, candlesticks, and miscellaneous *objets-d'art* in Mediterranean colors. At the top level is the school of ceramics and the small museum.

The structure of reinforced concrete is decorated, only on the side visible from the street, with glazed and plain terra cotta vessels pressed into the cement. This recalls the majolica cladding typical of Vietri domes. Traditional materials and humble objects of everyday use recreate in modern style the atmosphere of this region. Outside, the plain foundation of gray concrete contrasts with the warm colors of the terra cotta and with the large, triangular windows which allow glimpses of the spiral.

LUIGI CENTOLA
Architect

BASILICATA & PUGLIA

Editor's Note: Basilicata is commonly known as Lucania. There has not been such a place as Lucania since ancient times, but everyone always calls it that and always will, apparently. It is now for insufficiently cogent historical reasons officially called Basilicata. There are inflammatory articles about it in the local newspapers all the time.

CASTEL DEL MONTE
18 km south of Andria

Castello
Begun 1240, Federico II
Closed Mondays

The famous *castello* northwest of Alberobello was built as part of Federico II's major construction franchise of southern castles and fortifications in the 13th century. Federico II (or Frederick II) is the guy who made peace with the Arabs without violence in the time of the Crusades and for this was excommunicated by the Pope, which gives you an idea of how ahead of his time he was. Federico also wrote the still-used treatise on falconry and reigned over a modernist court which favored the use of Italian instead of Latin. Anyway, this *castello* near Bari is, I believe, the most metaphysical structure—*il castello incantato*, as some have called it—in a country not unknown for its metaphysical environments. Just catching glimpses as you drive in a long circular fashion up the *monte* will convince you that you are approaching something unearthly. Some of the locals call it the Flying Saucer (and these are people who, if they can afford it, live in *trulli*, round prehistoric stone houses that vanguard constructions have never matched. Only Dr. Seuss's cartoons, with their cylindrical elevations and coned roofs, come close. It's a zone that may as well be considered extraterrestrial.)

Bookstalls on the way up to the pine-strewn promontory sell books written about the castle's unique octagonal minimalist scarps. Most of the books note the building's confluences with Arab astronomy—the idea that the fortress was used as an observatory of angels, based on its incredibly precise workmanship and positioning; other theories rely on early Gaia theories working in tandem with Ptolemaic geometry. But if new-agers are attracted to this amazing structure, they forget that it was also an exclusive jail for Federico's powerful rivals. Therein lies a certain postmodern attraction, for tourists so inclined.

Lie down in the center of the court and look up at the sky, severely framed by the clean cut of the fortifications. Inside, an unexpected subtlety—and pleasant surprise amid the severity of the place—is the line of imbedded columns. Each one is a different marble, some in lugubrious orange and yellows. Also check out the *telamoni* (male columnar figures) in *torre* seven. Bring a date.

PIER CONSAGRA
Artist

Editor's Note: Trulli *are rounded structures of various sizes, typically with a gleaming whitewashed base surmounted by a conical beehive roof made of courses of limestone. They occur throughout this area of Puglia, with a particular concentration of them in the old quarter of Alberobello, one of the most fascinating places in all of Italy.*

Some locals also compare the castello *to a royal crown resting on the land.*

MARATEA

Costa di Maratea
Between Gulf of Policastro and Apennine Mountains

As visually striking as the Amalfi coast a hundred miles to the north, but with far more affordable amenities for the traveler, the slender Costa di Maratea lies between the wind-whipped Gulf of Policastro and the rugged western slope of the Apennine Mountains.

The Maratea region, a twenty kilometer-long finger of the rural province of Basilicata, enjoys a reputation for ends-of-the-earth wildness that dates far back into antiquity. Virgil tells us that it was here that Aeneas' helmsman Palinurus washed ashore after falling asleep on watch—and here that the local inhabitants promptly butchered the unfortunate stranger. In more recent years, the tall, cave-riddled hills overlooking the Mediterranean have served as hiding places for bandits and antifascist guerrillas. The odds of being robbed or injured here were solid enough that for many years few outsiders came to the region—which was just fine by the locals, who kept to their vineyards and gardens and worked the fertile sea unnoticed.

With the completion of a modern inland highway, the A 3, in the early 1980s, Maratea began to attract visitors, most from the interior of Basilicata and neighboring provinces. Twenty years later, it has become a destination for visitors from farther north in Italy, but it remains well outside the international package-tour orbit.

Extending from the River Noce to the border with Campania, Maratea is a congeries of small towns and ports. The largest, Maratea Superiore, perches precariously on the ridges of two mountains, one of which sports a kitschy, seventy-foot-tall statue of Christ, arms fully extended. My friend Renato Formisani, the captain of the lovely sailboat *Flora*, grumbles that the statue faces inland. "Jesus ought to be looking out for us sailors," he says. "We need the protection more than the landlubbers." (Renato offers half- and full-day cruises aboard the ocean-going *Flora*; ☎0339 751 36 48.)

The Porto di Maratea boasts a fine marina full of both pleasurecraft and fishing vessels, the latter of which provide a bounty of fresh seafood for restaurants in Maratea and the nearby village of Fiumicello Santa Venere. The Porto di Maratea also offers a broad public beach, but the swimming is better and the coast more scenic below the Marina di Maratea, five kilometers to the south, and at Acquafredda, ten kilometers to the north.

Both are reached by an especially tortuous leg of the via Nazionale, the narrow coastal highway reminiscent of U.S. 1 in the vicinity of Big Sur.

A number of fine hotels serve the Maratea area. In town, the best of them is the four-star Locanda delle Donne Monache (via Carlo Mazzei 4, ✆0973 87 74 87), a converted nunnery nestled atop a spur of rock with sweeping views of the coast and mountains. The winding road to the hotel is not recommended for acrophobics, who in any event will be uncomfortable just about everywhere in the vertiginous Maratea area. The Grand Hotel Pianeta Maratea (loc. Santa Caterina, ✆0973 8719 66) has less impressive views and, though both modern and well-appointed, lacks the charm of its older neighbor. The less expensive Hotel Settebello (via Fiumicello 52, ✆0973 87 62 77) is somewhat nondescript but has an outstanding restaurant and easy access to the beach.

In Acquafredda, the northernmost of Maratea's towns, is my favorite hotel, the Villa Cheta Elite (via Timpone 46, ✆0973 87 81 34). This early 19th-century villa, ringed by gardens full of fruit trees and flowers, overlooks a small cove with a horizon-to-horizon view of the Gulf of Policastro; the *prix fixe* restaurant is outstanding. The nearby Hotel Villa del Mare (via Nazionale 18, ✆0973 87 80 07), with its good restaurant and beautifully-kept grounds, overlooks the oak-lined, switchback path down to the turquoise cove. Keep an eye out for the vipers that abound hereabout. They enjoy sunning themselves on the beach just as much as we do.

GREGORY MCNAMEE
Author and editor

MATERA

100 km east of Potenza

I Sassi

Neolithic Age

Tours arranged through information office

This prehistoric village, almost completely desolate, is set within a stark landscape of rock quarries and crows. It sits in a wild ravine, with buildings cut directly into the rock. Caves become homes and churches; streets, ramps, stairs and tiled roofs form a manmade topography barely distinguishable from the natural. The Strada dei Sassi is a haunting, panoramic street skirting the gorge, lined by caves, where each turn reveals another astonishing act of bravado from the village's ancient unsung troglodyte builders. The ensemble is a chaotically beautiful work of urban lyricism.

During the day, take a stroll through I Sassi and have lunch and a siesta inside an abandoned cave-dwelling.

The nightly *passeggiata* occurs at the upper, modern town. Stroll or sit and be hypnotized by the reflections of the sunset off the ancient labyrinth below.

THOMAS SILVA

Architect

Perhaps my most unusual, though in ways most moving, recollection derives from the impoverished southern regions of Puglia and Lucania. My reason for visiting was to examine the distinctive architecture of the *trulli* in such towns such as Alberobello and Locorotondo. I would not have incorporated Lucania had I not read, a few years earlier at the urging of an anthropologist colleague, Carlo Levi's extraordinary book, *Christ Stopped at Eboli*. Not even the book could have prepared me for what I found at Matera, Lucania's provincial capital. In a deep and barren gorge below the modern town lies the eerie, desolate, and now abandoned Città Vechia, nearly indistinguishable from

the clay escarpments out of which it was carved. Walking
the grim and forbidding labyrinth of its byways, over the
rooftops of houses, I felt as though I had stepped back-
ward in time. Here, I experienced a most elemental expression of human existence: its fragility and indomitability.

ROBERT HANNA
Landscape architect

RECOMMENDED READING
Carlo Levi, *Christ Stopped at Eboli: The Story of a Year*, translated
by Frances Frenaye, Noonday Press, 1995.

RIONERO IN VULTURE
40 km north of Potenza

D'Angelo Winery
Via Provinciale 8, ☎ 0972 72 15 17

If you're passing through the small Basilicata town of
Rionero in Vulture, on the southeastern flank of the
ancient volcanic cone Monte Vulture, take a moment to
stop at the D'Angelo winery to sample its version of the
local specialty, a robust dark wine called Aglianico del
Vulture. Other Basilicata vintners, among them Sasso in
Potenza and Paternoster in Barile, also produce Aglianico
—but D'Angelo wins hands-down advantage by virtue of
its superbly scenic setting.

GREGORY MCNAMEE
Author and editor

VENOSA
165 km north of Potenza

The province of Basilicata, in the instep of Italy's boot, has
historically been a poor place, so much so that only a few
years ago residents of neighboring lowland Puglia—themselves none too affluent—customarily referred to their
country cousins as *indiani*, Indians.

The adjective, meant to evoke the poverty of Calcutta

and Pine Ridge alike, does not well suit much of Basilicata today. Far from being the bestial backwater of Carlo Levi's famed memoir *Christ Stopped at Eboli*, most of the province has, in just the last twenty-odd years, become a garden for the European Union; where individual farmers worked a few meters of stony soil to produce enough olives, tomatoes, and peppers to see their families through the winter, the volcanic hillsides are now carpeted with vast mechanically-harvested fields of vegetables and grains, and the province is strangely awash in lire.

But not in other currencies. Basilicata still lies far outside the usual tourist orbit, which means that should you visit, you will have the province pretty much to yourself. It also means, in the little town of Venosa, that you will draw an audience of curious onlookers wondering why on earth anyone would have chosen to negotiate the steep roads leading to their hilltop town.

There are, as it happens, good reasons to travel to Venosa, especially if you have an interest in history. The town is famed for being the birthplace of the Roman poet Horace, or Orazio, who left it in about 50 BC. A Gatsby for his time, he scarcely looked back at the rustic place then called Venusia, city of Venus, joined to Rome by the ancient via Appia, the traces of which can be seen in the fields north and west of town. As if to avenge their slighted ancestors, whom Horace considered bumpkins, the Venosini of today honor the poet only with a bronze, dove-bespattered statue in the main piazza. And this despite the fact that much of the town's present air of well-ordered prosperity is due to a series of government grants intended to mark, in 1993, the two thousandth anniversary of the poet's death—grants the townspeople apparently decided, quite reasonably, would better serve the living.

After Horace's time, wealthy Roman absentee land-owners erected a sprawling bath and resort complex, complete with a large amphitheater, on a finger of plateau below the southern approach to the modern town. The ruins of this structure are among the best-preserved in the region, and they are now protected as an archaeological park. Adjoining them are the ruins of the Abbey of the Holy Trinity, built by Benedictine monks in 1046 on the site of a Roman temple. Within the restored nave lies the tomb of the Norman crusader Robert Guiscard, whose remains were brought back to Venosa after his death on Cephalonia, in 1085, as well as the tomb of his unfortunate half-brother Drogo, whose death, it is said, Robert arranged. Also among the ruins are bas-relief stones depicting menorahs and stars of David, in quiet acknowledgment of the long Jewish presence in the town. (Many Venosini, though their ancestors converted to Christianity generations ago, continue to observe Jewish customs and holidays.) Jewish and early Christian catacombs, which local legend holds stretch all the way to Rome, lie in limestone caves about two hundred feet south of the church. You do not need a guide to visit these catacombs; suffice it to say that some of the people you'll encounter hereabout are residents of the local mental hospital, and that the caves themselves are full of harmless but alarm-inducing bats.

History is not the only reason to spend time in Venosa. It makes a convenient base of operations for day trips to Monte Vulture, an extinct volcano in whose bowl lie the crystalline pools of the Laghi di Monticchio; to the subprovincial capital of Matera (see p. 333), where postmodern homes are now being built in caves inhabited since Neolithic times; and to the Gravine di Puglia, narrow stream-laced canyons haunted by wolves, falcons, and vipers, wild places that recall the ancient Mediterranean better than any ruin.

A city of about twelve thousand inhabitants, Venosa has few hotels, among them the lovely, modern hotel Orazio (via Vittorio Emanuele 142, ☎ 0972 311 35). The city also has a fine new restaurant, Il Grifo (via dei Fornac 21,

☎ 0972 359 75), in the center of town, alongside Venosa's small Norman castle. The chef, recently returned to his hometown after twenty years of working in Rome, does wonders with local produce and game. Put your fate in his hands by telling the waiter, in local dialect, "*Cosa raccomanda voi*," or "whatever you recommend." Gastronomic marvels will ensue.

GREGORY MCNAMEE
Author and editor

SICILY/ SICILIA

- Palermo
- Messina
- Trapani
- Mozia
- Alcamo
- Gibellina Vecchia
- Marsala
- Castelvetrano
- Mazara del Vallo
- Selinunte
- Piazza Armerina
- Agrigento
- Gela
- Syracuse
- Noto

SARDINIA/ SARDEGNA

- Sassari
- Thiesi
- Santu Antine
- Serra Orrios
- Nuoro
- Oristano
- Nuraghe su Nuraxi
- Cagliari

SICILY / SICILIA

GIBELLINA VECCHIA
71 km southwest of Palermo

Il Cretto di Burri
1981, Alberto Burri

The road to Gibellina Vecchia winds through thick, wild country. As the car negotiates the mountain switchbacks, you can sometimes glimpse a large, white mass on a distant hillside. Then the rhythm of the landscape is interrupted and suddenly, you're upon it: a huge slope of white concrete broken by narrow passages where ancient streets once defined the town.

Il Cretto covers the entire hillside. It was created by the artist Alberto Burri as a memorial and protest piece commemorating the 1968 earthquake that decimated the town. No bodies lie beneath the concrete unless a few were left buried by the earthquake. Still, the piece can be interpreted as a tomb commemorating lives lost and a way of life lost. (The protest is against the government, which chose to abandon the original town site and rebuild farther down the hillside, using new architects.)

Without the distractions of street life, your mind focuses on moving about the maze. The pitch of the original street stretches your legs and feet, and suddenly you wonder how old people stiffened by arthritis and age got about. At some points, looking across the concrete, you can see undulating waves that record the rises and falls of the hillside—and marvel at the artist's ability to create such movement out of such mass. Standing at the very bottom and looking up, you sense the weight of the concrete, a few moments ago light and reflective, now pulling towards you in a way that recalls an earthquake.

LANA BORTOLOT
Journalist

Editor's Note: Il Cretto *literally means "The Crack," perhaps to be interpreted as the opening of the earth. Burri was previously known for a series of works he called* Cretti, *monochrome pieces in a sort of paste that dried and formed a pattern of cracks.*

An annual theatrical festival, "Orestiadi di Gibellina," has been established at the new Gibellina.

MOZIA

Located on the island of San Pantaleo; 11 km north of Marsala
Accessible by ferry opposite the island

On the west coast of Sicily, north of Marsala, is the island of Mozia. Take the ferry and review the history of the site. Walk around the island and visit the Whitaker Museum (☎0923 71 25 98) to see many artifacts and a superb white marble charioteer from 500 BC that bridges the enormous gap between that period and the time of Michelangelo. Have lunch before leaving.

ANDREA CALLARD
Artist

NOTO

33 km southwest of Siracusa

The city of Noto was built on its present location after the previous city, now called Noto Antica, was utterly destroyed in an earthquake in 1693. The new Noto rose slowly, first as a temporary city, and later, beginning in the 1730s, as one of the most exquisite baroque cities in the world. Native-born Sicilian architects like Rosario Gagliardi exploited the plan, laid out as a sloping Renaissance grid, to create a miniature urban center crowded with aristocrats' palaces, monasteries, convents and churches with expressive, scenographic baroque façades, unified by the golden stones of which they were made. Time, earthquakes, and neglect have taken their toll. The nave and dome of the Cathedral of San Nicolò collapsed in a rain storm in 1996 and are in the process of being reconstructed. Other buildings are being repaired as well. Yet even with some buildings closed, a visit to this tiny town just in from the Ionian coast is an unforgettable journey into the exuberant culture of 18th-century Sicily, a trip well worth taking.

STEPHEN TOBRINER
Art and architectural historian

RECOMMENDED READING
Stephen Tobriner, *The Genesis of Noto, an Eighteenth Century Sicilian City*, Zwemmer Press, London and U.C. Press, Berkeley, 1982. Republished in Italian as *La genesi di Noto, una città italiana del Settecento*, Dedalo, (Bari), 1989.
Stephen Tobriner, "Noto's Corso Remembered, 1693–1993" in *Streets: Critical Perspectives on Public Space*, Z. Çelik, D. Favro, R. Ingersoll, eds., University of California Press, 1996, pp. 135–150.
Stephen Tobriner, "Safety and Reconstruction after the Sicilian Earthquake of 1693—the Eighteenth Century Context" in *Dreadful Visitations: Confronting Natural Catastrophe in the Age of Enlightenment*, ed. Alessa Johns, Routledge, 1999, pp. 49–77.

Corrado Costanza
Via Silvio Spaventa 9, ☎ 0931 83 52 43

🍽 Go to Corrado Costanza for all kinds of *granita*—in particular *granita di mandorla*—just south of the Palazzo della Città.

STEPHEN TOBRINER
Art and architectural historian

Caffè Sicilia
Corso Vittorio Emanuele 125, ☎ 0931 83 50 13

🍽 Among the best *dolci* in Sicily: Corrado and Carlo Assenza's Caffè Sicilia.

STEPHEN TOBRINER
Art and architectural historian

PALERMO

La Kalsa
Northeast of Stazione Centrale

People who appreciate the romance of ruined buildings should visit the Kalsa district. Still shattered from World War II bombing, building roofs are torn open to the skies, exposing abandoned innards. But then, in the house next door, a lace curtain in a window, a pair of beaten shoes on the doorstep: a sign of life next to the uninhabitable.

Kalsa is abandoned cars, churches, animals. It's also laundry hanging from windows, people hanging from balconies, kids playing in the street, tiny storefront windows with sun-faded boxes of cereal selling bread and onions and Parmalat.

It's a place to wonder about past and current lives.

LANA BORTOLOT
Journalist

San Giovanni degli Eremiti
1132–1148, Roger II
Via dei Benedettini

San Giovanne degli Eremiti (Saint John of the Hermits) is the most intimate space in Palermo. To get here, walk through the ravaged Kalsa district, cross a few hair-raising intersections and come upon this quiet ancient church, its architectural oddities evident through the twisted trees. The church is austere and astonishingly beautiful, but the cloister with its faded frescoes, tiny spiraled columns, fruit trees and tangled garden is both a sanctuary and a fairyland. In March, the kumquats are ripe; there is nothing so magical as picking a few from the trees and sitting on the low stone bench beneath a flowering almond tree to eat them.

LANA BORTOLOT
Journalist

La Martorana
Piazza Bellini

Tiny La Martorana best shows off Palermo's eccentric
ancestry and architecture. Originally a Norman church, it
has a baroque façade, and adjacent, a strange, red, three-
domed, Arab-influenced chapel. But the real treasures are
inside: 12th-century Byzantine mosaics on the apse, walls,
and columns. If you can't make it to Monreale, come here
in the morning when the light shines through the high windows and the crowds are thin.

LANA BORTOLOT
Journalist

Vucciria Food Market
Area south of San Domenico and north of San Antonio

It's chaotic and crowded, and chances are you probably
won't even come away with anything to eat. But it's where
everyone in Palermo comes to poke the produce, sniff the
fish, and bargain for the best price. Best of all is night time,
when the market breaks down, and only a few vendors
remain, strangely illuminated by bare bulbs hanging hap-
hazardly, pirated from adjoining power lines. They pack up
slowly, eating dinner made from what didn't sell that day,
feeding their scraps to the lingering, hopeful street dogs.
When the streets are nearly empty, kids set fires to the
packing crates in small *piazze*, and a few at a time, people
emerge from alleys and doorways to kindle the fires.
Within minutes, the scene changes. Some straggling vendors will come, and shedding the weight of a day's com-
merce, melt into the crowd and become dark silhouettes
against the impromptu fires.

LANA BORTOLOT
Journalist

PIAZZA ARMERINA

46 km north of Gela

Villa Romana del Casale

4th century AD
5 km southwest of Piazza Armerina

Located in south central Sicily, this fourth-century AD villa of wonderfully complex design contains the most extraordinary mosaic floors in all of Italy. The majority of the mosaics follow a single theme: the hunting, capturing, and transporting of wild animals (from Africa) to supply the circuses of imperial Rome. In addition, there are mosaic portraits of the owner and his family as well as a group of bikini-clad women athletes. A little out of the way of the usual tourist route, but well worth the effort.

ARTHUR LEVERING
Composer

SELINUNTE

29 km southeast of Mazara del Vallo

Selinunte, near the extreme southwestern tip of Sicily, offers a remarkable glimpse into the massive human effort that went into building Sicily's great Greek temples. Unlike the well-touristed and well-manicured temple sites elsewhere in Sicily, Selinunte is a jumble of broken columns, capitals and blocks weighing up to one hundred tons, scattered about like building blocks of the gods. If you look closely at the chunks, you can see the marks of the lifting devices and try to imagine the effort of hundreds of men moving the massive marbles.

Temple G is a poignant monument to an unknown god (the dedications of the temples are unknown, so each is identified only by a letter). What would have been the second largest temple in the Greek world is now a chaos of unfinished columns, one jammed up against another, their sheer mass holding them in place like frozen Pick-up Stix.

Only one of the intended fifty stands, a lone silhouette against the sky.

Complete the trip by going to Rocche di Cusa (about eleven kilometers northwest), where Selinunte's stones were quarried. Here, amid ancient olive trees, abandoned pieces of the temples lie in various stages of progress, as though workmen planned someday to return to finish.

LANA BORTOLOT
Journalist

SYRACUSE / SIRACUSA

Fear of the Mafia, fear of Sicilian dialect, and a host of other potential problems in Palermo often keep American visitors from going to Sicily. Even for those intimidated by Palermo, however, Syracuse and other towns in the eastern part of the island are not to be missed. In addition to the Greek theater for which the town is best known (think back to the stories of Archimedes and the siege of Marcellus you read about in Latin class in school), there are also Christian catacombs. Finally, there is great baroque art, from some of the most exuberant architecture anywhere, to the haunting Caravaggio *Burial of Saint Lucy* (at the Museo Regionale d'Arte Medioevale e Moderna, located in the Ortygia section: Palazzo Bellomo, via Capodieci 16.) A short ride away is the amazing planned city of Noto (see p. 340), entirely rebuilt after the great earthquake of 1693.

JOHN MARCIARI
Art historian

Parco Archeologico
In the Neapolis section
Closed Mondays

In Siracusa is a cave called the Ear of Dionysus. It is a great
place to sing or to be silent. There is also a beautifully preserved Greek theater with scheduled theater experiences.
The Museo Archeologico Regionale Paolo Orsi (located in
Tyche, viale Teocrito 66) has large terra cotta burial jars
and densely arranged artifacts in a modern building based
on the hexagon. There is a stunning limestone sculpture of
a woman nursing twins, Night and Death. There's also a
numismatic collection with beautiful money: portraits on
the coins document rulers, important women and the idea
of dolphins.
ANDREA CALLARD
Artist

Ortygia
Accessible by two bridges from mainland

Duomo
Piazza Duomo

In the peninsular Ortygia, Syracuse's historic zone, stone-
faced buildings have been intricately carved by the wind.
A cathedral sits on the ancient site of the temple of
Athena. The temple columns became church columns.
Under the door is an ancient altar with the stone cutters'
iron oxide marks still visible. Outdoors, posters advertise
sexy underwear.
ANDREA CALLARD
Artist

SARDINIA / SARDEGNA

ITALIAN GHOST TOWNS

a. Nuraghe su Nuraxi, in the town of Barumini
   61 km north of Cagliari
b. Santu Antine (best preserved site)
   7 km southeast of Thiesi, off the Carlo Felice Road
c. Serra Orrios
   22 km east of Nuoro

Towns, for millennia in Italy, have been centers of civilization to which we are heirs. But signs persist of an earlier
kind of civilization, quite different. The cave dwellings of
Matera, the archaeological remains of even earlier peoples
in the cliffs along the western edge of Liguria, and the early
dwellers in the Dolomite mountains of the Veneto are all
mysteriously remote from us.

As are the villages of the strange *nuraghi* of the strange
geological antiquity called Sardegna.

An estimated seven thousand *nuraghi* remain, scattered
throughout the moon landscape of the island. They look
like the fantasy of a science fiction writer, but they are prehistoric, dating from long before the time when Ichnusa—
the name given in legend to this fish-shaped island—was
written about by the earliest lettered peoples, Phoenicians,
Greeks, Carthaginians, and Romans. They are massive,
even now, up to eighteen meters high and 33 meters wide,
conical structures of limestone or granite or tufa, grey and
mortarless, clustered together usually, but often solitary in
the dry landscape of a sere island flora. All are empty. If
you find one that has part or almost all of the dome-like
roof intact, you can make a noise inside and set up vibra-
tions that seem to enliven the space in the haunting echoes
that revive the ghosts of the former occupants. You sense
their unseen presence. These people from the past are seen
in museums in the forms of small metal figures, perhaps

four centimeters in length, like the old-fashioned lead soldiers of our own culture, found in diggings around Sardegna. Odd little humans, mute until your cry startles their spirits and they reply in echo form. And the light . . . bright Mediterranean sunshine pierces the smoke holes above or the cracks in the walls, from which lizards creep to bask in the sun and heat. High on the hills these fortress towns, small and large, defy the destruction that Sardinians have wreaked on wave after wave of subsequent occupiers. Greek temples, Roman temples, Spanish palaces—all intruders have weathered badly their rejection by the Sardinians through the centuries. The *nuraghi* remain, ready to be enlivened by the visitor's voice. Their entrances are narrow, but the inner space is charged with secrets and still vibrant expectancies.

CHARLES MATZ
Professor of Humanities

Editor's Note: The regular Greek name for Sardinia was Sardo. Its legendary name was Ichnusa (or Ichnussa). Several ancient authors, both Greek and Roman, say that this name was derived from the Greek word for a footprint, and give fanciful explanations.

INDEX OF RECOMMENDED READING

Diane Cole Ahl, *Benozzo Gozzoli*, Yale University Press, 1996.

Bernard Andreae, "L'accecamento di Polisemo" in *Forma Urbis*, iv, 12 (December, 1999).

Bernard Berenson, *Italian Painters of the Renaissance*, o.p.

Ranuccio Bianchi Bandinelli, *Sovana, topografia ed arte*, Rinascimento del libro, Firenze, 1929.

Bruce Boucher, *Andrea Palladio: The Architect in His Time*, Abbeville Press, 1994.

Robert Brentano, *Rome Before Avignon: A Social History of Thirteenth Century Rome*, University of California Press, 1991.

Joseph Brodsky, *Watermark*, Farrar Straus, 1992.

Robert Browning, "Fra Lippo Lippi" (poem).

Robert Browning, "A Toccata of Galuppi's" (poem).

Jacob Burckhardt, *The Civilization of the Renaissance in Italy*, Penguin, 1990.

Andrew Butterfield, *The Sculptures of Andrea del Verrocchio*, Yale University Press, 1997.

The Poems of Catullus, translated by James Michie, Vintage Books, 1969. Currently available from Bristol Classical Press, 1989.

Sir Kenneth Clark, *Piero della Francesca*, o.p.

Isabella and Livio Dalla Ragione, *Archeologia Arborea: diario di due cercatori di piante*. Ali&no, 1997.

Margaretta Darnall and Mark Weil, "Il Sacro Bosco di Bomarzo" in *Journal of Garden History*, iv (1984), pp. 1-91.

Esther Gordon Dotson, "Shapes of Earth and Time in European Gardens" in *Art Journal*, xlii (1982), pp. 210-216.

Francesco Paolo Fiore and Manfredo Tafuri, eds., *Francesco di Giorgio, architetto*, Electra, Milano, 1993.

David Freedberg, *The Power of Images: Studies in the History of Theory and Response*, University of Chicago Press, 1991.

S. J. Freedberg, *Painting in Italy 1500–1600*, o.p.

Walter Friedlaender, *Caravaggio Studies*, o.p.

Rona Goffen, *Giovanni Bellini*, Yale University Press, 1989.

Rona Goffen, ed., *Masaccio's Trinity*, Cambridge University Press, 1989.

Rona Goffen, *Piety and Patronage in Renaissance Venice: Bellini, Titian, and the Franciscans*, o.p.

Rona Goffen, *Spirituality in Conflict: Saint Francis and Giotto's Bardi Chapel*, o.p.

Robert Graves, *I Claudius*, Vintage Books, 1989.

Robert Graves, *Claudius the God and His Wife Messalina*, Vintage Books, 1989.

Marcella Hazan, *Marcella's Italian Kitchen*, Knopf, 1995.

Ludwig Heinrich Heydenreich, *Architecture in Italy: 1400–1500*, o.p.

Hugh Honour, *Companion Guide to Venice*, 4th edition, Boydell & Brewer, 1998.

Horace, *Horace in English*, Kenneth Haynes & D.S. Carne-Ross, eds., Penguin Classics, 1996.

Aldous Huxley, "The Best Picture" in *Along the Road: Notes and Essays of a Tourist*, Ecco Press, 1989.

Henry James, *The Portrait of a Lady*, Viking Penguin, 1984. Originally published in 1881.

Marilyn Lavin, *Piero della Francesca*, Harry N. Abrams, 1992.

Marilyn Lavin, ed., *Piero della Francesca and His Legacy*, National Gallery of Art, 1995.

Claudia Lazzaro, *The Italian Renaissance Garden: From the Conventions of Planting, Design and Ornaments to the Grand Gardens of Sixteenth Century Central Italy*, o.p.

Carlo Levi, *Christ Stopped at Eboli: The Story of a Year*, translated by Frances Frenaye, Noonday Press, 1995.

J. G. Links, *Venice for Pleasure*, 6th edition, Bishop Museum Press, 1999.

Roberto Longhi, *Three Studies*, translated by David Tabbat and David Jacobson, Sheep Meadow Press, 1996.

Giulio Lorenzetti, *Venice and Its Lagoon*, Istituto Poligrafico dello Stato, Roma, 1961.

Paul MacKendrick, *The Mute Stones Speak: The Story of Archeology in Italy*, W.W. Norton & Company, 1984.

John McAndrew, *Venetian Architecture of the Early Renaissance*, o.p.

Mary McCarthy, *The Stones of Florence*, Harcourt Brace, 1989.

Alexander Gordon McKay, *Houses, Villas and Palaces in the Roman World*, Johns Hopkins University Press, 1998.

Eugenio Montale, *Cuttlefish Bones: 1920–1927*; translated by William Arrowsmith, W.W. Norton & Company, 1992.

Jan Morris, *The World of Venice*, Harcourt Brace, 1995.

Alex Munthe, *The Story of San Michele*, o.p.

John Julius Norwich, *A History of Venice*, Vintage Books, 1989.

Iris Origo, *Images and Shadows: Part of a Life*, David R. Godine, 1999.

Roberto Pane, *Il Chiostro di Santa Chiara in Napoli*, L'Arte tipografica, Napoli, 1954.

John Pope-Hennessy, *The Piero della Francesca Trail*, o.p.

Donald Posner, *Annibale Carracci: A Study in the Reform of Italian Painting Around 1590*, o.p.

Regione Lombardia, Assessorato all'Urbanistica, eds. *Il Recupero Paesistico Dell'Adda di Leonardo*, Milano, 1998. Available in Italian and English.

L. Richardson Jr., *Pompeii: An Architectural History*, Johns Hopkins University Press, 1997.

Jonathan B. Riess, *Luca Signorelli: The San Brizio Chapel, Orvieto*, George Braziller, 1995.

Jonathan B. Riess, *The Renaissance Antichrist: Luca Signorelli's Orvieto Frescoes*, Princeton University Press, 1995.

Mark Rudman, *Provoked in Venice*, Wesleyan University Press, 1999.

Jean-Paul Sartre, "The Prisoner of Venice" in *Situations I*, Schoenhofs Foreign Books, 1989.

Irving Stone, *The Agony and the Ecstasy*, New American Library, 1996.

Cornelius Tacitus, *The Annales of Tacitus*, reprinted by Cambridge University Press, 1993. Originally published in the 2nd century ad.

Giuseppe Tassini, *Curiosità Veneziane*, 8th edition reprinted by Filippi, 1970. Originally published in 1863.

Alfred Lord Tennyson, "Frater Ave Atque Vale" (poem).

Stephen Tobriner, *The Genesis of Noto, an Eighteenth Century Sicilian City*, Zwemmer Press, London and U.C. Press, Berkeley, 1982. Republished in Italian as *La genesi di Noto, una città italiana del Settecento*, Dedalo, (Bari), 1989.

Stephen Tobriner, "Noto's Corso Remembered, 1693-1993" in *Streets: Critical Perspectives on Public Space*, Z. Çelik, D. Favro and R. Ingersoll, eds., University of California Press, 1996, pp. 135–150.

Stephen Tobriner, "Safety and Reconstruction after the Sicilian Earthquake of 1693—the Eighteenth Century Context" in *Dreadful Visitations: Confronting Natural Catastrophe in the Age of Enlightenment*, ed. Alessa Johns, Routledge, 1999, pp. 49–77.

Salley Vickers: *Miss Garnet's Angel*, Carroll & Graf, 2001.

Virgil, *The Aeneid*, Penguin Classics, 1991.

INDEX OF CONTRIBUTORS

Beth van Hoesen Adams, artist and printmaker. City of San Francisco Award of Honor in Graphics, 1981; California Society of Printmakers Distinguished Arts Award, 1991. pp. 50, 224, 274

Ross Anderson, architect. pp. 37, 220, 265, 282

Nicholas Arcomano, former Senior Attorney, BMI; and vice-president and counsel, SESAC, Inc., specializing in copyright law. Member of the Copyright Society of the U.S.A.; member of ALAI (International Organization for Protection of Literary and Artistic Property); former Contributing Editor to *Dance Magazine*. pp. 107, 131

Cameron Elizabeth Barrett, assistant editor, *Where Rome Magazine*. Former assistant coordinator and lecturer for Elderhostel (an organization offering short-term residential learning experiences abroad for American seniors) in Verona, Rome, Florence, and Sorrento. pp. 182, 209

Lidia Matticchio Bastianich, restaurateur. Star of *Lidia's Italian Table* on public television; owner of Felidia, Becco, Lidia's Kansas City, and Lidia's Pittsburgh; and cookbook author. She also has a sauce line and travel company (www.lidiasitaly.com). pp. 28, 39

Jack Beal, painter. pp. 68

Frederick Biehle, architect. Fellow, American Academy in Rome, 1987; adjunct professor, Pratt Institute; coordinator, Pratt Rome Program;

partner with Erika Hinrichs via Architecture Studio. pp. 287

George Bisacca, Conservator of Paintings, the Metropolitan Museum of Art. pp. 16, 131

Chester Biscardi, composer. Catalog includes works for opera, chorus, voice and piano, orchestra, chamber ensembles, and solo piano; music performed worldwide. He is currently Director of the Music Program and holds the William Schuman Chair in Music at Sarah Lawrence College. pp. 154

Lana Bortolot, journalist based in New York City and Rome. pp. 339, 342, 343, 344

Elizabeth Boults, San Francisco bay area designer. pp. 153, 159, 240

Katey Brown, art historian, University of Georgia Studies Abroad Program. pp. 20, 166, 219, 223

Margaret A. Brucia, Latin teacher. Fellow, American Academy in Rome, 1991–1992, in post-classical studies; NEH seminar in Rome, 1993. pp. 160, 168, 201, 250, 277

Gregory S. Bucher, classicist. Fellow, American Academy in Rome, 1993–1994, 1995-1996; Fellow, American School of Classical Studies, Athens, 1994–1995; PhD. Brown University, 1997; Fellow, Center for Hellenic Studies, 2000. pp. 140, 279

Virginia L. Bush, art historian. Art consultant and private lecturer on art history. pp. 227

Michael Cadwell, associate professor, Knowlton School of Architecture, The Ohio State University. pp. 64

Andrea Callard, artist. pp. 292, 296, 320, 340, 346

Caren Canier, painter. Associate Professor of Art, Rensselaer Polytechnic Institute; Fellow, American Academy in Rome, 1978. pp. 251, 258

Claudia Cannizzaro, coordinator for the Fellows program of the Civitella Ranieri Center, an artist residency program in Umbria. pp. 208, 236, 266, 269

John Carswell, curator and art historian; also professor of fine arts. Director of the Smart Museum, University of Chicago; Director of the Department of Islamic Works at Sotheby's in London; author of numerous books and publications. pp. 111, 143

Luigi Centola, architect. Educated in London and Naples; Fellow, American Academy in Rome, 1997, in architecture; projects, exhibitions, and placed competitions, worldwide. pp. 308, 327

Adele Chatfield-Taylor, President of the American Academy in Rome. pp. 45, 139

Keith Christiansen, Curator of Italian Paintings, the Metropolitan Museum of Art, pp. 76, 77, 109, 119, 129

Jean Conlon, photographers' agent. Co-author of Beauty is No Big Deal and Super Baby; board member of Friends Without a Border, a humanitarian organization which has built a pediatric hospital in Angkor for Cambodia's land mine victims. pp. 221

William B. Conlon, painter. Director of Visual Arts at Fordham University at Lincoln Center; recipient of the National Endowment for the Arts Fellowship; retrospective at the Museum of Art, Carnegie Institute. pp. 221

Pablo Conrad, writer and editor, living and teaching in Brooklyn. pp. 112, 173

Pier Consagra, artist. pp. 150, 329

Francesca Dell'Acqua, art historian. Specializes in archaeology of the Middle Ages and particulary in the study of glass and window-glass. pp. 24, 58

Eric Denker, art historian and senior lecturer, National Gallery of Art. Also serves as Curator of Prints and Drawings at The Corcoran Gallery of Art. pp. 95, 119

Mary Ann Haick DiNapoli, genealogist. Educator and licensed New York City tour guide. pp. 21, 83

Judith DiMaio, architect. Associate professor of Architecture and Director of the Undergraduate Major, Yale University. Head of Judith DiMaio Studio, New York, since 1988; academic director and professor for the University of Notre Dame's Rome program, 1979–1982. pp. 23, 31

Simon Dinnerstein, artist and professor of studio art, New School for Social Research & Parson's School of Design. pp. 176, 224, 264, 278

Paul DiPasquale, sculptor. Public monuments: Arthur Ashe Monument, Oliver Hill, Esq., Governor and Mrs. Godwin; author and recipient of "Fathers in Prison" Grant; Social Justice Award, Virginia Commonwealth University. pp. 239, 295

Kathe Dyson, traveler. Divides her time between New York and Italy; operates a winery and vineyard in Tuscany. pp. 28, 54

Geraldine Erman, artist. Rome Prize, American Academy in Rome, 1990, in sculpture. pp. 32

Robert Evans, architect. pp. 149, 151, 172, 174, 178, 180

Lawrence Fane, sculptor. pp. 194

Susan Farricielli, product designer. Founded a.k.a. prototype, specializing in three-dimensional design and product development. Visiting Artist, American Academy in Rome, 1999. pp. 226

Richard L. Feigen, art dealer. President, Richard L. Feigen & Company; author of Tales From the Art Crypt (Knopf, 2000). pp. 27, 37, 54, 245

Gail Feigenbaum, curator of painting (specializing in Baroque Art), New Orleans Museum of Art. Fellow, American Academy in Rome, 1980; formerly worked at the National Gallery of Art. pp. 194, 199

Alan Feltus, painter, Assisi, Italy. pp. 110, 113, 125, 206, 208, 209, 212, 213, 235, 236, 237, 247, 255, 256, 257, 258, 260, 270

James Fenton, writer. Author of Leonardo's Nephew: Essays on Art and Artists. pp. 164, 172, 230

Helen Costantino Fioratti, interior designer. Painter, illustrator (furniture), antique dealer, president of L'Antiquaire & The Connoisseur, Inc. at 36 East 73rd Street. Author and lecturer on furniture and Italian decorative arts. pp. 29, 33, 36, 39, 48, 50, 54, 55, 57, 58, 109

Philip Freeman, classicist. pp. 294

M. Paul Friedberg, landscape architect. pp. 271, 275

Jan Gadeyne, archaeologist and art historian of Roman antiquity. On the faculty of Temple University Rome and American University of Rome; visiting professor at Cornell University Rome. Assistant field director of the excavations of a Roman villa at Artena. pp. 300, 301, 302

Cecelia Galiena, director of the Civitella Ranieri Center, an artist residency program in Umbria. pp. 232, 253, 260, 262

Katherine Allston Geffcken, professor of Latin and Greek, Emerita, Wellesley College. pp. 231

Linda W. Rutland Gillison, associate professor of classics, University of Montana-Missoula. Also directs the university's Italy Study Program. pp. 283, 285, 289

Giancarlo Giubilaro, operations manager of the Civitella Ranieri Center, an artist residency program in Umbria. pp. 220, 233, 237, 243

Rona Goffen, Board of Governors Professor of Art History, Rutgers University. Author of books on Giotto, Bellini, Masaccio, Titian and the Frari. pp. 22, 28, 37, 38, 48, 68, 70, 71, 76, 82, 87, 91, 93, 97, 98, 99, 106, 113, 118, 126, 135, 139

Norma Wynick Goldman, adjunct professor in the Interdisciplinary Studies Program of College of Lifelong Learning at Wayne State University. Retired from the Department of Classics. pp. 217, 306, 322, 324, 325

Alexander Gorlin, architect. pp. 41, 278, 310

Robert Berkeley Green, artist and teacher. Works in the Smithsonian, the Carnegie Mellon, the Spencer and Yale art museums; retired from the University of Kansas. pp. 320, 325

Michael Gruber, architect. Richard Meier & Partners. Fellow, American Academy in Rome, 1996. Modelmaker for the Getty Center. Creator of Mr. Tree paper trees. pp. 304

Beatrice H. Guthrie, executive director of Save Venice for thirteen years. *Cavaliere* of the Italian Republic. pp. 85, 100, 103

Robert Mitchell Hanna, landscape architect at R.M. Hanna Landscape Architects. Adjunct professor at the University of Pennsylvania; Fellow, American Academy in Rome, 1976. pp. 333

Marcella Hazan, cookbook author and educator. Consultant in Italian cooking; author of five award-winning books; conducted own cooking school for nearly thirty years. pp. 72, 73, 75, 76, 82, 83, 84, 86, 92, 93, 103, 106, 108, 109, 110, 118, 126, 138

Ursula Heibges, classicist. Retired professor of classics; Fellow, American Academy in Rome, 1965–1966. pp. 202, 203, 204

James J. Hennessey, professor of painting, Maryland Institute. Rome Prize, American Academy in Rome, 1962–1964, in painting. pp. 313

Pamela Potter Hennessey, art historian and assistant professor of art history, Ursinus College. Received Smithsonian, Winterthur, and U.S. Capitol Historic Society fellowships. pp. 313

Martie Holmer, artist. Faculty, Rhode Island School of Design. pp. 267, 301

Edith Isaac-Rose, painter and teacher, co-director, Art Workshop International: Assisi, Italy (800-835-7454). Pollock-Krasner and Adolph and Esther Gottlieb Awards, among others. pp. 216, 225, 234, 249

Emilie Johnson, curatorial assistant, the Corcoran Gallery of Art. pp. 87, 91

Robert Kahn, architect. pp. 148, 175

John Kearney, sculptor. pp. 240, 241, 319

Lynn Kearney, artist and curator. Director of Contemporary Art Workshop, Chicago. pp. 224, 236, 291, 293

Pamela Keech, artist, historian, curator, and sculptor; President of the Society of Fellows of the American Academy in Rome. pp. 247, 265

John F. Kenfield, associate professor of Greek art, Rutgers University. Fellow, American Academy in Rome, 1977; Fellow, American School of Classical Studies, Athens. pp. 266, 312

Dave King, writer. Free-lance editor and Adjunct Professor of English, Baruch College. pp. 110, 165

Susan Kleinberg, artist. pp. 23, 43, 68, 81, 91, 100, 309

Gordon Knox, director of the Civitella Ranieri Center, an artist residency program in Umbria. pp. 232, 253, 260, 262

David Konstan, professor of classics, Brown University, President of the American Philological Association, 1999. pp. 316

Swietlan N. Kraczyna, artist and printmaker. Teaches at Sarah Lawrence College and Syracuse University programs in Florence; one of the founders of il Bissonte International School for Advanced Printmaking in Florence. pp. 26, 56, 216

Peter Harris Kross, D.V.M., veterinarian. pp. 195, 199

James M.Lattis, historian of astronomy. Director, Space Place at

University of Wisconsin-Madison. pp. 205

John C. Leavey, painter. pp. 28, 162, 177, 206, 208, 231, 233, 234, 241

Arthur Levering, composer. Fellow, American Academy in Rome, 1997. Awards from Barlow and Hecksher foundations, NEA, Composers Guild, and others. pp. 293, 305, 309, 315, 327, 344

Robert Livesey, architect. Director of the Knowlton School of Architecture, The Ohio State University. pp. 41, 160, 162, 164, 222, 226, 274, 277, 309

Barbara Lynn-Davis, art historian and writer. Multiple awards, most recently a Certificate for Distinction in Teaching from the Faculty of Arts and Sciences, Harvard University. The selections included here are drawn from her manuscript, *Illuminations: A Travelers Guide to the Art of Italy*. pp. 98, 162, 176, 183, 202

Thomas F. Madden, professor of medieval history, Saint Louis University. Author *of The Fourth Crusade, A Concise History of the Crusades*, and numerous other studies on Venice during the Middle Ages; editor of *Medieval and Renaissance Venice*. pp. 72, 102

John Marciari, professor of art history, Loyola College. Fellow, American Academy in Rome, 1998. pp. 174, 235, 345

Michael Marlais, Gillespie Professor of Art History, Colby College. Author of *Conservative Echoes in*

Fin-de-Siecle Parisian Art Criticism (1992). pp. 276

Judith Martin, journalist. Author of the *Miss Manners* books and newspaper, internet and magazine columns; also novelist. pp. 93, 127

Charles Matz, Professor of Humanities. Southampton College of Long Island University. pp. 347

Margaret Spencer Matz, architect. Graduated with honors from The Cooper Union School of Architecture. pp. 93, 113

James McGarrell, painter. Work in the Metropolitan Museum of Art, Whitney Museum, and Museum of Modern Art, among others. pp. 268

Gregory McNamee, author and/or editor of twenty books. Traveler and travel writer. pp. 330, 334

Melissa Meyer, artist. Teacher at the School of Visual Arts, New York; Rome Prize, American Academy, 1980. pp. 179, 180, 181, 186

D. B. Middleton, architect. pp. 59, 173, 205, 278, 279, 315, 319, 321, 325

Jan Morris, writer. pp. 135

Gianfranco Mossetto, merchant banker. Professor of public finance and art economics at Cà Foscari University, Venice. pp. 71, 81, 139, 175

Gwynn Murrill, sculptor. Rome Prize, American Academy in Rome. pp. 217

Helen Nagy, art historian. Professor of art history, The University of Puget Sound. pp. 244

Helen F. North, Centennial Professor of Classics Emerita, Swarthmore College. pp. 101, 108, 118, 141, 157, 158, 188

John Julius Norwich, author of *A History of Venice* and *Venice: A Traveler's Companion*. pp. 97, 100, 107, 115

Jane Oliensis, director of Humanities Spring, a summer program for Classical and Renaissance study in Assisi. pp. 49, 250, 251, 252

Jacqueline Osherow, poet. Author of four collections of poetry. pp. 34, 44, 49, 77, 81

Paul Pascal, professor Emeritus of Latin. pp. 102 and Editor's Notes throughout

Andrew Patrick, geologist and earth science teacher. Conducted research in paleoclimatology; curatorial scientist for the Ocean Drilling Program, 1997–1998. pp. 303, 311, 321

Mary Jane Phillips-Matz, musicologist and biographer. Author of *Verdi, A Biography*, which won the Royal Philharmonic Prize and the ASCAP Deems Taylor Prize. pp. 112, 128, 133

Sam Posey, race car driver, artist and designer. Competed in the Indianapolis 500, the United States Grand Prix, and the 24 Hours of Le Mans, where he set the lap record with a Ferrari that had a top speed of 248 mph. pp. 167, 200

Dana Prescott, artist and writer. On the art faculty of Temple University Rome; twice a Visiting Artist at the

American Academy in Rome; director of the Rhode Island School of Design in Rome for eight years. pp. 27, 37, 44, 45, 53

Gillian Price, author of three guides on the Italian Alps, one on Tuscany, and one on Sicily (forthcoming). Also translator at the Venice Film Festival. pp. 84

Ernst Pulgram, historical linguist. Hayward Keniston Professor of Classical and Romance Linguistics, Emeritus. pp. 178, 182, 187, 188, 189

Theodore K. Rabb, professor of history, Princeton University. Author or editor of more than a dozen books; contributor to the *New York Times*, the *Times Literary Supplement*, and other publications. Nominated for an Emmy for *Renaissance*, a PBS series. pp. 36, 96

Leslie Rainer, conservator of wall paintings. Recipient of the Rome Prize for Conservation and Historic Preservation, 1998–1999. pp. 32, 34, 148, 153, 244

Anton Rajer, conservator. pp. 282, 288, 292

Saskia Reilly, author of *Living, Studying and Working in France*; also a journalist. pp. 268

L. Richardson Jr., James B. Duke Professor of Latin, Emeritus. Fellow, American Academy in Rome, 1950, in classics; field archaeologist in 1952–1955; and trustee in 1969–1991. pp. 243, 317, 318

Carole Robb, painter. Faculty of New York Studio School. Rome Prize, Accademia Britannica, 1979. pp. 294

Mark Rudman, poet, essayist, and translator. Adjunct Professor at New York University. Rudman received the National Book Critics Circle Award in Poetry for *Rider* in 1994. pp. 133, 215, 280

Wayne Ruga, social architect. Loeb Fellow, Harvard University, 1998, Visiting Artist at the American Academy in Rome, 1999. pp. 296

Carol Saper, private art dealer. pp. 220, 221

Celia E. Schultz, classicist. Latin scholar; visiting lecturer, Bryn Mawr College, Whiting Fellowship, 1998-1999; visiting lecturer, Johns Hopkins University. pp. 182

Charles P. Segal, Walter C. Klein Professor of the Classics, Harvard University. Rome Prize, American Academy in Rome, 1961–1963; also classicist in residence, 1986. President of the American Philological Association, 1994. pp. 181, 182, 230

Joan Silber, fiction writer. Author of novels *Household Words* (PEN-Hemingway award winner) and *In the City*; also the story collection *In My Other Life*. Work has appeared in *The New Yorker*, *Ploughshares*, the *Voice Literary Supplement* and other journals. pp. 237

Susan Silberberg-Peirce, photographer and Greco-Roman art historian; associate professor of art history, Colorado State University. pp. 319, 320

Thomas Silva, architect. Fellow, American Academy in Rome, 1989. pp. 333

Sally Spector, artist. Author and illustrator of *Venice and Food*, Arsenale Editrice, Venice (1998). pp. 71, 138

Frederick Steiner, professor of Planning and Landscape Architecture, Arizona State University. Author of *The Living Landscape*, *To Heal the Earth* (with Ian McHarg), and *Ecological Design and Planning* (with George Thompson). Fellow, American Academy in Rome. pp. 162, 165, 167

Chip Sullivan, associate professor of landscape architecture. Fellow, American Academy in Rome, 1984-1985. pp. 153, 159, 240

Wayne Taylor, artist, architect, and Professor Emeritus, School of Design, North Carolina State University. Rome Prize, American Academy in Rome, 1960–1962, in architecture. pp. 281

Sallie Tisdale, writer. Author of six books, most recently, *The Best Thing I Ever Tasted*. pp. 32

Stephen Tobriner, professor of architectural history, University of California Berkeley. Member of several earthquake reconnaissance teams and author of forthcoming book about the collapsed Cathedral of Noto. pp. 340, 341

John Varriano, professor of Art History, Mount Holyoke College. Author of *Italian Baroque and Rococo Architecture* and *Rome, A Literary Companion*. pp. 266, 270

William E. Wallace, professor of art history, Washington University. Internationally recognized authority on Michelangelo and his contemporaries. pp. 38, 40, 59, 69, 107, 140

Marianne Weil, sculptor. Lived and worked in Pietrasanta, Italy 1974–1991. Teaches at SUNY-Stony Brook and Suffolk County Community College. pp. 227

Fred Wessel, artist and professor, Hartford Art School, University of Hartford. Director of Workshops in Italy (http://workshopsinitaly.com). pp. 42

Rebecca J. West, professor of Italian Literature and Cinema Studies, The University of Chicago. Author of *E. Montale: Poet on the Edge* (1981), and *Gianni Celati: The Craft of Everyday Storytelling* (2000). pp. 198, 200

Andrew Wielawski, sculptor. Works in museum and private collections throughout the world; lectures on Art World Economics at numerous universitites. pp. 238

Ann Thomas Wilkins, associate professor of classics, Duquesne University. pp. 20, 23, 46, 48, 185, 305

David G.Wilkins, chair and professor of the history of art and architecture, University of Pittsburgh. pp. 23, 25, 48, 51, 176, 185, 201, 241, 305

John Wilton-Ely, art historian. Professor Emeritus, University of Hull; author of *Piranesi as Architect and Designer*. pp. 218

David Winter, sculptor. pp. 315

Nancy A. Winter, archaeologist and librarian of the American School of Classical Studies, Athens. pp. 217, 221

John L. Wong, landscape architect, San Francisco, California. Rome Prize, American Academy in Rome, 1981. pp. 32, 41, 42, 53, 55, 86, 185

Susan E. Wood, professor of art history, Oakland University. pp. 46, 51, 312, 316, 318

Jack Zajac, painter and sculptor. Fellow, American Academy in Rome, 1958. Retired from the faculty of the University of California in Santa Cruz. pp. 262

GENERAL INDEX

Entries that appear in bold refer to
cities and towns.

Aalto, Alvar 205
Abbazia di Fossanova 279
Abbazia di Monte Oliveto
   Maggiore 221
Abbazia di Sant'Antimo 237
Abbazia di San Benedetto 285
Abbazia di San Galgano 233
Abbazia di Santa Scolastica 285
Abruzzo 300–302
Acciaioli, Niccolò 56
Adoration of the Golden Calf
   (Tintoretto) 77
Alba Fucens 300
*Allegories of Good and Bad
   Government* (Lorenzetti) 241
Angelico, Fra 234
Annunciation (Fra Angelico) 234
Annunciation (Pontormo) 26
Antique Markets (Arezzo) 213
Aquileia 187
Arca, Niccolò dell', 194
Arcetri 54
Arciconfraternita della Misericordia
   (Florence) 21
Arezzo 208–214
Arsenale (Venice) 101
Asilo Infantile Sant'Elia (Como) 160
Asolo 172
Assisi 247–249
Associazione Archeologia Arborea
   (Lerchi) 260–261
Autodromo Nazionale di Monza
   167

B
Badoer-Giustinian Chapel (Venice)
   100
Bagnaia 271
Bagni di Lucca 215

Bagni di Viterbo 296
Baldovinetti, Alesso 52
Baptistery (Castiglione Olona) 158
Baptistery (Siena) 242
Baptistery of San Giovanni (Naples)
   312
Bardi Chapel Frescoes (Giotto) 49
Barga 216
Bartolo, Taddeo di, 242
Basilicata 329–337
Bassano del Grappa 172
Bellini, Gentile 127
Bellini, Giovanni 96
Bevagna 250
Biblioteca Comunale (Siena) 240
Biblioteca Marciana (Venice) 113
Biblioteca Mediceo-Laurenziana
   (Florence) 40
Blue Grotto (Grotta Azzurra) 306
Boboli Garden (Giardino di Boboli)
   32
Bologna 194–200
Bomarzo 274–277
Brion-Vega Family Tomb (San Vito
   d'Altivole) 180
Brodsky, Joseph, Grave of (San
   Michele) 139
Brunelleschi 16, 20, 26, 49
Buontalenti 32, 53
Buori, Giovanni 86
Burano (Umbria) 251
Burano (Venice) 141
Burri, Alberto 339

C
Camera degli Sposi (Mantegna) 162
Camera di San Paolo (Parma) 201
Campania 303–328
Campi Flegrei 303
Campiello del Pistor (Venice) 71
Campo Santa Margherita (Venice)
   118, 119–125

Candi, Giovanni 108
Cannaregio (Venice) 76–85
Canova, Antonio 65, 179
Capella del Rosario (Venice) 91
Cappella Baglioni Fresco Cycle
    (Pinturicchio) 268
Cappella Brancacci (Florence) 34
Cappella di San Tarasio (Venice) 97
Cappella Sansevero (Naples) 316
Cappella Sassetti (Florence) 38
Cappella degli Scrovegni (Padua)
    176
Cappelle Medicee (Florence) 41
Caprarola 277
Capri 305
Caravaggio 165
Carmignano 54
Carnevale (Viareggio) 244
Carpaccio, Vittore 98
Carracci 199
Carrara 227–230
Casa di Canova 178
Casa Cononica (Montepulciano)
    222
Casa de Giulio Romano (Mantua)
    164
Casa del Fascio (Como) 160
Casa Giuliani-Frigerio (Como) 160
Casa Malaparte (Capri) 308
Casella d'Asolo 173
Caserta 309
Castel del Monte 329
Castel Sant'Elmo (Naples) 315
Castello (Castel del Monte) 329
Castello Caetani (Sermoneta) 288
Castello del Buonconsiglio (Trento)
    182
Castello di Miramare 187
Castello di Rivoli 148
Castelseprio 157
Castiglione del Lago 252
Castiglione Olona 158
Cava Scura (Ischia) 311
Cave of the Sibyl (Cumae) 309–310
Cavriglia 216

Le Celle (Cortona) 219–220
Centro delle Tradizioni Popolari
    (Città di Castello) 253
Ceramiche Artistiche Solimene SHC
    Vicenzo Solimene (Vietri sul
    Mare) 327
La Certosa del Galluzzo 56
La Certosa di San Lorenzo (Padula)
    318
Cerveteri 278
Chapel of the Cardinal of Portugal
    (Florence) 52
Il Chiostro Maiolicato (Naples) 317
Chiusi 217
Churches, Basilicas and Duomos
    Angelo Raffaele (Venice) 115
    Duomo (Aquileia) 187
    Duomo (Arezzo) 212
    Duomo (Florence) 16–19
    Duomo (Milan) 164
    Duomo (Naples) 312
    Duomo (Orvieto) 264
    Duomo (Syracuse) 346
    Duomo (Todi) 270
    Gesuati (Venice) 129
    Gesuiti (Venice) 81
    Madonna dei Bagni (Deruta)
        256
    Madonna dell'Orto (Venice) 77
    Madonna di San Biagio
        (Montepulciano) 222, 223
    Ognissanti (Florence) 36
    Orsanmichele (Florence) 22
    La Pietà (Venice) 129
    Il Redentore (Venice) 135
    Riola, Parish Center 205
    Sant'Agostino (San Gimignano)
        234
    Sant'Alvise (Venice) 76
    Sant'Anastasia (Verona) 183
    Sant'Apollinare in Classe
        (Ravenna) 204
    Sant'Apollinare Nuovo (Ravenna)
        203
    Sant'Apollonia (Venice) 95

Churches, Basilicas and Duomos
(continued)
Santa Chiara, Basilica di (Assisi)
248
Santa Chiara (Naples) 317
Santa Croce (Florence) 48
San Damiano (Assisi) 249
San Domenico (Arezzo) 212
San Domenico Maggiore (Naples)
316
Santa Felicita (Florence) 26
San Francesco (Arezzo) 208
San Francesco, Basilica di (Assisi)
247
San Francesco della Vigna
(Venice) 99
San Giobbe (Venice) 76
San Giorgio Maggiore (Venice)
139
San Giovanni Crisostomo
(Venice) 82
San Giovanni degli Eremiti
(Palermo) 342
Santi Giovanni e Paolo (Venice)
87–92
San Lazzaro degli Armeni
(Venice) 143
San Lorenzo (Florence) 40–41
San Lorenzo (Sansepolcro) 236
San Marco, Basilica (Venice) 112
Santa Maria dell'Assunta
(Torcello) 140
Santa Maria del Carmine
(Florence) 34
Santa Maria della Consolazione
(Todi) 270
Santa Maria del Fiore (Florence)
16–19
Santa Maria Foris Portas
(Castelseprio) 157
Santa Maria Formosa (Venice) 93
Santa Maria Gloriosa dei Frari
(Venice) 65
Santa Maria delle Grazie al
Calcinaio (Cortona) 218

Santa Maria Maggiore (Spello)
268
Santa Maria dei Miracoli (Venice)
85
Santa Maria Novella (Florence)
36
Santa Maria della Pieve (Arezzo)
208
Santa Maria della Salute (Venice)
131
Santa Maria della Vita (Bologna)
194, 195
San Michele (Carmignano) 54
San Michele a San Salvi
(Florence) 38
San Miniato al Monte (Florence)
51
San Moisè (Venice) 110
San Nicolò dei Mendicoli
(Venice) 115
Santa Restituta, Basilica (Naples)
312
San Salvatore (Venice) 69
San Sebastiano (Venice) 118
Santo Stefano, Basilica (Bologna)
198
Santa Trinita (Florence) 38
San Trovaso (Venice) 126
San Vitale (Ravenna) 203
San Zaccaria (Venice) 96–97
San Zan Degolà (Venice) 70, 71
San Zanipolo (Venice) 87–92
San Zeno Maggiore (Verona) 182
Cima da Conegliano 77
Cimabue 212
Circolo Canottieri, see Società
Canottieri
Città di Castello 253
Cividale del Friuli 188
Civita di Bagnoregio 278
Coducci, Mauro 82, 86, 96
Collegiata (San Gimignano) 234
Colleoni, Bartolomeo, monument
(Venice) 87
Colli (Florence) 51–52

Colonnata 217
Como 159
Correggio 201
Corridoio Vasariano (Florence) 23
Corte del Duca Sforza (Venice) 102
Cortona 218–220
Costa di Maratea 330
Il Cretto di Burri (Gibellina
    Vecchia) 339
Cumae 309

D
del Tasso, Marco 32
della Quercia, Jacopo 242
della Robbia, Luca 52
Deposition (Roccatagliata) 110
Deposition (Pontormo) 26–28
Deposition (Rosso Fiorentino) 236,
    245
Deruta 255
Desenzano del Garda 160
Doge's Palace (Venice) 112
Dorsoduro (Venice) 115–134
Duccio 241

E
Emilia-Romagna 194–207
Ercolano 310
Escrivà, Pedro Luis 315

F
Fanzolo 173
Fegato di Piacenza 201
Ferrari S.P.A. (Maranello) 200
Ferry Boat (Lecco) 162
Fiesole 55
Flagellation (Piero della Francesca)
    206
Flood Marker (Florence) 48
Florence 16–52
    Arciconfraternita della
        Misericordia 21
    Bardi Chapel 49
    Biblioteca Mediceo-Laurenziana
        40

Boboli Garden (Giardino di
    Boboli) 32
Campo di Marte 54
Cappella Brancacci 34
Cappella Sassetti 38
Cappelle Medicee 41
Cenacoli 38
Chapel of the Cardinal of
    Portugal 52
City Center East 48–50
City Center North 39–47
City Center West 36–38
Colli 51–52
Corridoio Vasariano 23
Flood Marker 48
Fondazione Horne 48
Galleria degli Uffizi 23–25
Grotta Grande del Buontalenti 32
Grotticina di Madama 32
Historic Center 16–24
Hotels
    Albergo Splendor 45
    Hotel Lungarno 30
    Pensione Sorelle Bandini 34
Maiano, Benedetto da 50
Mercato Centrale 39
Museo Archeologico 46
Museo Bardini 29
Museo La Specola 32
Museo Salvatore Ferragamo 30
New Sacristy (Sagrestia Nuova) 41
Ognissanti 36
Oltrarno 25–35
Opificio delle Pietre Dure 45
Orsanmichele 22
Palazzo Medici-Riccardi 43
Piazza Santo Spirito 34
Piazzale Michelangelo 51
Ponte Vecchio 25
Restaurants
    Antica Gelateria il David 39
    Beccofino 28
    Buscioni 54
    Caffè Rivoire 23
    Cammillo 28

Florence restaurants (continued)
  Cantinetta Antinori 30
  Dolci e Dolcezza 50
  Il Latini 37
  Osteria Santo Spirito 34
  Trattoria Garga 37
  Le Volpi e l'Uva 29
  Roman Roads 20
  Santa Croce 48
  Santa Felicita 26
  San Lorenzo 40
  Santa Maria del Carmine 34
  Santa Maria del Fiore (Duomo)
    16–19
  Santa Maria Novella 36
  San Miniato al Monte 51
  Santa Trinita 38
  Shops
    Beltrami 37
    Castorina 30
    Madova 28
    N'uovo 36
    Peter Bazzanti and Son 30
    Romanelli 30
  Società Canottieri (Circolo
    Canottieri) 25
  Sotterraneo 42
Foligno 257
Fondazione Querini Stampalia
  (Venice) 94
Fonti del Clitunno (Pissignano) 266
Food Markets (Bologna) 200
Fortini, Davide 32
Fossacesia 301
The Founding of Rome (Caracci)
  199
Franciabigio 231
Friuli-Venezia Giulia 187–189

G
Gaeta 281
Galleria Luce (Venice) 107
Galleria Multigraphic (Venice) 131
Galluzzo 56
Gambello, Antonio 96

Garden of the Fugitives (Pompeii)
  321
Genoa (Genova) 153
Genzano di Roma 279
Ghirlandaio, Domenico 36, 38
Giardino Giusti (Verona) 185
Gibellina Vecchia 339
Giotto 49, 176
Giudecca (Venice) 135
Gloria di San Niccolò
  (Montemezzano) 115
Gozzoli, Benozzo 43
Grado 189
Grotta Azzurra (Capri) 306
Grotta Azzurra (Portovenere) 154
Grotta di Tiberio (Sperlonga) 289
Grotta Grande del Buontalenti
  (Florence) 32
Grotticina di Madama (Florence) 32
Guardi, Giovanni Antonio 115
Gubbio 258–260
Guidoriccio da Fogliano (Martini)
  241

H
Hadrian's Villa (Villa Adriana) 294
Hellenistic Etruscan Tombs
  (Sovana) 243
Herculaneum (Ercolano) 310
Hotels
  Albergo Splendor (Florence) 45
  Antica Locanda Montin (Venice)
    125
  Antico Spessotto (Portogruaro)
    178
  La Chiusa (Niccone) 262
  Grand Hotel Pianeta Maratea 332
  Hotel Cipriani (Giudecca) 138
  Hotel La Fenice et des Artistes
    (Venice) 107
  Hotel Lungarno (Florence) 30
  Hotel Paradiso (Portovenere) 154
  Hotel Settebello (Maratea) 332
  Hotel Villa del Mare
    (Acquafredda) 332

Hotels (continued)
Locanda da Lino (Solighetto)
181
Locanda delle Donne Monache
(Maratea) 332
Motel Villa dei Misteri (Pompeii)
324
Orazio (Venosa) 336
Pensione Sorelle Bandini
(Florence) 34
Villa Cheta Elite (Acquafredda)
332
Villa Cipriani (Asolo) 172

I
Impruneta 57
Ischia 311
Istituto Universitaria di Architettura
di Venezia 64–65

J
Juvarra, Filippo 148

K
La Kalsa (Palermo) 342

L
Lago d'Averno 303
Lapi, Zanobi 53, 59
Last Judgment (Nardo di Cione) 37
Last Judgment (Tintoretto) 77
Last Judgment Cycle (Signorelli)
264
Last Judgment Mosaics (Torcello)
140
Last Supper (Ghirlandaio) 36
Laurano, Luciano 205
Lazio 271–296
Lecco 162
The Legend of the True Cross
(Piero della Francesca) 208
Leonardo da Vinci 162, 165
Lerchi 260
Libera, Adalberto 308
Licenza 280

Life of Saint Benedict (Signorelli &
Sodoma) 221–222
Life of the Virgin (Bartolo) 242
Liguria 153–156
Lombardo, Pietro 85, 86, 91, 100
Lombardo, Tullio 82
Lombardy 157–168
Longhena, Baldassare 131
Lonigo 174
Lorenzetti, Ambrogio 241
Lorenzetti, Pietro 209
Lucca 220
Lucignano 220

M
Madonna and Child Enthroned
(Negroponte) 99
Madonna and Child with Saints
(Piero della Francesca)
166–167
Madonna and Child with Saints
(Tiepolo) 130
Madonna and Four Saints (Bellini)
96
Madonna del Parto (Piero della
Francesca) 224
Madonna della Misericordia (Piero
della Francesca) 236
Madonna della Misericordia
(Vivarini) 93
Madonna di Senigallia (Piero della
Francesca) 206
Maestà (Duccio) 241
Magdalen (Piero della Francesca) 212
Magliano in Toscana 220
Maiano, Benedetto da 50
Maioliche 255–256
Manciano 221
Mantegna, Andrea 162
Mantua (Mantova) 162–164
Maranello 200
Maratea 330
Marble Quarries (Colonnata)
217–218
Marche 194–207

Marghera Channels (Mestre) 175
Martini, Francesco di Giorgio 218
Martini, Simone 241
La Martorana (Palermo) 343
Masaccio 36
Masèr 174
Masolino da Panicale 158
Matera 333
Mausoleo di Galla Placidia
    (Ravenna) 202–203
Mausoleo di Teodorico (Ravenna)
    204
Medici Villas 53
Mercato Centrale (Florence) 39
Mercato delle Gaite (Bevagna) 250
Mestre 175
Michelangelo 238
    Biblioteca Mediceo-Laurenziana
        (Florence) 40
    New Sacristy / Sagrestia Nuova
        (Florence) 41
    Sotterraneo (Florence) 42
Michelangelo's Road 238–239
Michelozzo 43, 53, 55
Milan (Milano) 164–167
The Miracle of the True Cross at
    the Bridge of San Lorenzo
    (Bellini) 127–128
Molise 300–302
Monaco, Lorenzo 38
Monastero Santa Anna (Foligno) 257
Monte Circeo 281
Montefollonico 221
Montemezzano, Francesco 115
Montepulciano 222
Monterchi 224
Montevarchi 225
Montughi 58
Monza 167
Mozia 340
Museums
    Accademia (Venice) 127
    Fondazione Horne (Florence) 48
    Galleria degli Uffizi (Florence)
        23–25

Gipsoteca at Casa di Canova
    (Possagno) 178
Museo Archeologica Nazionale
    (Sperlonga) 291
Museo Archeologico (Florence)
    46–47
Museo Archeologico (Terracina)
    293
Museo Archeologico (Venice) 113
Museo Archeologico Mecenate
    (Arezzo) 213
Museo Archeologico Nazionale
    (Naples) 315
Museo Archeologico Nazionale
    Prenestino (Palestrina) 283
Museo Bandini (Fiesole) 55
Museo Bardini (Florence) 29
Museo della Basilica di Santa
    Maria delle Grazie (San
    Giovanni Valdarno) 234
Museo Civico (Piacenza) 201
Museo Civico (San Gimignano)
    234
Museo Civico (Sansepolcro) 235
Museo Civico (Siena) 241
Museo Correr (Venice) 110–111
Museo Fortuny (Venice) 106
Museo La Specola (Florence)
    32–33
Museo Nazionale di
    Capodimonte (Naples) 315
Museo Nazionale Tarquiniense
    292
Museo dell'Opera del Duomo
    (Pisa) 230
Museo dell'Opera del Duomo
    (Siena) 241
Museo Salvatore Ferragamo
    (Florence) 30
Museo Stibbert (Montughi) 58
Pinacoteca di Brera (Milan)
    165–166
Pinacoteca e Museo Civico
    (Volterra) 245

N
Naples (Napoli) 312–318
Nardo di Cione 37
Naviglio Grande (Milan) 165
Naviglio Pavese (Milan) 165
Necropolis (Norchia) 282
Necropolis (Tarquinia) 292
Negroponte, Antonio da 99
Niccone 262
Nile Mosaic (Palestrina) 283
Norchia 282
Norcia 262
Noto 340
Nuraghe su Nuraxi (Sardinia) 347

O
Oltrarno (Florence) 26–35
Opera in the Roman Arena
    (Verona) 185
Opificio delle Pietre Dure (Florence)
    45–46
Oratorio di San Giorgio (Padua)
    177
Orcagna, Andrea 22
Ortygia (Syracuse) 346
Orvieto 264–266
Ostia Antica 282

P
Padua (Padova) 176
Padula 318
Paestum 319
La Palazzina di Caccia 148
Palazzo Cervini (Montepulciano)
    222
Palazzo Comunale (Montepulciano)
    222
Palazzo Comunale (Pienza) 226
Palazzo Contarini del Bovolo
    (Venice) 108–109
Palazzo Ducale (Mantua) 162
Palazzo Ducale (Urbino) 205
Palazzo Ducale (Venice) 112
Palazzo Farnese (Caprarola) 277
Palazzo Magnani (Bologna) 199

Palazzo Medici-Riccardi (Florence)
    43
Palazzo Piccolomini (Pienza) 226
Palazzo Pubblico (Siena) 241
Palazzo Reale (Caserta) 309
Palazzo Tarugi (Montepulciano)
    222
Palermo 342
Palestrina 283
Palladio, Andrea 99, 135, 139, 172,
    173, 174, 186
Palma Vecchio 93
Parco Archeologico (Syracuse) 346
Parco dei Mostri (Bomarzo) 274
Parma 201
The Passion of Christ (Niccolò
    dell'Arca) 194
Pavia 168
Piacenza 201
Piazza Armerina 344
Piazza Fontane Marose (Genoa) 153
Piazza Piò II (Pienza) 226
Piazza Santo Spirito (Florence) 34
Piazzale Michelangelo (Florence) 51
Piedmont 148–152
Pienza 226
Piero della Francesca
    The Flagellation 206
    The Legend of the True Cross
        208
    Madonna and Child with Saints
        166
    Madonna del Parto 224
    Madonna della Misericordia 236
    Madonna di Senigallia 206
    Magdalen 212
    The Resurrection 235
Pietrabbondante 301
Pietrasanta 226
Pinacoteca di Brera (Milan) 165
Pinturicchio 268
Pisa 230
Pisanello 183
Pisano, Giovanni 241
Piscina Mirabile (Campi Flegrei) 304

Pissignano 266
Pitigliano 231
Poggio a Caiano 231
Pollaiolo, Antonio and Piero del 52
Pompeii 321
Ponte degli Alpini (Bassano del
    Grappa) 172
Ponte Vecchio (Florence) 25
Pontormo, Jacopo 56, 231
    Annunciation 26–28
    Deposition 26–28
    Visitation 54
Portofino 153
Portogruaro 178
Portovenere 154
Possagno 178
Pozzo di San Patrizio (Orvieto) 265
Procession of the Magi (Gozzoli) 43
Puglia 329
R
Ravello 325
Ravenna 202
Restaurants
    Acqua Pazza (Venice) 106
    Al Cacciatore della Subida
        (Cormons) 188
    Al Mascaron (Venice) 93
    Alla Madonna (Venice) 75
    Alle Testiere (Venice) 92
    American Bar (Venice) 111
    Antica Gelateria il David
        (Florence) 39
    Antica Locanda Montin (Venice)
        125
    Antica Osteria L'Agania (Arezzo)
        213
    Antica Trattoria dell'Orso
        (Orvieto) 266
    Antico Capon (Venice) 118
    Antico Dolo (Venice 74
    Antico Ristorante Sibilia 294
    Bar Italia (Impruneta) 57
    Bar Michelangelo (Pietrasanta)
        227
    Beccofino (Florence) 28

    Bella Ciao (Galluzzo) 57
    La Bianchina (Bottai) 56
    Buca di Sant'Antonio (Lucca) 220
    Buca di San Francesco (Arezzo)
        213
    Buscioni (Florence) 54
    Caffè Rivoire (Florence) 23
    Caffè Sicilia (Noto) 341
    Cammillo (Florence) 28
    Cantinetta Antinori (Florence) 30
    La Chiusa (Montefollonico) 221
    La Chiusa (Niccone) 262
    La Colonna (Venice) 84
    Corrado Costanza (Noto) 341
    D'Angelo Winery (Rionero in
        Vulture) 334
    da Baffone (Burano) 251
    Da Delfina (Artimino) 54
    Da Guido (Magliano in Toscana)
        220
    Da Ivo (Venice) 108
    Didovich (Venice) 86
    Do Mori (Venice) 75
    Dolci e Dolcezza (Florence) 50
    Fiaschetteria Toscana (Venice) 82
    Giudea (Pietrasanta) 226
    Harry's Bar (Venice) 110
    Hotel Giotto (Assisi) 249
    Il Giardino da Felicin (Monforte
        d'Alba) 152
    Il Grifo (Venosa) 336
    Il Latini (Florence) 37
    Locanda Cipriani (Torcello) 142
    Locanda da Lino (Solighetto) 181
    Il Molino (Spello) 269
    La Mora (Bagni di Lucca) 215
    Nico (Venice) 126
    Osteria da Alberto (Venice) 74
    Osteria Da Fiore (Venice) 72
    Osteria di Rendola (Montevarchi)
        225
    Osteria La Solita Zuppa (Chiusi)
        217
    La Pergola (Paestum) 320
    Petronio (Manciano) 221

Restaurants (continued)
  Pozzi degli Etruschi (Volterra) 244
  Il Richiastro (Viterno) 296
  Ristaurante L'Erbhosteria del Castello (Rofelle) 232
  Ristorante La Medusa di Canese Manuela (Portovenere) 155
  Ristorante Al Covo (Venice) 100
  Ristorante Da Ivano (Genzano di Roma) 279
  Ristorante da Silvio (Bologna) 199
  Ristorante Fiorentino (Sansepolcro) 237
  Ristorante Il Pino (San Presto) 267
  Riviera (Venice) 118
  Russo Zi'ntonio (Sorrento) 325
  Taverna del Lago (Cavriglia) 216
  Trattoria ai Cugnai (Venice) 128
  Trattoria al Muleto (Milan) 167
  Trattoria da Mario (Casella d'Asolo) 173
  Trattoria Garga (Florence) 37
  Trattoria Leonida (Bologna) 198
  Trattoria Omero (Arcetri) 54
  Villa Cheta Elite (Acquafredda) 332
  Villa Cipriani (Asolo) 172
  Le Volpi e l'Uva (Florence) 29
  Zi Franco (Caprarola) 277
The Resurrection (Piero della Francesca) 235
Rio Terrà dei Catecumeni (Venice) 133
Riola 205
Rionero in Vulture 334
Rivoli 148
Rocca del Leone (Castiglione del Lago) 252
Rocca Pisani (Lonigo) 174
Rofelle 232
Rossellino, Antonio 52
Rosso Fiorentino 236, 245

S
Sacro Monte 149–151
Saepinum 302
Saint Barbara Altarpiece (Palma Vecchio) 93–94
Saint George and the Dragon (Carpaccio) 98–99
Saint George and the Princess (Pisanello) 183–184
Saint John the Baptist and Four Saints (Coregliano) 77–80
Saint John the Baptist Fresco Cycle (Masolino da Panicale) 158
Sala Anatomica (Bologna) 195
Samnite Village (Pietrabbondante) 301–302
Santa Croce (Venice) 64–75
San Francesco del Deserto 141
San Fruttuoso 153
San Gimignano 233–234
San Giorgio Maggiore (Venice) 139
San Giovanni Valdarno 234
San Giovanni in Venere (Fossacesia) 301
San Lazzaro degli Armeni (Venice) 143
San Marco (Florence) 38
San Marco (Venice) 102–114
San Michele (Anacapri) 306
San Michele (Venice) 139
Santi Pietro e Paolo (Sovana) 243
San Polo & Santa Croce (Venice) 64–75
San Presto 267
San Vito d'Altivole 180
Sanctuary of Monte Sant'Angelo (Terracina) 293
Sangallo, Antonio da, the Elder 223
Sangallo, Antonio da, the Younger 265
Sangallo, Giuliano da 53, 231
Sansepolcro 235
Sansovino, Jacopo 81, 99, 113
Santu Antine (Sardinia) 347

Sardinia (Sardegna) 347
Sarto, Andrea del 231
I Sassi (Matera) 333–334
Save Venice Treasure Hunt 103
Scamozzi, Vicenzo 174, 186
Scarpa, Carlo 64, 94, 178, 180
Scuola Grande di San Giovanni
    Evangelista (Venice) 70,
Scuola Grande di San Marco
    (Venice) 86
Scuola Grande di San Rocco
    (Venice) 68–69
Scuola Nuova Della Misericordia
    (Venice) 81
Scuola di San Giorgio degli
    Schiavoni (Venice) 98–99
Selinunte 344
Seravezza 238
Sermoneta 288
Serra Orrios (Sardinia) 347
Settignano 58
Shops
    Beltrami (Florence) 37
    Castorina (Florence) 30
    Colonna (Venice) 86
    Domus (Venice) 108
    Flea Market (Tivoli) 295
    Giossi (Naples) 314

    Leo Grilli Arte (Gubbio) 259
    M'Art di Nulli, Maria Teresa
        (Deruta) 255
    Madova (Florence) 28
    Maioliche di Pierluigi Monotti
        (Deruta) 255
    Majani (Bologna) 198
    Mascari (Venice) 73
    Mastri Librai Eugubini (Gubbio)
        260
    N'uovo (Florence) 36
    Ospedale delle Bambole (Naples)
        313
    Pastificio Giacomo Rizzo (Venice)
        83
    La Pescheria (Venice) 119

    Peter Bazzanti and Son (Florence)
        30
    Prada Outlet (Montevarchi) 225
    Presepi (Naples) 316
    Rigattieri (Venice) 103
    Romanelli (Florence) 30
    Tuttocasa (Venice) 82
    Veschini (Deruta) 255
Sicily (Sicilia) 339–343
Siena 240–243
Signorelli, Luca 221, 264
Società Canottieri (Circolo
    Canottieri) 25
Sodoma 221
Solfatara 303
Solighetto 181
Sorrento 325
Sovana 243
Spaccanapoli (Naples) 313
Spello 268
Sperlonga 281, 289–291
Storie di Tobiolo (Guardi) (115)
Stupinigi 148
The Supper at Emmaus
    (Caravaggio) 165
Swimming Pools (Venice) 138
Syracuse (Siracusa) 345–346

T
Tarquinia 292
Teatro Olimpico (Vicenza) 186
Teatro Poliziano (Montepulciano)
    222
Teatro Verde (Venice) 139
Tempietto Longobardo (Cividale del
    Friuli) 188
Tempio (Possagno) 179
Tempio Voltiano (Como) 159
Temple of Jupiter Anxurus (Tempio
    di Giove Anxur) 293
Temple of Sibilla (Tivoli) 295
Terme di Mevania (Bevagna) 251
Terracina 281, 293
Terragni, Giuseppe 160
Tintoretto, Jacopo 68–69, 77

Tivoli 294–295
Todi 270
Tomb of Alvise Diedo (Venice) 91
Tomba del Triclinio Frescoes
    (Tarquinia) 292
Torcello 140
Torre Annunziata 325
Trentino-Alto Adige 172–186
Trento 181
Trequanda 243
Treviso 182
Tuscany (Toscana) 208–245

U
Udine 189
Umbria 247–270
Urbino 205–207

V
Valle d'Aosta 148–152
Vanvitelli, Luigi 309
Varallo 149
Vasari, Giorgio 23, 32, 208
Venetian Islands 135–143
Veneto 172–186
Venice
    Accademia 127
    Angelo Raffaele 115
    Annunciations 69
    Arsenale 101
    Bacari 73
    Badoer-Giustinian Chapel 100
    Basilica di San Marco 112
    Biblioteca Marciana (La Zecca)
        113–114
    Brodsky, Joseph, Grave of (San
        Michele)139
    Burano 141
    Ca' Rezzonico 129
    Campiello del Pistor 71
    Campo Santa Margherita 118,
        119–125
    Cannaregio 76–85
    Capella del Rosario 91
    Cappella di San Tarasio 97

Castello 86–101
Colleoni, Bartolomeo, monument
    87
Corte del Duca Sforza 102
Doge's Palace (Palazzo Ducale)
    112
Dorsoduro 115–134
Fondazione Querini Stampalia 94
Galleria Luce 107–108
Galleria Multigraphic 131
Gesuati 129
Gesuiti 81
Ghetto 77
Giudecca 135
Hotels
    Antica Locanda Montin 125
    Hotel Cipriani 138
    Hotel La Fenice et des Artistes
        107
Istituto Universitaria di
    Architettura di Venezia 64–65
Last Judgment Mosaics (Torcello)
    140
Madonna dell'Orto 77
Museo Archeologico 113
Museo Correr 110–111
Museo Fortuny 106
Palazzo Contarini del Bovolo
    108–109
Palazzo Ducale, see Doge's Palace
La Pietà 129
Il Redentore 135
Restaurants
    Acqua Pazza 106
    Al Mascaron 93
    Alla Madonna 75
    Alle Testiere 92
    American Bar 111
    Antica Locanda Montin 125
    Antico Capon 118
    Antico Dolo 74
    La Colonna 84
    Da Ivo 109
    Didovich 86
    Do Mori 75

Venice restaurants (continued)
    Fiaschetteria Toscana 82
    Harry's Bar 110
    Locanda Cipriani (Torcello) 142
    Nico 126
    Osteria da Alberto 74
    Osteria Da Fiore 72
    Ristorante Al Covo 100
    Riviera 118
    Trattoria ai Cugnai 128
Rio Terrà dei Catecumeni 133
Saint Barbara Altarpiece 93–94
Saint George and the Dragon
    (Carpaccio) 98
Saint John the Baptist and
    Four Saints (Conegliano) 77
Sant'Alvise 76
Sant'Apollonia 95–96
Santa Croce 64–75
San Francesco del Deserto 141
San Francesco della Vigna 99
San Giobbe 76
San Giorgio Maggiore 139
San Giovanni Crisostomo
    82–83
Santi Giovanni e Paolo (San
    Zanipolo) 87–92
San Lazzaro degli Armeni 143
San Marco 102
Santa Maria dell'Assunta
    (Torcello) 140
Santa Maria Formosa 93–94
Santa Maria Gloriosa dei Frari
    65–68
Santa Maria dei Miracoli 85
Santa Maria della Salute
    131–132
San Michele (Island of the
    Dead) 139
San Moisè 110
San Nicolò dei Mendicoli 115
San Polo 64–75
San Salvatore 69
San Sebastiano 118
San Trovaso 126

San Zaccaria 96–97
San Zan Degolà 70–71
San Zanipolo 87–92
Save Venice Treasure Hunt 103
Scuola Grande dei Carmini 129
Scuola Grande di San Giovanni
    Evangelista 70
Scuola Grande di San Marco 86
Scuola Grande di San Rocco
    68, 69
Scuola Nuova Della Misericordia
    81
Scuola di San Giorgio degli
    Schiavoni 98–99
Shops
    Colonna 86
    Domus 108
    Mascari 73
    Pastificio Giacomo Rizzo 83
    La Pescheria 119
    Rigattieri 103
    Tuttocasa 82
Swimming Pools 138
Teatro Verde 139
Tomb of Alvise Diedo 91–92
Torcello 140
Traghetti 102
Venetian Islands 135–143
La Zecca, *see* La Biblioteca
    Marciana
Venosa 334
Verona 182
Veronese, Paolo 91, 118, 174
Verrocchio, Andrea (del) 87
Via Garibaldi (Genoa) 153
Viareggio 227, 244
Vicenza 186
Vietri sul Mare 327
Vignola 271, 277
Villa Le Balze (Fiesole) 53
Villa Barbaro (Maser) 174
Villa Bianca (Seveso) 160
Villa Emo (Fanzolo) 173
Villa Gamberaia (Settignano) 53, 59
Villa Gregoriana (Tivoli) 295

Villa Iovis (Capri) 305, 306
Villa Lante (Bagnaia) 271
Villa Medicea (Artimino) 53
Villa Medicea (Poggio a Caiano) 53,
    231
Villa Medicea della Petraia
    (Castello) 53
Villa Medici (Fiesole) 53, 55
Villa dei Misteri (Pompeii) 322–324
Villa Oplontis (Torre Annunziata)
    325
Villa d'Orazio (Licenza) 280

Villa Romana del Casale (Piazza
    Armerina) 344
Viterbo 296
Vittone, Bernardo 151
Vivarini, Bartolomeo 93
Volterra 244

Z
La Zecca (Venice), see La Biblioteca
    Marciana
Zevio, Altichiero da 177

TRAVEL BOOKS FROM THE LITTLE BOOKROOM

City Secrets Rome
Edited by Robert Kahn
Tour Rome in the company of its most passionate admirers
as the world's foremost artists, writers, architects, archaeologists, and historians reveal their favorite discoveries in
this ultimate insider's guide: a renowned painter shows the
way to a hidden garden, a poet laureate shares the address
of a little-known trattoria, a classicist suggests an ecclesias-
tical shopping spree. Detailed maps. ". . . the best literary
gift to Italian travelers since the Baedeker and Henry James."
—FINANCIAL TIMES
Clothbound $19.95 ISBN 1-892145-04-9
Upcoming volumes in the City Secrets series: *City Secrets
Dublin, City Secrets Amsterdam, City Secrets Paris,
City Secrets New York, City Secrets Miami, City Secrets
North Carolina.*

City Secrets London
Edited by Robert Kahn
Beyond the public London of pomp and circumstance
exists a private London that endlessly inspires its artists
and writers. Infused with the spirit of history and literature—yet undeniably of-the-moment—the city's loveliest
old corners and hippest new addresses are now revealed:
the lopsided seventeenth-century premises of the wine
merchant who supplies claret to the Queen, Oscar Wilde's
favorite restaurant, a barge trip by canal to Camden
Market, a connoisseur's afternoon.
Clothbound $19.95 ISBN 1-892145-01-4

The Historic Restaurants of Paris
A Guide to Century-Old Cafés, Bistros, and Gourmet
Food Shops
by Ellen Williams
The vanished world of nineteenth-century Paris still awaits

behind the doors of select restaurants and gourmet shops that have delighted customers for more than a hundred years. Crossing these thresholds, the discriminating diner and shopper can step into a gilded Belle Epoque setting favored by Manet and Degas, a vintage confectioner that supplied bonbons to Monet, or a shaded café terrace frequented by Zola. From tiny pâtisseries, cozy bistros, and rustic wine bars barely known outside the quarter to bustling brasseries, elegant tea salons, and world-famous cafes, *The Historic Restaurants of Paris* is an indispensible guide to classic cuisine served in settings of startling beauty. Hardcover $14.95 ISBN 1-892145-03-0

Artists in Residence
by Dana Micucci with photographs by Marina Faust
Open to the public, the homes and studios of eight celebrated 19th-century painters—Vincent van Gogh, Claude Monet, Gustave Courbet, Eugène Delacroix, Gustave Moreau, Rosa Bonheur, Jean-François Millet, and Charles-François Daubigny—provide intimate insights into their work and personalities as well as pleasurable day-long itineraries in and around Paris. Sumptuous portraits of these painters' lives and times is supplemented by detailed travel information.
Paperback in slipcase $19.95 April 2001
ISBN 1-892145-00-6

Harpo Speaks. . . about New York
by Harpo Marx with Rowland Barber
introduction by E. L. Doctorow
One hundred years ago, little Adolph "Harpo" Marx was literally tossed out the window of Miss Flatto's second grade classroom and onto a life on the streets. His unceremonious exit from the New York City public school system set in motion a chain of events which he describes with a mixture of sweetness and hilarity in this memoir of a child's

life in an immigrant family at the turn of the century.
". . . This enchanting memoir will make you regret every
day you ever wasted going to school."—JOHN GUARE
Hardcover $16.95 May 2001 ISBN 1-892145-06-5

Here is New York
by E. B. White with a new introduction by Roger Angell
In the summer of 1949, E. B. White checked into The
Algonquin Hotel for the weekend and, sweltering in the
heat, wrote the remarkable *Here is New York*. *The New
York Times* has chosen it as one of the ten best books ever
written about Manhattan. *The New Yorker* calls it "the
wittiest essay, and one of the most perceptive, ever done on
the city." Based partly on his memories of Manhattan
when he first came to the city as a young writer, this legendary work by one of America's literary masters is now
back in print with a new introduction by Roger Angell.
". . . Just to dip into this miraculous essay—to experience
the wonderful lightness and momentum of its prose, its
supremely casual air and surprisingly tight knit—is to find
oneself going ahead and rereading it all. White's homage
feels as fresh now as fifty years ago."—JOHN UPDIKE
Hardcover $16.95 ISBN 1-892145-02-2

The Impressionists' Paris
Walking tours of the artists' studios, homes, and the sites
they painted
by Ellen Williams
This guidebook pairs some of the most beloved masterpieces of Impressionism with the exact locations where
they were painted. Itineraries include the artists' studios,
apartments, and grave sites. Listings for restaurants, many
dating from the Impressionist era, round out the tours.
"This pocketable hardcover book is a small marvel. It is
fun to look at and fun to read."—JOHN RUSSELL, *THE NEW
YORK TIMES*
Hardcover $19.95 ISBN 0-9641262-2-2

Picasso's Paris
Walking tours of the artist's life in the city
by Ellen Williams
A century after his arrival there as an unknown Spanish
teenager, Paris still bears the mark of Pablo Picasso's
enduring presence. Four walking tours follow the painter
from the gaslit garrets of fin-de-siècle Paris to the Left
Bank quarter where he sat out the Nazi Occupation.
Dining recommendations include many of Picasso's
favorite haunts; with full-color reproductions of Picasso's
paintings, archival photos, vintage postcards, and maps.
Hardcover $19.95 ISBN 0-9641262-7-3

The Little Bookroom
5 Saint Luke's Place New York NY 10014
phone 212 691 3321 fax 212 691 2011
book-room@rcn.com
Distributed by Publishers Group West and in the United Kingdom
by Macmillan Distribution Ltd.

SPECIAL SALES

Little Bookroom publications are available at special
discounts for bulk purchases for sales promotions or
premiums. Special editions, including personalized covers,
excerpts of existing guides, or corporate imprints can be
created in large quantities for special needs. For more information contact The Little Bookroom, 5 St. Luke's Place,
New York, NY 10014. Inquiries from the United Kingdom
and European Community should be sent to Granta Books,
2/3 Hanover Yard, Noel Road, London N1 8BE.

BIOGRAPHIES

ROBERT KAHN is an architect in private practice. His work has been widely published. He has taught design, most recently at Yale University. In 1981 he was awarded the Prix de Rome by the American Academy in Rome. He lives and works in New York.

THE AMERICAN ACADEMY IN ROME, a center for independent study and advanced research in the arts and humanities, is located on the Janiculum, the highest point within the walls of Rome. For the scores of artists, art historians, classicists, architects, and writers who have been awarded a Rome Prize, "the beauty and resources of the place, the quality and variety of the friendships, the depth of Rome, and the time and freedom to work," mark their stay there as among the top two or three experiences of a lifetime.

SAVE VENICE INC. is an American non-profit organization based in New York with a second office in Venice, Italy and chapters in California and Boston. The mission of Save Venice is to preserve the art and architecture of Venice and to safeguard its cultural heritage by raising funds and providing educational programs. Founded in 1971, Save Venice has provided funding for the restoration of more than one hundred important works of art and buildings in Venice.

Paul Pascal, Professor Emeritus of Classics, University of Washington, and Fellow of the American Academy in Rome (1952), served as the fact-checker for this volume. It was a task to which he brought great erudition and enthusiasm, often exploring well beyond the contribution at hand. His notes to our editorial staff were filled with information revealed by his researches or brought forth from his heroic store of knowledge: folkloric arcana, linguistic twists, the odd historical anecdote. Too delightful not to share with our readers, many of these are included here as Editor's Notes. "I think of myself as Dr. Johnson defined a lexicographer," Professor Pascal told us, "a harmless drudge."